Mark Whittaker is the author or co-author of eight books. In 2005, he won the Walkley Award for Magazine Feature Writing for a story in *The Weekend Australian Magazine* about the people who ran into a burning daycare centre to save the children inside. Mark lives on the New South Wales south coast with his wife and sometimes co-author, Amy Willesee, and their two children.

Also by Mark Whittaker

Sins of the Brother: The Definitive Story of Ivan Milat and the Backpacker Murders (with Les Kennedy)

The Road to Mount Buggery: A Journey through the Curiously Named Places of Australia (with Amy Willesee)

Love and Death in Kathmandu: A Strange Tale of Royal Murder (with Amy Willesee)

Bomber: From Vietnam to Hell and Back (with Tony 'Bomber' Bower-Miles)

BRAVE

MARK WHITTAKER

MACMILLAN
Pan Macmillan Australia

For Amy

First published 2011 in Macmillan by Pan Macmillan Australia Pty Limited
1 Market Street, Sydney

National Library of Australia
Cataloguing-in-Publication data:

Whittaker, Mark.

Brave / Mark Whittaker.

9781405039871 (pbk.)

Heroes – Australia – Anecdotes.
Courage – Anecdotes.
Australia – Biography – Anecdotes.

920.0994

Typeset in 13/15.5 pt Granjon by Post Pre-Press, Australia
Printed in Australia by McPherson's Printing Group

Some of the people in this book have had their names changed to protect their privacy.

Contents

The narrative compression of storytelling, especially in the movies, beguiles us with happy endings into forgetting that sustained stress is corrosive of feeling. It's the great deadener. Those moments of joyful release from terror are not so easily had.
Ian McEwan, *Enduring Love*

I don't usually look at the news. Every time I see some poor wonderful person going in to save somebody I look at them and say, 'I love ya, and you're brave, but your life is never going to be the same again.'
Sharon O'Leary

ONE

The Roundhouse

All is quiet as childcare worker Amanda Zimmerman tiptoes the darkened playroom, through scattered mattresses and snoring bodies on their 1 pm nap. Santa is coming later this afternoon, so the prospect of cake and a concert for the parents had made her two- and three-year-olds – the Possums – a little harder than usual to get down. Sophie Delezio, a determined little thing, had been the last to go, about ten minutes earlier.

Without warning, there is an explosion of glass. Amanda swings around to see a car crashing through the change room wall. The car is airborne, flying at her head. In that frozen moment as she faces death square in the radiator grille, she wonders how her partner will pay the mortgage without her.

She takes a reflex step back, and watches the driver's face gliding by in the descending white Commodore which misses her by the length of her forearm. The back wheels clip the top of a waist-high room divider made of wood and fabric. The car crashes to the floor and slams into sliding glass doors at the back of the room. Somehow, the reinforced glass and wire mesh hold, and the car stops.

Amanda can see it has flown over most of the children, but she knows it has come to rest on top of where at least one of them had been sleeping, and others had been all around. Worse, the driver's foot appears to be stuck hard on the accelerator. The back wheels are spinning, screeching, burning rubber. Amanda and colleague Laura Hayman grab the first of the thirteen children in their care, taking them out the bathroom door to the playground. By the time Amanda returns, thick black smoke has filled the room. She gets down low and looks for another child who she knows is right in front of her. She can't find him. She sees another, picks him up and takes him outside. While there, she tries to smash open the glass doors to let the car run out into the playground but the doors are strong. A man is there and she asks him to do it, before she runs around to the front door.

She has entered a world where there is no time for thought, no emotion, just doing. She hits the fire alarm, ties something around her face and crawls back in to find more children.

The curtains had all been drawn for the nap. The only light in the room is from a fire at the back of the car. 'By that stage there was only a couple of centimetres of air left on the ground,' she will later recall. 'All I could see was Molly [Wood, aged two and a half] on fire. I went back in twice but had to keep leaving because the car kept sounding like it was going to explode. It kept getting faster and the flames kept getting higher and higher, right up to the top of the ceiling by this stage. I was half a hand length away from Molly's bed. Every time I went in I was trying to just grab it to drag her out. When I saw it the next day I couldn't believe I couldn't do it. But it was pitch black smoke, and you just didn't know.

'Molly was at the back of the car. Behind the boot. She

wasn't even underneath it. She was never underneath it. That's what all the papers got wrong. But that was where the main part of the fire was, where it started, and then her bed caught alight, her nappy and all that kind of stuff.'

While all this is happening, Amanda suspects there is another child under the car, but she doesn't know who. The nightmare is just beginning. About half a dozen children are still trapped inside, under and around the flaming car. And there are six babies in the adjacent cot room.

Over the seven minutes or so after the crash on 15 December 2003, more than twenty hitherto ordinary civilians going about their business on a perfect beach day will be driven to step outside their world into this other reality. Their actions will determine whether those children live or die. Their memories of those minutes remain vivid yet somehow vague and often contradictory, etched into minds being flooded with a cocktail of stress hormones.

*

Scott Black was in awe of the day's perfection. He'd been at the Balgowlah shops and was heading home to nearby Manly at the bottom end of Sydney's northern beaches. His dark blue Mercedes was cruising through Fairlight, the sort of suburb where nothing much happens, but the California bungalows and cute-as-a-button cottages edge up towards a million bucks – those without ocean or harbour views, that is. As he came through an S-bend, near the golf club, he drew up behind a white Commodore that was slowing as if it was about to turn right without indicating. Then the Commodore eased forward like the driver had changed his mind. Not a problem. It was too nice a day for the 46-year-old to worry about bad driving.

There was a screech of rubber. The Commodore accelerated hard and lurched left. It mounted the gutter, still accelerating, crossed the footpath and a narrow strip of garden. It was heading straight towards an old house set slightly lower than street level. The garden seemed to act as a ramp and the car launched straight through the Commodore-sized window of what Scott knew to be a childcare centre.

You are kidding. You are kidding. What the fuck is going on? He looked around but there was no one. No pedestrians, no cars. *Did somebody else see this? Where is everybody?*

He popped his seatbelt, and fumbled with his mobile as he turned left into a parking area that ran around the back of the centre. He expected to see that the car had burst out the back wall, it had been going so fast.

But he saw women screaming out a door, children in their arms.

There's smoke coming out of the place, too. Jesus!

And there was the absolute flat-out whine of an engine revving into the red zone. He ran in through a storeroom door off to the left. Inside, smoke was at about head height. Little spot fires burnt to his right where the noise was coming from. Wearing T-shirt, shorts, sandals and sunnies, he ducked down to look for children. Scott had spent seven years on offshore oil rigs and he knew what 140 decibels sounded like. He knew what hot machinery could do. He had seen a man die in front of him, the victim of an engine tearing itself apart. A thick scar on his left forearm came from one such motor. 'This was howling a lot hotter than things I've run out in oil-rig land. Listening to that car I did not want to get any closer to it than I had to. Something was about to happen . . . It was pretty hard to deal with. Personal confession: fear of catastrophic circumstances prevented me getting closer than what I was.'

As he left the building, he recognised a guy he played rugby against when they were kids, Ian Cooper. Ian, 46, who owns restaurants, was working from his home across the road when he heard the bang. The two picked up a table and tried to smash a window to let smoke out, but the thing just bounced.

'You've got to help us,' a teacher said. 'There's kids in there.'

Great, in we go. Scott handed his Ray Bans to a teacher and crawled back in.

*

While Ian and Scott were sure they were first on the scene, elderly neighbours Neil Nutley and Vic Eisenhut didn't see them when they jumped the safety fence into the playground – a feat which now astonishes them. Also running across Balgowlah Road with them were neighbours Ray Garner and Belinda Glynn. Believing they were the first there, all four ran in through the storeroom door with no idea what was causing the terrific thundering.

Belinda, 35, only got in about a metre. The smoke was too thick. Too black. 'I couldn't see anything,' she'd recall. 'I just didn't have the guts to go in with the noise building up like it was going to explode.'

Neil, Vic and Ray went further before retreating.

Physiotherapist Adam Semciw had stopped on his way to the beach and followed a group in on hands and knees. The 24-year-old with long blond hair had no idea what was making the horrendous noise. He picked up a T-shirt or something off the floor to put over his mouth to breathe. About six metres in, one of the two people in front of him turned around. 'I was at the point where I just needed one excuse to get away, and that was it. Everybody turned back and walked out.'

*

Ray Garner made his way around to the foyer at the front of the building, found a fire extinguisher, and continued on into the playroom. Amid the noise and smoke, he found the back of the car on fire, its wheels still spinning. 'There was nobody else around. I think I might have been the first one in, so I went to the back of the car and blasted the fire extinguisher around the back wheel where most of the flame was and over the car-pet area . . . I'm not sure if it was petrol spilling but it was all flame.' He put the fire out, but kept blasting for what felt like minutes until the extinguisher ran out. As soon as it did, the fire reignited. He had no idea that, according to Amanda Zimmer-man's account, Molly Wood was lying right in front of him.

Meanwhile, Amanda had retreated to the foyer after her second unsuccessful attempt to get Molly. Staff members Margaret Lawrence and Liz Strange had already braved the fumes and noise while getting babies out of the cot room, but they weren't sure if they had them all. Someone told Amanda there were still babies in there. She grabbed a man who she didn't know and they crawled past the back of the car, to the cot room. 'The only light you could see on the floor – because you couldn't see anything standing up – was Molly on fire.' The smoke was so low they couldn't see whether any babies were in the cots, so they crawled around, sucking air from the floor, shaking each cot and listening for crying over the howl-ing engine. But all Amanda heard was the sound of the man she'd dragged in vomiting.

*

Andrew Anast, 33, a mechanic at Peninsula Holden, was road-testing a car when he saw the smoke. He went around the back and heard the noise. When somebody said it was a car in there, he jumped the fence to leave. 'Maybe because I work on cars every day and I know the weight of them, because I put them on hoists, and with the fuel and the high speed of that engine running, it was my worst nightmare. That noise was the eeriest thing I've ever heard. It's just knowing that this thing is in there, causing all this damage. It was a monster. Like the damn thing was alive.'

Then someone else said, 'The kids are on their nap.' Hearing that changed something inside him. Andrew jumped back over the fence. *You're gunna do it.* He later describes this in a stern voice, like he's talking to a stubborn child.

There were men trying to break open the glass doors at the back. 'I wasn't game enough to go near it,' Andrew says. 'I was afraid the car was going to come flying out. I warned them, I said, "Please, you watch you don't knock that door down. You don't know what the car is wedged up against. You knock the door down, it might take you out."'

Meanwhile, Scott Black was inside, having handed one kid over at the storeroom door. For all the sights and toxic smells, the noise dominated his senses. The engine was howwwwling. *That'd be right. Now the bloody car's gunna blow up.* He looked to the door and the barefooted Ian Cooper was in the doorway. 'Get in here.'

Ian motioned that he was going the more direct route to the car, but fire and a metre-high wall blocked his way. Then BOOOOM. The engine blew something. It started winding down.

Scott ran outside as the glass doors were at last being prised open. Many of those outside could not comprehend a car inside. Belinda Glynn thought they had all been talking about some sort of toy, like a supermarket coin-operated car.

As the doors came down, neighbour Vic Eisenhut's first thought was that it was the shell of a car for playing on. *What a stupid place to put it, right next to the door.*

As smoke belched from the doors, many people streamed in. Recollections differ. Some would be certain that the engine was still revving when the doors first opened. Those who went around the driver's side found a pocket of children who had been trapped between the metre-high dividing wall, the car and the flames at its rear. Each recalled finding and passing children out.

Vic got down and crawled into the playroom and into all the rooms. He sat up, towards the back, and became disorientated in the smoke but came across a woman's feet and followed her soles. Together they found a redheaded child and brought him or her to safety.

Andrew Anast delivers his story with a gentle sense of wonder: 'I grabbed a child at the back door. Right next to the front bumper of the car. I passed him through to one of the ladies. There was another little girl crawling around. Grabbed her, passed her through. Poor buggers, they were just crying. One of them was in a nappy. I can remember trying to see, in this toxic-smelling black smoke, thinking, "Andrew, you're going to see something here that's going to live with you for the rest of your life. It's happening right now, it could all blow up, but you're doing it."' He has two kids of his own. One of them was in kindy that day. *Jesus, the driver's still in the car. Get him out! Wake up to yourself. This is it. This is the real thing.*

*

Scott Black was lying on the ground on the driver's side, pulling wood-and-fabric debris from under the car, some of it flaming, expecting that if there were any kids left in the building, they'd be under here. Andrew Anast trod on him as he opened the door and fumbled with the driver's seatbelt. *Fuck the driver. Where are the kids?* Having seen the accident, Scott had a feeling the driver could have been motivated by malice.

Neighbour Belinda Glynn saw a small girl being brought out. 'I'm all wet,' the girl cried, like she was going to get in trouble for it. Belinda picked her up from a guy who went straight back in. 'You know, I remember his face but I haven't seen that guy since. He was bald on top, youngish, probably thirty, thirty-five, light-coloured eyes, quite lean. I remember thinking, "How does he go back in?"'

Physiotherapist Adam Semciw helped Andrew carry the driver onto the lawn. 'His eyes were open but he wouldn't respond to anything. The others went back and I sat with him, trying to place him on his side in the safety position. He had blood coming out of his mouth. Gasping, shallow breaths. White skin. I thought I was watching a man die. He started bleeding and frothing at the mouth.'

Belinda remembers sitting with the driver alone. 'He had foam and blood coming out of his mouth, his glasses were kind of hanging off, and the guys just dumped him and ran back inside. There was still really thick smoke. I tried to turn him over.' She didn't know first aid. *Holy shit, what do I do?* She found it hard to even look at the old man. It was upsetting her too much. It was equally hard looking at the childcare centre, such was her feeling of helplessness. Her eyes went around to Balgowlah Road where she saw a fire truck out the front and firemen standing there looking at the window at the front of the building. *Why are they standing around out there?*

Amanda Zimmerman was the only one who knew there were children under the car, but in the chaos the message didn't reach those inside. She knows she told a policeman who had turned up. Several other witnesses recalled that the policeman declined to participate in the rescue. But Amanda disagrees: 'He went inside. I dragged him in by the arm through the bathroom door. He was very young and I didn't see him afterwards. He looked sick. I was screaming at him. "Do something. Do your job." I pushed him through the door and I went in, but it was just the same in there, so I came out and I think he came out not long after.'

Several rescuers recalled yelling from the double doors, 'How many more? Have we got them all?', and not getting any definitive answer.

Amanda remembers shouting, 'There's a child under the car', but some officious idiot pushed her away to the back fence like she was hampering the rescue effort.

*

Kerry Griffiths, the mother of a five-year-old at the Roundhouse, had seen the smoke while driving home from her shift as a social worker at a hospital. As she pulled in around the back, she saw her son being led away safely with all the four- and five-year-olds – the Gumnuts – who'd been in a separate room. She had turned towards the toddlers' room when the glass doors came down. The blackness and smoke would snap-freeze in her brain. And the car, right where she knew the Possums slept. Staff screamed, 'Turn it off. Turn it off.' Then 'Get our babies out. Get our babies out.'

She felt like she froze for half an hour. *Oh fuck oh fuck oh fuck.* Her speech had gone, all she had was this mantra.

As the driver was carried out, Kerry saw a staff member. 'How many are we missing?'

'We don't know.'

'Is the list where it's meant to be?'

'Yes.'

Kerry ran in, thinking she could look for kids and get the rolls at the same time. There were people all over the car, pulling debris from underneath. She heard someone yelling there was a kid under the car. She looked and couldn't see through the debris on her side. She was near the back of the car when it flared again. Flames shot up. A male voice screamed, 'Get out. It's going to blow up.' That was the first time she felt fear, crippling terror, but like most of the others in there she knew she couldn't leave. She'd never forgive anyone if they left her son to die. She went around to the driver's side and started throwing debris out. She screamed, 'Is there anyone there?', which would seem pretty stupid to her in hindsight. She found a child wedged between some shelving and the car and as she bent to pick the child up, she heard another crying. She ran out shouting: 'There's another child.'

Ray Garner had helped Andrew carry the driver out before returning with another extinguisher which Amanda had handed him. He quelled the flame, but as soon as the extinguisher ran out, it flashed again. With the doors open and the engine stopped, however, the smoke had thinned. Standing near the back passenger-side door, he looked under the car and saw two small bare feet amid the debris, toes pointing to the ground. It was a sight that would stay with him. The head, not visible, was over near the middle of the car.

'There's a kid under this car. Let's get it up.' That was his recollection, though others would recall more forceful language.

Because the tyres had shredded, the car was sitting low. Its floor was pressed against the child's body, so they couldn't drag her out. The back of the car was still on fire, so Ray jumped straight to the front wheel arch and started lifting by himself.

Ian Cooper, who Ray also knew from schoolboy rugby, joined in with Scott, Andrew, council worker Nick Christophides, neighbour Michael Altenburger in his Speedos, and others, all concentrated around the front.

As the ragtag collection began to lift, gagging still on the toxic fumes, they were greeted by the vision of two firemen walking into the chaos in boots, masks and helmets.

Firemen Wade Laverack and Anthony Farrell went around to the back of the vehicle along with council worker Ties Bruijns. The men heaved and the car went up onto its side. The child was lifted out and Nick Christophides recalls someone yelling, 'There's another one under here.' Many who were there, exhausted, would recall only one lift. Others two. Some would recall only one child recovered. But out of the wreckage came two tiny bodies, Sophie Delezio and Molly Wood, suffering major burns and clinging to life. Facing decades of treatment ahead.

*

The driver regained consciousness in the ambulance. 'Was I in a prang? Was any other person injured?' he asked.

The rescuers, dazed and exhausted, with searing eyes and crap-filled lungs, drifted out onto the lawn as the professionals took over. One more child was coaxed from a cupboard by a spaceman-like fireman.

Andrew Anast needed to find out what it was all for. He went up to an ambulance officer. 'I've got to know if anybody was killed. I've just got to know that all the kids are safe.'

'They're all alive,' he was told, though he couldn't quite believe it.

The ambos examined him and said he had to go to hospital.

Andrew didn't want to go. He said he'd be okay.

'No, we've got to take you,' the ambos said. 'Your nasal hairs are singed. Your throat's black.'

He sobbed all the way there, thinking about the kids and how life can change so badly. Just beautiful and sunny and all of a sudden it's like hell.

He wasn't in physical pain, but couldn't stop replaying the scene. His wife visited him that night, and before she left, he said, 'Go into the kids' room and kiss them. Please, you've got to do that.'

Three other rescuers were taken to hospital: Ray Garner, Neil Nutley and Vic Eisenhut. The two elderly neighbours,

12

Neil and Vic, had both repeatedly entered the playroom, then gone over to their place to fix drinks for everybody afterwards.

*

When I speak to Andrew Anast eighteen months after the rescue, it still troubles him. He fears the worst for his kids. He dreams of disasters. He lives near the airport and looks at planes rocketing off and he hopes he doesn't see the day when one of the damn things comes down.

Most of the other men report no ongoing anxieties. Maybe they suffered a few lost nights sleep and a few bad dreams, but they say they're fine. Ian Cooper gets angry when a car speeds down the street. He wants to give the driver a good talking to.

Ray Garner couldn't sleep for three or four nights. He put that down to excess adrenaline, but says he's suffered no long-term effects. 'Every time I think about the two little feet under the car I get a bit emotional. But other than that . . .'

Belinda Glynn worked as a night secretary at a legal firm. She packed herself off to work that night after the accident, thinking no one would believe her excuse. She 'lost it' towards the end of the week and rang a number given to her by the council for counselling, but the guy on the line didn't help. 'He just shut me down and said, "Look, I've got some important stuff I've got to deal with." I'm beginning to think now a counsellor wouldn't have acted like that.' Belinda developed repetitive strain injury. 'I don't know if that was how my body dealt with it. I couldn't use my arms.'

Kerry Griffiths got home on the night of the fire at about 7 pm and her son Liam almost recoiled at the sight of her, covered in soot and blood. Liam had a few problems over the coming months but they worked through them. Kerry became teary, couldn't sleep and was 'hyper-vigilant' around kids. Even today if a child gets too close to a road, she reacts.

'People would come up to me and say, "It's so lucky you were there", or, "You were meant to be there". Every time someone says something like that, I'm like, "Well, no, I couldn't do anything to stop those two children being hurt that badly." I couldn't cope with that. Every time somebody says something positive, it just grinds me into the ground, which is interesting because I know none of the men feel like that. They all say, "We're absolutely fine." I don't think they are, but . . .'

When I ask Amanda Zimmerman what had given her the courage to keep going back inside, she answers: 'Because I knew there was someone under there. And it's my responsibility. That's how I felt. That's the kind of thing I stupidly do and pay the price for.'

I ask later what she meant by 'pay the price'.

'I didn't lose my job, but I can't work there any more,' she says. 'It's hard to go back there. I found the months in counselling hard to do. All the staff, they've all gone through it. Half of them have left and the others are still having counselling and stuff. It wrecked everybody's lives in lots of ways — people's relationships. I couldn't work there any more. You don't get paid enough to nearly die. We were allowed time off, however much we needed, but enough's enough. Parents always looking at you, tears in their eyes, not wanting to talk to you about it, but really wanting to talk to you about it . . . I just had to go.'

*

A funny thing happened when Manly Council put on a ceremony to thank the heroes of the disaster, and then, a year afterwards, when the fire brigade handed out 25 Commissioner's Commendations to the civilians involved. As they came to meet each other at the various ceremonies, some became suspicious of the involvement of others.

'I know what I saw and I didn't see him there' was a

common comment. It was usually spoken with scepticism, sometimes nearing hostility, but rounded off with the acceptance that everybody gave as much as they were able.

Scott Black has had people come up to him: 'Are you the one telling people you were the first on the scene?'

'Well, I'm not actually telling anyone that, but it just so happens I was.'

Despite inconsistencies in the fourteen accounts that have made up this story, the differences can be easily accommodated by the smoke and confusion, with people running in and out of four doors like some old silent slapstick. The most uniformly remembered person at the scene was Andrew Anast, whose maroon overalls and manic demeanour stood him apart, yet he'd arrived relatively late. He had, however, stood outside until the doors came down so everybody had a chance to see him.

It appears that two staff members got the Commissioner's Commendations after having turned up only when the disaster was over. But far from there having been less than 25 heroes, it seems possible that there were more.

Almost all those interviewed recalled crawling about on the floor in the blackness and bumping into someone who they had not seen since. He was short and dark, or tall and dark, or bald, or blond. He was young or middle-aged and he definitely never turned up for any award.

*

Eighteen months after the Roundhouse fire, the driver of the car, Donald McNeall, then 69, had criminal negligence charges against him dismissed by a magistrate. The accident was caused by a seizure. His body had stiffened. His foot had pushed down hard on the accelerator where it stayed until he was dragged out by the rescuers.

I was sent to the court to take a look by my editors at the *Weekend Australian Magazine*. They wanted the story of Sophie and Molly from start to finish, but the first person I interviewed the following week was Scott Black, and from that time on, it was all about the civilian rescuers who'd come from everywhere to help. They very kindly and eloquently opened up their minds, offering a little slice of that incredible seven minutes in their lives. I admired their bravery as much as the way they were able to admit their fears and acknowledge their limitations.

Two years later, something made me think of them again and I Googled their names trying to find out if they'd ever been awarded anything. Knowing nothing about how bravery awards worked, I found myself at a website called 'It's An Honour'. There, I learned that some, but not all, had been given something called a Group Bravery Citation.

This didn't sound very exciting. The Group Bravery Citation was listed at the bottom of the awards hierarchy. Aside from the fact that it was a nonsense to suggest that these people had acted as a group, I thought the Roundhouse rescuers deserved better.

But that award also induced curiosity. If they only got a group citation, what did you have to do to get the medal at the top of the hierarchy, the Cross of Valour? I learned that only five of them have been handed out since the award's inception in 1975 when it replaced the George Cross as the civilian equivalent of the Victoria Cross.

I set out to find those five people to see what it took to get one. I managed to talk to four of them and saw that, yes, their stories were remarkable, but the surprise was the extent to which they had all suffered for their acts of valour. They had not just ridden off into the sunset as we might expect.

There is something that changes a person in these moments

when the brain is expecting death and pumps out a potent brew of chemicals to increase physical performance, to prepare for expected wounds, and to make sure it never forgets.

Along the way I came across other award recipients and it soon became apparent that many of them had done things every bit as extraordinary, had souped up their bodies on all the adrenaline, cortisol and noradrenaline, and been affected every bit as deeply. And their stories were always a lot more interesting than the official citations or news clippings indicated.

You sometimes see these people on television, usually just after the incident or perhaps on the day they receive a medal. You might get their story told in two or three sentences before the interviewer asks the compulsory question: 'Do you think you're a hero?' The interviewee modestly denies they are a hero, before a third party – usually the rescued person or a loved one – is forced to affirm that, 'Yes. He's my hero.' The news format has neither the time nor the space to convey what happens to the man who rushes into a burning house and manages to save one child but then learns there was another one in there; what happens when that man's spouse gets up him for risking his life for the sake of some stranger; what happens when the demons start coming for him in his dreams.

These people don't need to be put on pedestals but they do seem to feel a need to be understood. I tended to gravitate towards the people who'd had a bit of time since their incidents and so were able to put the trajectories of their lives into a better perspective. It often took them years to get back on track. Many of them have turned it into a positive – 'post-traumatic growth' – but there are a few who will never recover physically and/or mentally from what they went through to save someone else.

There are an awful lot of brave people out there. While only five have been awarded a Cross of Valour since 1975, several hundred have received the next highest honour, the Star of Courage, more than 2000 have received the Bravery Medal, and almost as many again have received the Commendation for Brave Conduct. Many thousands of others have received different forms of recognition and no doubt there are thousands more again who have risked their lives to save others and gone unrecognised.

What follows is but the smallest sample of some of the extraordinary stories of people who have had the question asked of them – how far would you go to save a life, or to right a wrong?

TWO

Darrell Tree

Life was going well on Darrell Tree's farm in August 1988. After a few tough years of drought and bushfire, the winter rains had come and the often golden landscape was lush and green. The 39-year-old wheat and sheep farmer was helping local mechanic Joe Honner, 32, pull up old telephone poles from the edge of Darrell's 1600-hectare property, Damperdale, on South Australia's Eyre Peninsula. Darrell had bought the poles from Telecom and was going to cut them into fence posts.

Darrell was working with his eighteen-year-old nephew Anthony Dolphin whose dad had been killed in an accident on the Adelaide wharves just nine days earlier. Anthony had come back to the area for his father's funeral and was staying with the Trees. Darrell's sons, aged four and seven, had come along for the day, too, in the back of the Land Rover ute.

In the crane, Joe, an affable redhead, had his three-year-old son Ryan with him as well. Darrell had asked Joe if he wanted to put the boy in the Land Rover with his kids, but Joe declined. 'Ryan's a cluey kid. He'll be okay.'

And so they worked. Darrell would wrap a chain around a pole. Joe would wriggle it around with the crane then winch the cable in, lifting the pole clean out of the hole. They'd done twelve of the 32 poles by around midday. Darrell and Anthony had gone ahead to the next pole while they waited for Joe to lay the twelfth pole on the ground and catch up in the slow old 'Blitz' crane – a Bedford truck with a crane mounted on the back.

At the thirteenth pole, Anthony untied a strainer wire helping support the pole and Darrell was about to put the chain around it when they heard a peculiar humming noise – like a welder's torch – coming from the approaching crane. They looked over and saw sparks coming out from under the crane.

Darrell looked up and saw the jib of the crane touching live powerlines that intersected the redundant poles they were working on. He ran to the vehicle. A blue arc as thick as a man's thigh wavered around the front wheels while a paler glow seemed to hover off the ground around the rear.

'What is it?' Joe yelled from the cabin.

'You're on the powerline,' Darrell said.

In an instant, Joe had jumped clear and both he and Darrell retreated from the weirdly glowing vehicle. But in that instant, Joe realised his enormous mistake.

'Ryan!' he called out. He had left his son alone in the cabin. He turned and headed back to get him.

Blue arcs of power zapped out from the crane onto the wet grass. Darrell knew enough about electricity to know that as soon as Joe touched the machine he was a goner. So he stood in front of his friend and in-law – Joe's brother was married to Darrell's sister – to stop him.

He tried to get it into Joe's head that the boy was safe so long as he stayed put (think of a bird sitting safely on a powerline), but if he touched the ground at the same time as the crane, he was dead. Joe, however, was frantic. Darrell argued with him, desperate to convince him that the boy was okay so long as he stayed where he was. Anthony watched his uncle repeatedly cutting Joe off as Joe pushed towards the crane. They ended up circling the vehicle.

'Daddy!' called the three-year-old above the fizzing electricity.

Joe charged forwards again and Darrell grappled him back. 'Don't do it, Joe. It'll kill you both.'

The boy stood in the truck, crying and bewildered. He raised his arms to be lifted. 'Daddy!'

After what seemed to Darrell like half an hour, but was probably only two or three minutes of fierce argument, Joe seemed to settle.

'I'll go and get a rope,' said Darrell. 'We'll lift him off with that.' His idea was that they could stand on either side of the crane and the boy could grab the rope and swing down. Ryan could have safely stayed where he was, but Darrell felt he had to be seen to be doing something in order to calm Joe down. 'I'm going to get the rope, okay?' Darrell turned to run to the ute. But the next time he looked back, he saw Joe running to the crane.

'No! Don't do it!'

In an instant, Joe was at the old Bedford, reaching in to grab Ryan's shirt.

Joe's head arched back, his body shuddered and his teeth were bared by facial muscles contracting into a terrible grimace. Joe had his hands around Ryan so now Ryan was being electrocuted, too. His body was bent over backwards, vibrating.

Suddenly, Darrell was faced with a whole new scenario. There was no time to grab a rope. If he didn't act, Joe and the boy were dead. But if he touched Joe, he was just going to wind up stuck to him, with all of them being killed. He knew that electricity renders a person immobile – sending their muscles into spasm by firing up the body's nerve system. And that the flow of positively charged atoms sticks a person to the power source. Touching Joe meant certain electrocution, but Darrell knew what he had to do. He sprinted towards the crane, dropped his shoulder and smashed into Joe.

Next thing Darrell knew, he was lying on the grass, waking, with his whole left side numb. He felt lethargic and strange. He had just survived 19,000 volts.

The next part of the story was not mentioned in Darrell's official citation. When I first interviewed him, Darrell never mentioned it to me either, presumably out of sensitivity for the feelings of Joe's family.

The citation says that Joe Honner remained unconscious after he touched the truck, but Darrell and Anthony say that as Darrell got back to his feet, Joe got up too.

The boy was still in the cabin, safe again now that he wasn't being earthed by his father. But Joe was just as determined to grab him despite what he'd just experienced. He staggered towards the crane.

'No! Stop!' Darrell yelled, moving his weary, shaky body in front of Joe. Anthony watched the two men wrestle until Joe – who was the larger of them – overpowered Darrell and pushed him back onto the mudguard of the crane. The electricity hit Darrell again. He blacked out and fell.

Joe ran in, stepped over Darrell – lying at the door of the crane – and grabbed his son again. Anthony watched as the power pulsed through Joe for a second time before he collapsed on top of Darrell.

Joe had moved Ryan out onto the mudguard which sloped beneath the door, and the three-year-old was now slipping slowly down it. When the boy was about a foot off the ground, Anthony saw electricity arc from his foot into the wet grass.

Ryan kept sliding and he hit the ground, coming to rest leaning between the tyre and the mudguard with the blue arcs pulsing through his body.

Anthony, the only one left standing, ran to fetch a piece of plastic conduit he'd just taken off the pole's strainer wire. He knew that the conduit would not carry a current. He thrust it in between Ryan and the truck, thinking he could lever the boy away.

Next thing he knew, he was sliding along the grass, on his back, having been thrown metres away by the shock. The conduit should have been a perfect insulator, but Anthony later figured there must have been enough moisture on it to carry the charge.

He ran back to Darrell and Joe, both on the ground. Darrell was conscious again. 'Don't touch me,' he said, aware that the electricity was periodically arcing out and booting him.

'I'll go and call the ambulance.' Anthony jumped in the Land Rover with Darrell's two boys still safely inside and he drove hard to a farmhouse owned by Darrell about a mile away. He got there and didn't know the ambulance number so he rang his mum for her to call triple-0.

Darrell had, meanwhile, managed to get to his feet, free from the crane. Whatever damage he had just done to his body was hardly registering, because now he could see young Ryan on the ground next to him with electricity arcing into his left elbow and his head, then coming out through his feet so strongly his sandshoe was smoking.

Despite what had just happened, Darrell knew he had to do something. He knew, too, that if he reached in and just grabbed the boy, he'd be stuck to him and they'd both fry. But he thought that if he went in crouched up, the current – by sending his back muscles into spasm – might fling him backwards and clear of danger.

So that's what he did.

He bent his back but leant a little backwards, knowing that he'd want to fall that way. He knew what was about to happen and he was scared. Very scared. Even before his hand touched the boy, he could see the sparks reaching out for his fingers. But he kept going, gripped the boy's shirt hard . . . and everything went blank again.

When Darrell regained consciousness for the third time, he was three metres clear of the crane. Ryan was a little further away. His plan had worked.

He crawled to Joe and found he wasn't breathing. Darrell pinched Joe's nose closed, opened his mouth and put his lips to Joe's, filling his unconscious friend's lungs with air. As captain of the local Country Fire Service brigade, Darrell had done the St John's Ambulance course but he'd never had to apply it before. It took a few minutes of steady breathing, but suddenly Joe took a small gulp. Then a larger breath.

Darrell moved over to Ryan's limp body with a desperate hope that he was alive but expecting him dead. The boy wasn't breathing. He had to try something so Darrell began breathing into his mouth, too. And it almost came as a surprise when he also spluttered back to life.

Anthony returned to find his uncle working on Ryan. Darrell handed the now crying boy over and went back to the father, still lying by the side of the crane.

The power was off. The fuses had tripped at last and it was all safe. But Darrell heard Joe let out a big sigh, and suddenly he stopped breathing. Darrell got down to work again, breathing into his mouth, pumping at his heart. Anthony watched the intensity of the moment, but after about five minutes, Darrell stopped and turned to his nephew. 'We better go.' Joe Honner was dead.

They put the boy in the ute and Darrell drove about fifteen

kilometres towards the nearest town, Elliston, before they met the ambulance coming the other way with Anthony's mum on board, too. She took over the ute.

Darrell's body was numb. The current had blasted hundreds of little holes out of his flesh where the electricity went in and out. Most were small, like someone had poked him with a red-hot needle – especially around his ankles and his left arm – but some were bigger, and one on his back near his shoulderblade was the size of a twenty-cent piece.

At the hospital, Darrell remembers nurses putting cream on him before he flaked out.

*

Darrell had nineteen stitches put in his left arm, 37 stitches in his back, five on his right foot and five on his left. His left little toe was amputated because it was burnt to charcoal.

When the numbness started to subside, weeks later, he complained to the doctors about terrible headaches, stomach pain, chest pain. His back was still numb so that didn't worry him too much.

Doctors took X-rays and found he'd broken four vertebrae. The back muscles had contracted so fiercely when he'd grabbed Ryan, the compression had cracked the bones.

'The pain was coming out the front of my body,' says Darrell. 'My back was numb. It destroyed my nerves.'

Darrell had a wife and four young children to support and a farm to look after. He lay there in his hospital bed, worrying about all the work that needed doing. The shearing had been done, but the bales needed loading. It was time to start spraying the winter crop.

Neighbours helped. Anthony stayed on at the farm for a while until Darrell could return. But Darrell would never be able to work the place properly again.

'I'm a farmer and your back's got to be good to be a farmer,' he says. 'So I was virtually buggered. First of all I just did the basics, then I employed somebody. The drought came back and when you're in drought there's not a lot of farm work to do, you've just got to look after your stock. I cut a lot of corners.'

He'd just drive the header but wouldn't get out to grease it, hoping that it kept going. It did that first year, but he ended up paying for it the second year when equipment started to fail. He ignored the fences so they grew steadily worse. It was all building the stress. Throw in sleep deprivation from the back pain and the nightmares and it was not a happy situation.

His children – Crystal, two, Liam, four, Kym, seven, and Natasha, eight – found it hard. Suddenly they didn't have a dad to play with any more.

In 1989, a year after the accident, Darrell became the first-ever recipient of the Cross of Valour. A spokesman for the then governor-general, Bill Hayden, said that since it had never been awarded before, it was felt that the first recipient should have shown such extraordinary courage that there could be no controversy. There was none.

The Trees were taken to Canberra. They dressed up and hobnobbed for a day. The award was greatly appreciated, but Darrell was still very much in the depths of despair. It couldn't stop him wallowing in the doubts about whether he could have done something different. All the what-ifs. 'The acknowledgment was good,' he says. 'But people who have these accidents should have support straight after. I got a bit of compensation out of SGIC [State Government Insurance Commission] but that took eighteen months. What am I supposed to do in the meantime?'

I ask how he fared psychologically.

'It's pretty hard mentally. You know what happens when you're up, people knock you down. People say you're mad for risking your life for other people. It's hard. You get plenty of it, too, don't worry.'

His wife, Josie, is a little more forthcoming. 'He was in bed all the time and in a lot of pain and it was *very tough for me for five whole years*,' she says, putting a full deep-voiced emphasis on every one of those last words. 'After the accident we went through hell. But I've moved on and he's moved on. He's in a lot of pain now, of course. I've had to go everywhere on my own. He just sort of stays home, does a bit on the farm. He potters around and doesn't do a lot of lifting. He's riddled with pain all the time.'

'What happened after five years to make things better?' I ask.

'He sort of realised what was really happening in our life and with our kids. He wouldn't take any medication 'cause he's not one of those people that likes taking medication. He tried a lot, but it just sent him mad, if you know what I mean. I don't want to go into it because it was pretty horrific what I went through, trying to shoot himself and all sorts of things. I couldn't say one thing about the kids. He'd throw chairs and he'd get up through the night and bash the walls. "Why? Why me?" All that sort of stuff. My neighbours had to sort of help me. I don't like bringing it up, but I did go through a lot for five years.'

It hadn't always been like this. Darrell's great attraction for Josie had been his wonderful kindness, right from the time they'd met at Josie's sister's wedding. In those days, people weren't really invited to weddings. Everybody pitched in with the food and everybody turned up. They were great community gatherings. So the two met and dated for four years before they married. 'He was very caring and loving. He was a gentleman and he still is. He's a top man,' says Josie. 'He was such a placid man, he'd help you out. I used to help him reaping and seeding and fencing, laying troughs and lamb tailing. And he used to help me doing dishes, washing floors, vacuuming and folding the washing. We worked together. But once the accident happened, that was it. He lost interest in everything, in farming, you name it. But he just kept going and going and going. I tried to push him. The doctor told me that was the best thing to do to make him realise that life goes on.

'I actually went over to the doctor in the early hours one morning and spoke to her. She called Darrell over about nine o'clock and about four months after that he came to his senses and realised he was going to lose me and the kids if things didn't change. He still hasn't been a hundred per cent but he's been a hell of a lot better.'

*

Darrell went on to meet other bravery award recipients and he learned that a lot of them suffered similarly. I ask if it was any consolation to him when he realised that.

'A little bit. I just wish it never happened, that's all. It destroyed my life. I guess everybody feels the same way. Everybody suffers. There's no easy way out.'

I say that what really astounds me about his actions was the act of saving Ryan, having already been knocked unconscious twice.

'What can you do? Sit there and watch a boy die? It's worthwhile in the sense that I saved him.'

Have you ever regretted it?

'If Ryan had died I would have regretted it.'

What's your relationship with him now?

'I haven't had much to do with them [Ryan and his mother]. I just leave them alone. Meeting up probably brings back memories for them, too, as it does for me. They choose not to come to me so . . . His mother wasn't too happy with everything that went on. You can understand, I guess.'

I ask what he meant by 'wasn't too happy'.

'For a start she blamed me for driving the crane. She reck-
oned I drove the crane into the powerlines.'

Darrell has received updates from Ryan's uncles and
learned that Ryan went to uni, taught in Ireland and has done
a stint living in Kuwait. It is some consolation that he is getting
on with a full life.

*

In the last few years, Darrell's back has started going bad again,
but the boys have come home. He tried telling his sons to go
into mining where all the money is – that farming's a mug's
game – but they both wanted to come back for the lifestyle.
He confines himself to checking the water troughs and doing
a few odd jobs. Every night he needs a hot bath for pain relief
so he can get a little sleep.

Now in his early 60s, he and Josie plan to retire to Cow-
ell on the Spencer Gulf in the next few years. They're putting
their house on a truck and moving it holus-bolus to a block
they own there.

While reinterviewing Darrell in October 2010, he tells me
about Joe returning to the crane for the second time to rescue
his son.

'Very stupid, but courageous as well,' I say.

'Hmmmmm.'

'He deserved a bravery award, too, would you say?'

There follows a long, empty silence which he declines to fill.

I realise how easy it would be for Darrell to hold a bitter resentment towards Joe. All the guy had to do was stay
calm, tell his kid not to move, and wait for the fuse to blow.
They would have all walked away with nothing more than a
dramatic story to tell. Instead, he's been obfuscating the dead
man's true role for all these years, not wanting to besmirch his
memory. And that takes a whole different sort of courage.

THREE

Allan Sparkes

Jai Galloway and his two mates decided it was too wet for school. They didn't want to walk all the way there, get 'satched', then have to sit around in soaking clothes all day. Better to ditch their bags, get their boogie boards and sneak down to the creek. It had been bucketing for days — heavy, flooding rain that was running quickly off the nearby hills.

The creek, which on most days was a dry ditch through a park, had become a swirling brown torrent. The boys had a brilliant morning floating down the swollen stream or running at it and skimming across it on their boards, but after a few hours they were cold and had had enough. All three got out, but as his two mates walked away towards the industrial estate on the other side of the road, Jai spotted a little whirlpool. *Cool.*

'Wait a bit,' the twelve-year-old called out, 'I'm just gunna skim across this.' They didn't hear him. *Shit, eh*. He lined up the vortex and ran at it, intending to bounce off the far lip.

When his mates, Dwayne Teece and Gareth Owen, turned around to see where Jai was, he wasn't there any more.

*

Allan Sparkes, an overweight 38-year-old detective with thinning hair, was making tea – white, two sugars – back at the Coffs Harbour police station, pretty chuffed about his morning's work. He and his partner, Gavin Dengate, 29, had just got back to the office after retrieving some stolen jewellery for an old lady in a nursing home. It was only a couple of rings and gold necklaces, but they'd been given to her by her late husband and were the only treasures left from her marriage. The old dear had been very grateful. It was one of those jobs that made him feel good to be a policeman.

Still at the sink, Allan heard two beeps on the police radio, signalling an urgent message was about to come through. 'Any car in the vicinity of Ann Street and Marcia Street, there is a report that a child has been swept into a stormwater drain.'

Detectives don't normally respond to such calls, but Allan and Gavin looked at each other, tipped their cups into the sink, and headed for the car. They knew every minute might count.

There was an awful lot of water around. Earlier in the morning, Allan had been to the beach and seen that the ocean was a foaming froth of chocolate as creeks spewed out from the banana-clad hills surrounding the New South Wales north coast town. The weather station recorded that 195 millimetres fell on the town in the 30 hours to 3 pm that day.

Allan and Gavin were first on the scene. They saw a park on one side of Ann Street and the industrial estate on the other. They found two sodden thirteen-year-olds at a panel beater's shop across the road from the park.

'He was right behind us one minute,' one of them said. 'The next minute he was gone.'

The boys took the coppers across the road to the creek and pointed down to the little whirlpool. It was the only place Jai could have gone. The whirlpool marked the spot where the creek got funnelled into the underground stormwater system which appeared to head under Ann Street and the industrial estate, towards Coffs Creek, a mangrove-lined estuary about 800 metres away. The kid's chance of survival seemed remote.

A manhole out the front of the panel beating shop looked like it was connected to the stormwater system, so the coppers pulled up the cover, unstrapped the pistols from their ankles and dropped into it.

They found that the manhole went down to a pipe about 90 centimetres in diameter – a little smaller than a standard hula hoop. And as Allan peered into the dark pipe, he could see something about 80 metres away. He couldn't make out what it was, but he knew that if that was the kid, they had to get to him fast. There'd been a lull in the rain, but if it picked up again – which it looked like it would – then he'd be swamped in there. So Allan went back up the manhole, got a rope from the panel beater, tied it around his waist and dropped straight back in.

Water came almost halfway up the pipe's diameter, and when Allan got in there – all six-feet-two (188 centimetres) and 110 kilograms of him – it backed up behind him and gave a hell of a push. He'd only gone a few metres when he decided the rope was too light for this torrent. Gavin pulled him back the ten or fifteen metres and, by this time, a State Emergency Services (SES) truck had arrived. The SES guys had a more solid rope. And while Allan stripped off his shoes, shirt and tie, one of the SES blokes tied a bowline in the rope and looped it over him. They gave him a torch and down he went again, feet first, with little more than a plan to tug three times when he wanted to be pulled out.

The torrent washed him like a leaf down to the obstruction in the pipe. He got there in seconds to find that it was just debris. *Shit, this kid is gone.*

Now he had to look after himself. He tugged on the rope three times, but the torrent was damming up behind his girth so the pipe was suddenly a lot more than half full. Gavin, meanwhile, had crawled down the pipe and could see Allan was in trouble. He signalled for the dozen or so men – police and SES – now on the surface to start pulling.

Allan was on his back, being dragged headfirst into the flood. In order to breathe, he lifted his head to create an air pocket around his face. He gulped and spluttered a breath, then straightened out again to streamline his bulk against the torrent. He felt the men pulling the rope, his body edging up the pipe, then he lifted his head again to find more air.

In the blackness, with the walls closing in, he doubted he was going to make it. He'd overreached. *This is the end.* But he'd flatten again and feel the tug until he needed air, and he'd lift his head once more to find it. Eighty metres was a long way to be pulled like that. The darkness eased eventually and, suddenly, he was back in daylight. He was almost surprised to be alive, but there was no joy in survival. They'd lost the boy.

Moments after he climbed out of the manhole, however, a call came over the police radio. Screams had been heard 600 metres away next to the Pacific Highway. The police jumped in their Commodores and raced through the ugly little industrial area of Marcia Street to the highway corner where traffic was already building. A manhole cover lay flipped up on the road. As the police car door opened, Allan heard a noise that was to etch itself into his brain – the shriek of a child screaming for his life.

Examining the manhole, all they could see was water bubbling up to the surface. The scream seemed to be rising up in the bubbles. People yelled down the manhole, but, having been in a pipe himself, Allan knew that was futile. Gavin appeared with a ladder and stuck it down the hole.

While there were SES and other rescue specialists there, the two detectives took it upon themselves to step up, or rather, down. They'd asked for scuba gear but there was no time to wait. The risk of more rain continued to hang over this kid's life. Allan took off his slacks, leaving him now only in sodden boxers, as he and Gavin descended the ladder.

They took deep breaths and dropped down into what seemed like an underwater chamber. There was no current to speak of. They felt around and found that there was some sort of passage under a beam. So, still holding their breath, they crawled under it. They didn't know what might be on the other side – if they were heading to an air pocket or a fast-flowing death trap. They just went forwards. This was the only way in. There was no time for thinking.

Past the beam, they lifted their heads and popped up in an air pocket. Shining a torch, they saw it was a small junction area where six pipes converged and emptied into the pit area that they were standing in. The pipes were raised up, so those with a heavier flow poured in on top of them. Some didn't have much flow at all.

And over the din of the cascading water, the boy's scream reverberated off the concrete walls. He hadn't let up at all. They knew he was up one of the six pipes, but with the roaring water and the echoing squeal, it was impossible to tell which one.

They each started crawling a little way into the various pipes to see if they could hear him more clearly. Allan went up one and thought the scream sounded a little louder.

'I think he's up here,' he called to Gavin. 'I'll keep going up this pipe and see if I can find him.' There was no room for the two of them, so Gavin, now knowing the direction of the pipe, decided to go back to the surface to see if he could find another way into it, perhaps upstream of the boy.

Allan had a rope tied to him, but it was more hindrance than help, so he took it off to start dragging himself up the pipe against the current. His toes and fingers gripped the slime as he edged towards the scream that just never let up. Always in his head was the thought that it would start raining again. 'That was what upset me the most,' he'd recall, 'the fear of being so close and not getting him. Just this pitiful horrific scream going on.'

People were yelling things down from above and ambulance officer Mick Marr, who'd now swum down into the junction to replace Gavin, relayed them on. 'Have we got him yet? Can you see him?'

Allan was trying to focus on the job and sent back a few expletive-laden comments to please be quiet till he got there.

On the surface, council engineers had arrived with maps and were talking about digging up the road with a backhoe. The scuba gear was on the way in the likely event the detectives failed to bring the boy up.

And there was Allan, about 30 metres up this pipe, when he saw a little white face in his torchlight maybe ten metres away. Allan's pipe joined the boy's pipe at a T-intersection. As it turned out, had Jai not grabbed whatever it was he had hold of, his pipe dropped off at 45 degrees into a grille and certain death. Allan had to convince the petrified child to stop screaming and climb into his pipe.

The boy reluctantly did as he was told and was washed down into Allan's arms. Allan locked him up in a bear hug to let him know he was safe. He wedged himself in the pipe so they didn't move and told the kid, 'Say, "thank you, God".'

'Thank you, God,' came a little voice in reply.

Allan started to cry and so did the boy. He could see Mick peering up the pipe and he let himself be washed down towards him.

*

Jai Galloway's near-hysterical mother, Val, arrived at the scene just as they were bringing him to the surface. The television cameras captured the small dark-haired boy in Speedos and a lurid purple, blue and yellow singlet being pulled by the arms out of the manhole as the crowd cheered.

The first thing he said to Val as they were reunited was, 'Sorry, Mum, I lost my glasses.' The shaking child could barely see without the expensive Coke-bottle things, but his head darted left and right, taking in all the fuss – the fire engines, the ambulances, the people and the traffic. The news cameras flashed. Jai was wrapped in a space blanket and rushed to hospital.

*

Allan emerged from the drain, covered in mud, with blood on his back and shoulders. He returned to the police station where the Scientific Unit had a shower in its office. 'I remember just sitting in the cubicle, weeping with a whole range of emotions. My wife, Deb, brought a fresh set of clothes in and I had the afternoon off with her. We went to lunch and we went to the hotel. Everyone saw it on the news. Gavin was there. We were hailed as heroes. So I went to bed feeling pretty good about things.'

Allan had a feeling of absolute euphoria for the next 48 hours, after having plumbed the depths of thinking the boy was dead, facing death himself, then saving Jai and himself. There was a lot to get his head around. He kept seeing it all, over and over, in his mind.

The incident had occurred on a Friday and two days later, on the Sunday, he had to report in at the Goulburn police academy for a homicide investigators course. He was still seeing the events crisp and clear in his head every time he shut his eyes. He couldn't sleep and now other events started piling up on top of this one.

Allan's euphoria promptly faded and the emotional flood-gates opened. All the traumas seen in twenty years of police work were suddenly let loose to prey upon his sleep-deprived mind. Ten months earlier, a camouflaged gunman had ambushed two policemen, one of whom Allan knew, at Crescent Head. 'We were called down there to rescue people in the vicinity and then we had to go and search for the gunman.' They found the gunman's body then found the bodies of the policemen – Peter Addison and Bob Spears. 'That was a very, very sad and terrifying time that stayed with me.'

Emotionally, he'd been able to keep the lid on that one. This latest incident, however, popped the cork: he continued working, though, because he thought he could get through it.

'I had severe depression and I wasn't getting any sleep. I was sick and becoming suicidal. Only those at the point of taking their own life understand the pain. It's an indescribable pain. It's not like a physical pain, but your whole body and mind are just hurting so bad. And nothing will stop it. I have great sympathy for those who have taken their own life because I know what they were thinking. They were craving that delicious feeling that the pain would stop. I didn't want to die, but I just couldn't deal with the pain. I used alcohol as a crutch and that just made things worse.

'I went to my commander and said, "I need help." It was a major thing for anybody to say they needed help. I believed I could carry out my work to a basic level. I was trying to battle through. But he decided that because my work performance was suffering he would transfer me out of investigations back into uniform on general duties. That was going to leave me even more exposed to being the first response at dramatic events. My wife and child could have been in danger because of my health. I don't think I'm unique in this, but I never told Deb how sick I was. Her mum had just passed away and I didn't want to burden her any more.'

On 6 October 1996 – five months and three days after the incident – contemplating ways and means of killing himself, he knew he could go no further. Allan handed his gun and his handcuffs to a work mate. 'Take me home.'

It was the saddest day of his life.

Next morning, the police psychiatrist told him he had to make a decision: 'If you want to live I can help you. And if you want to die, I can't help you. You have to make a choice.' Allan chose life and was prescribed Mellaril (thioridazine, an antipsychotic drug then widely used to treat psychosis and schizophrenia). The psychiatrist said the medication would stop Allan from making any cognitive decisions and allow him to sleep.

'I was out of my mind with sleeplessness by this stage because of the cesspool going on in my head. With the Mellaril, all I could do was get up, make a coffee, walk to the edge of the beach, have a cigarette and sleep. I was a walking zombie. I slept and slept and slept. After two weeks I thought, I can't go on like this. I stopped taking the Mellaril. I said to the psychiatrist, "I have to be able to think again." He put me on a strong antidepressant and I got on to the process of recovering my body and soul. I felt like Humpty Dumpty – a shattered eggshell that had to be put back together again.'

In January 1998, Allan received a letter telling him he'd been discharged from the force, medically unfit. There was a three-month appeal window but he was in no state to fight it. He felt it was a diabolical betrayal – to do what he did only to be shafted. He lived for the coppers and here he was, with a wife and baby, thrown on the street.

Soon after, he received a letter telling him he'd been awarded the country's highest bravery award, the Cross of Valour. He was only the third person to receive one.

Allan was disappointed his partner Gavin Dengate received the second highest honour, the Star of Courage. 'He did just about everything I did that day, but I only saved one person. He saved two, because he saved my life when he entered that first pipe to get me out.'

*

Jai Galloway didn't last any longer at school than Allan Sparkes lasted in the force. He was kicked out at thirteen. According to his mum he'd been a normal kid before the accident. He liked the beach and fishing. He'd wagged school a couple of times and got in trouble for not doing assignments, but that was it.

She tries not to blame the incident for what followed but she says that the trouble started in the months after. 'For quite a few years he was – how can I put it? – it was like he didn't really care.'

She attributed his change to the different crowd he was hanging out with. 'Maybe I should have been there more with him. I couldn't be there and work, being a single mum. I blamed myself. I was a mess for quite a while. Just the not knowing if he was going to survive and how I would have taken it had they not got to him.'

For his part, Jai says he has lost all memory of life before the accident. His previous life seemed to get obliterated by the video that played in his head every time he shut his eyes . . . He's back in that freezing pipe waiting to die, going smash against an unseen corner then smash into another, and crash into a junction. He sees daylight, grabs a grille and screams at passing cars with his fingers poking through, before he is swept away, and again resigns himself to oblivion, until . . . Smash! He hits something else and hangs on to it, screaming in the blackness. Screaming, screaming, screaming.

Every time he shut his eyes.

He still doesn't like to link that giant plug hole to all the crap that followed in his life.

I seem more intent on making the point than him, but he says that after the accident, for some reason, crime felt good. 'Mum would growl at me for doing something wrong and I'd yell at her. I'd lock myself in my room then jump out the window and that night I'd be out stealing something to make myself feel better about what I'd done to make myself so cranky. After I'd done something wrong, I'd just feel better about things. I don't know why. It's weird to feel better after stealing something off someone. That's not usual, but that's how it felt to me. Like, if I stole a car, I felt proud of it. Mum used to say, "You can't keep doing this. You'll go to jail." And I said, "Mum, I don't care any more."

'I used to just steal a car, go for a rally drive out bush then come back and burn it in the middle of town so the next morning everyone could see it. I don't know why, but I felt good about putting it where I did. I was putting myself on display to get myself locked up. I might as well have written "Jai was here" on it. There was a lot of crime going on when I was in town. Everything that happened, the coppers were on my door.'

I ask what sort of crime he'd been into.

'The main stuff was car theft, bashing people, break and enters, robberies. Stuff like that. Everything except for the real big shit like killing people and bank robs. I didn't go that far.' He has a laugh, before continuing: 'If I was walking on a street at night and I saw another bloke, I'd walk over, start talking to him. As he starts to walk away I'd call him back for a minute and ask for a smoke, and as he's getting a smoke out for me I'd turn around and hit him. Drop him on the spot and start bashing into him. Then my mates would come over and start doing it. Today, I look back at all the bad stuff I've done and I regret nearly every single thing.'

Jai never thought he'd wind up in 'the big house', but in what seemed like the blink of an eye, he found himself having done four stints by the time he was 21. When he got out in May 2005, his mum told him that if he went back again she was going to disown him.

'That just automatically went straight to the top of my head and I just stopped everything. I haven't even thought about doing something wrong again. I can't afford to go to jail, lose my missus, lose my mum. I'd be buggered. I'd have no one.'

During his life of crime, he had never talked about the incident in the drain but around the time of his last stretch inside, he found that he could start to get it out.

*

Eleven years after Jai Galloway's accident, Allan Sparkes is down in the dry creek bed where it all began. It's the first time he's been back. Jai is meant to meet us here after a Centrelink appointment but he hasn't shown up.

'I used to give references for him in his various court matters — about the trauma that it caused and the impact on his life. I think they got tired of hearing it from me in the end,' says Allan, as we fill in the hours, waiting. But Allan never tired of writing the references and offering his opinion that Jai wasn't responsible for his actions. It saddened him every time he had to do it. And he was frustrated that he couldn't do more to help the guy, but he was in no state to be helping others when he was flat out looking after himself. Allan understood Jai because he knew the demons that had been let loose in his own head. Others didn't understand. Some of his former police colleagues had told him it would have been better had he left the little shit to drown.

A couple of years after the incident, Allan told the psychiatrist he wanted to get off the medication. The shrink told him the best way to rebuild the mind was to rebuild the body.

And so, two months after receiving the Cross of Valour from then governor-general Sir William Deane, he vowed to his daughter Nikola that he'd never smoke again. He tore up his packet and threw it in the bin. He began a rigorous training regime that saw him spend as much as eight hours a day exercising. He dropped his alcohol consumption to negligible levels and turned fat into muscle.

He got his life back on track and set up a private investigations business. Past 50, he looks fitter and healthier now than he did in the photos from 1996. He wound up the business in 2008 and bought a boat in the United Kingdom, spending eighteen months sailing it back home with the family, only returning because Nikola wanted to finish high school in Australia.

*

Eventually we make contact with Jai. He's at the Aldi supermarket and he wants some money to be in a photo. I tell him we can't pay him as such, but I offer to pay for his groceries. We meet him outside the supermarket and he leads us in. He is short with a slouching, loose gait that takes its inspiration, I gather, from the American ghettos via various juvenile institutions. Inside there are two trolleys chock full of groceries that come to 170 dollars.

He tells us he was never going to meet us at the creek. He hasn't been back there since a week after the incident when he wrote, 'Jai was here, 3/5/96 never to return.'

We head off to the beach to take some photos. Jai and Allan are talking about the consequences of that day. Allan says he wants to have coffee with Jai in coming weeks. 'I want you to tell me your story. I've never heard your side of the story.'

'What do you mean my story?' asks Jai.

'What happened to you.'

'I got sucked down the drain and I turned into a prick.'

'But do you understand why?'

'No.'

'Have you heard of post-traumatic stress disorder?'

'I've heard of it.'

'I think that's what you had.'

Allan explains his post-traumatic stress disorder arising out of the shooting and the rescue and how he was unable to work after it. 'I'm quite sure you had the same illness as me. You just reacted differently.'

Jai says a doctor once diagnosed him with attention deficit disorder. The doctor gave him some drugs for that, but he got into even more trouble when he was on them.

Jai seems a little wary, but they agree to catch up next time Jai's in town for his Centrelink appointment.

He lives up the mountain now, about 45 minutes out of town. His sister Tammie, who lives in the same village, attributes his change to his girlfriend Chloe, a local girl. 'She's got her head on straight,' Tammie says.

The one-time tough guy still won't get into a bath and, if he has done the dishes, he has to get Chloe to pull the plug out of the sink because he can't stand to see the water spinning down that hole.

FOUR

Victor Boscoe

Searching for Cross of Valour recipient Victor Boscoe, I ring one of the few Boscoes in the Brisbane phone book. She turns out to be Victor's cousin and she tells me Victor has disappeared off the face of the earth and if I find him to please tell him to give her a ring.

He hasn't quite disappeared to that extent. He still has his old job as a fireman at Brisbane airport and that's how I eventually find him. But, he explains, 'I've pulled out of life for a while. No, shouldn't say that. I've pulled into a different life. I'm just rebuilding my life after everything that happened.'

I apologise for bringing it all up again so many years later but he says he is happy to talk. 'I'm a firey. I deal with everything every day, so feel free to ask.'

It was September 1993 and the nuggety firefighter was out shopping with his wife, Narelle. The 45-year-old had been off sick with a virus for the previous three weeks. His resting pulse had sat on 200, and just climbing the stairs had made him want to pass out. But a diet from a Chinese herbalist – broth of chicken bones and green vegies with lots of snow peas – had got him back on track. This was the first day in weeks he'd felt even half decent. He wanted to buy some chewing gum.

Victor and Narelle were walking through an arcade in the Westfield Shopping Centre in Strathpine, northern Brisbane, when, as they passed Franklins, normality suddenly shifted. Two men came towards them with guns. One had a balaclava on, the other was pulling one down over his face. 'Everybody get down.' It was like some sort of show at a theme park as the men waved their weapons about.

Two security guards, about five metres from Victor, walking out of Franklins, were the targets. The robbers shouted at the crowd. 'Get back! Keep back!' Onlookers screamed. Victor retreated into a fruit shop, behind a crate of oranges on display out the front. He heard a loud bang at the back of the shop and spun around to see what it was. While his back was turned, there was another bang from the direction of the bandits – a muffled crack, like a small-calibre gun.

Then it was over. The robbers fled (with 70,000 dollars, it turned out). Victor came out of the fruit shop and saw one of the security guys lying on the ground and presumed he'd been shot. He figured there were plenty of people around to give first aid to the guy. Even with his training, there wasn't much he could do for a bullet wound. But if this was going to be a murder investigation, the police would need a description. So he took off in pursuit of the robbers down a narrow service corridor as his wife pleaded with him to stop. She, too, thought the bang had been a gunshot. 'Don't worry,' he told her, 'nothing's going to happen.'

He followed the men to the car park. As it happened, he saw them get into a car parked one along from his own vehicle. *I haven't seen them with the balaclavas off yet.* So he jumped in his Commodore and followed them to the exit. By the time the bandits pulled into traffic, heading south on Gympie Road, he was about seven cars behind them in the queue of cars waiting to get out of the car park. When he reached the exit, they were long gone. So much for his car chase. He was about to head back to Narelle when a car came screaming past on the far side of the road, heading north. It was them. They'd gone down to a roundabout and come back the other way. And now they pulled into a little shopping centre car park diagonally opposite Victor on Gympie Road.

So when a break came in the traffic, Victor drove across the median strip and quietly pulled into the car park, just past a Sizzlers restaurant. He parked where they'd have to drive by to get back out. He took out a newspaper and pretended to read while he watched them get out of their car. Their balaclavas were off now, and he saw that one of them had a shotgun under his overcoat and another was carrying a large metal canister. They walked towards him, and he looked at their faces, took in their details: height, hair colour, clothing. They came closer. They looked at him, but he wasn't too worried because they were sussing out everything. He was sure they didn't suspect him. But they came closer and closer, stopping when they got to a white Mitsubishi Cordia parked nose to nose with his own car. They opened the doors and got in.

I've got enough to take to the police. He put down the paper and kicked over the engine. They were looking at him again. He looked back at them, and quietly pulled away, happy that he had got a good description.

Victor was going to drive back to his wife, but he couldn't get across the three lanes of northbound traffic on Gympie Road, so he turned left and stayed in the left lane with a view to going around the block, left, left and left again. Suddenly, the bandits whom he had left behind in the car park screamed past him in the right lane. They did 'a split-arse turn' from the right-hand lane, in front of some other cars ahead in the left lane, hard into Samsonvale Road – the same street Victor was planning to turn into.

At the rate they were going, Victor expected they'd be long gone by the time he reached the same corner. He went around it, but there they were – facing him on the opposite side of the road, pulled over with one wheel of the Cordia up on the kerb and a pistol pointing at him from the driver's window. He was the target now.

He had to make a decision and make it fast. He figured that if he drove past them, he was a sitting duck. So he floored his Commodore, bounced over the raised median strip and pointed the car directly at the pistol. He doesn't remember fear. Just a sense that he had to avoid injury, calculate his risks and act.

The bullbar missed the driver by centimetres when it slammed hard into the little Japanese car. His plan was to throw the shooter off, then drive away, but as Victor recovered from the impact, he saw the second thief now standing on the footpath pointing a shotgun across the bonnet at him. Victor ducked, putting his head on the passenger seat. He grappled for the gear stick poking into his guts. He had to get it into reverse. But as if changing gears down there wasn't hard enough, he'd had a brand new engine put in a few weeks earlier and they'd put in the wrong gear box, so he had to rev it a little in neutral before he could change gear. It was a bastard of a car to drive at the best of times.

He got it into reverse and drove back. Boom! The shotgun sounded like a cannon as the pellets hit the door. Windows shattered. Even though Victor's head was down on the seat, he could still see the gunman standing on the footpath above him. Point blank. As the shotgun swung towards him again, he had to get the revs up a little, push the stick back into drive, and go forwards again. Bang! And as the gun swung forwards, he went back into reverse. Bang! Then forwards. Bang! The gun followed him and shots rang out, glass fragments flew all around. About six shots were fired in all. Victor had missed the full blast from all of them – just – but he was bleeding with glass and lead pellets in his head, hands, arms, back and legs. His right arm throbbed and his back felt like it was on fire.

Having given Victor a good blast, the bandits abandoned the Cordia and ran to a van that was waiting for them. (Witnesses reported that a man had pulled up in it during the shooting, got out and just walked away down the street.)

The two bandits sped off.

Victor sat up, did a U-turn then turned left, heading north on Gympie Road in pursuit of the van. He was angry now. Getting hurt had pissed him off. *Shit!* The bullbar was scraping on the wheel. He got out and pulled it away. Resuming the chase, he drove up a hill, hurting real bad. He was looking down a tunnel, his speed climbing. And he doesn't remember the next bit. But he must have backed off and turned around, because the next thing he recalls was returning to the shopping centre, coming down the hill on remote control. The pain was intense. He had the feeling his right arm had been blown off. The only way he knew it hadn't been was that he could see his right hand on the steering wheel with the fingers moving. The little finger was a bloody mess, having taken a pellet or a shard of glass.

He was barely conscious when he got back to the Westfield car park. There were holes through the car, blood dripped down the door. His wife wasn't happy either. He had put somebody else's problem above his own life and the wellbeing of their four children.

People milled around as police took statements. A stranger took it upon herself to call him a fucking dickhead right out of the blue. A day earlier he might have agreed with her, but the comment bit hard. It was an attitude he found repeated often, if not expressed so crudely. Just as many people, however, wanted to shake his hand.

That night, home from hospital, all bandaged up, feeling pain like he'd never felt before and dosed up on goodness knows what, he sat alone with his thoughts and it felt like he was looking down on himself with his shoulders all blown away and the ribs exposed. It was an uncomfortable experience.

*

The police had suspects in the frame soon after. Victor went down and identified two guys from a book of photographs. He was sure it was them, even though the pictures showed them with near-shaved heads and he'd seen them with wigs on. The men were arrested and charged.

Then, a few days later, the police warned him that they had an inside source and that the accused men's associates were planning a home invasion on him. This changed everything. What he'd done up to this time had been calculated risk. And it was all his own risk. Now it was unpredictable and his family was in danger.

When I ask Victor what was the worst part of the whole ordeal, he nominates the entire aftermath. From the out-of-body experience onwards. 'During the incident I backed myself to do whatever I could do. I could handle that. But the aftermath took away my life as I knew it.'

With the perpetrators facing trial based partly on his evidence, Victor suffered nightmares and was always paranoid that people were watching. He'd never sit with his back to a door. The all-pervading fear of a home invasion never left them. One of his older kids moved out for safety's sake. And he's sure all the children suffered, but they didn't let on to him.

He took up bodybuilding – obsessively – and the Korean martial art, hapkido. 'Damien, my instructor, said to me that the day I learned to master this will be the day I do not need to use it.' But that mastery was still a way off.

The reaction of colleagues in the fire service was surprising. 'I had my fire station manager tell me I was an absolute disgrace to the fire service and that I must never cooperate with the media on any stories about it. And if I said anything to anybody about what he'd just said, he'd deny it all. He would never say what was so wrong with what I did. I didn't know what his problem was.' The boss stayed on Victor's case so bad he almost flipped. 'I was huge, over a hundred kilograms, ten per cent body fat, and my boss was chest high. I was on the juice,' he says, making a syringe motion, hinting at steroid use. 'A ball of rage. It crossed my mind to throw him out the second-storey window. I had to contain myself.

'Of my colleagues, some thought what I had done was good, most were indifferent and some thought I was an effing idiot. I got the same from the church I was going to at the time. They thought I was taking over the police job by trying to capture these people and had overstepped as a Christian. They said I needed intensive Bible studies to bring my thinking back in line with true Christian ways. I told them to get stuffed and walked away.'

But the worst part was his family disintegrating around him. His wife and children stayed with the church. They grew apart. Within two years of the incident, the marriage of 26 years was over. He won't blame it entirely on that day, but says it was 'in the mix'.

'I lost everything. My ex walked because I left the church, my kids walked.'

He read a lot of self-help books and kept working on the hapkido and, just as the instructor had predicted, when he mastered it, everything else fell away. 'I found an inner peace and tranquillity in my own soul from being able to look after myself.'

*

Victor Boscoe was awarded the Cross of Valour in 1996. He was greatly honoured, but he suffered doubts about whether he deserved it. How could you compare what he'd endured to the horrors faced by soldiers in trenches? Some of his colleagues had openly questioned whether he deserved it, too.

But at the investiture ceremony an old digger came up and shook his hand, then saluted him, saying he would have been proud to serve with him. It had a deep impact.

Victor isn't happy that I'd heard he'd sold his Cross of Valour. He hadn't wanted it to become public and explains that he needed the money for his divorce.

How did it feel to sell it?

'It ripped the heart out. I got the money together about twelve months later to go and buy it back, because the buyer said he'd hold it for me for twelve months, but he'd sold it on and wouldn't tell me who bought it. It was the worst thing I've ever done. Honest. To me, it wasn't worth money, it was worth my life . . . It was worse than getting divorced.'

Nevertheless, approaching 60 years old, he is upbeat about his life. 'I've spent the last five years working my heart out and I've built myself up financially to where I'm okay and emotionally I'm okay.' He got himself a part-time job in the building industry on his days off from the fire service. He started going out dancing and now has 'a good friend', Cheryl.

'She's a lovely understanding lady who appreciates what I've done. She's proud of me and her friends are the type of people who appreciate this. And we just get on good as friends.'

Would he do it again?

'My philosophy today is I've done my share, but having said that, I'm still a firey and I'm still who I am. If somebody's in trouble, I'd look at doing something, but I'm not going to kill myself for somebody else by doing something I know I can't do.'

He's not seen his eldest son or eldest daughter for years, nor one of his grandchildren.

'My other two daughters I have a reasonably good relationship with. It's not a close relationship but it's a good relationship. I'm not allowed to see the others. I keep a very small group of friends whereas before I used to know people everywhere. I was gregarious. Now I stay at home and play music.'

Victor wanted to learn guitar but his fingers were too short, so a friend suggested Latin percussion. 'It turned out I was a natural.' He plays congas, bongos, timbales, cabasa, cowbells, cymbals, guiro and a bell tree. He's played in a few bands and now he's getting together his own group. I find it hard to summon images of him wearing the frilly Latin sleeves, but life is full of surprises.

'You've got to keep growing,' he says.

FIVE

Jim Runham and Dean Hepburn

*Don't worry if your man screams at night or throws himself
down when a plane flies over the back garden.*
British army advice to the wives of soldiers evacuated
from Dunkirk

It is interesting how many people, when they see a bloke coming at them with a gun, think, like Victor Boscoe, that it is some sort of show. Their logical brain cannot make the leap from the everyday world into the primal business of survival. And that's what it was like for 37-year-old school teacher Jim Runham as he made his way out through the glass doors of his local building society in Ipswich, west of Brisbane, in November 1993, the day his life got tossed to the wind.

Jim was leaving the branch with his intellectually disabled son, Sam, thirteen, when a guy passed them in the doorway wearing a big afro wig. It was obviously a wig, but what made it look all the more preposterous was the little baseball cap on top struggling to contain the great coils of fake black hair. Jim paused outside the glass doors to watch the clown inside.

Without hesitating, Bozo jumped the counter and was suddenly waving a revolver around, and Jim's logical brain concluded that it must be a training exercise. But when the joker aimed the gun at the head of a female teller, Jim saw her stiffen and her face contort with terror, and he knew then that it was real. (Unbeknown to him, it was the teller's second armed robbery, and would end her career in banking.)

Jim turned to a guy selling newspapers from a path-side shop counter. 'Get the police. There's a bank robbery going on.'

He knew there was a security guard outside the National Australia Bank a few doors up on Brisbane Street, so he said to his son, 'Go get the policeman. Tell him to come down. Bad man is robbing the bank.' Sam, despite his disability, understood and headed off to get the guard.

It felt like just seconds before the bank robber walked out the door, and straight past Jim, so close that he'd later wish he'd just tripped the guy. Thinking that the police wouldn't be long, Jim decided to tag along and do his civic duty so he could tell them what sort of car he got into, which way he went.

Jim wasn't the most mobile of fellows. A car accident at a school camp had left him with a bad leg and a back injury. Since the accident, he'd only been able to teach part-time because he couldn't stand in front of a class for the required hours.

The thief crossed the road. Jim, hobbling behind on a walking stick, could never have kept up but for the robber deciding to count his booty as he sauntered down the street. He stopped to talk to a man outside the dole office. 'This fella is cool,' Jim thought, catching up to him now.

When the guy got to the corner of Brisbane and East streets, he looked back and saw Jim, realised he was being followed, and broke into a trot. Jim shuffled up a gear, too, and crossed East Street. The robber turned into a walkway between two buildings. About halfway down, he stopped and looked back again. Jim was right there behind him. Without thinking, the school teacher found himself talking: 'I think you better give it up, mate.' He would later be astounded at what a stupid thing it was to say to a guy with a gun who'd just robbed a bank.

The robber stopped and walked back towards Jim, telling him where to go. He reached into his bag and pulled out the revolver. As Jim watched it come out – black barrel, about fifteen centimetres long – he toyed with the idea that the gun might be fake. It looked real, but hope triumphed over reason as he back-pedalled four or five steps before falling.

The guy walked towards him, pointing the gun at his face, just metres away.

Jim looked into his eyes. *What's he gunna do?* But there was nothing there. It was like looking into an abyss. There was no sign of emotion. No fear. Nothing.

He's going to do this. It was all happening too fast to feel fear. *What do I have to do to stay alive?*

He ducked left just as the guy fired from about three steps away. The noise of the blast bounced around the enclosed area and totally dominated Jim's sense of what was going on. The bullet had hit an iron railing right where he'd just been. The concussion jarred him, turning thin air thick and creating a sensation that would haunt his bones for years – like being pushed in the sternum firmly backwards.

Shit, the gun is real.

The robber took off down the walkway, and Jim paused to gather his composure. He thought he was okay. He didn't realise a bullet fragment had lodged in his gammy leg because he didn't have full feeling down there.

The guy had gone around a corner and Jim feared he might be waiting there to jump him. Then, around that same corner came a woman with a white top, black skirt. 'What's going on?' she asked.

'He's just robbed a bank and took a shot at me. Ring the police.' Now confident that the guy was not waiting in ambush, Jim resumed the pursuit, leaving the walking stick behind. He was driven, he would later say, by a sense that it just wasn't right that this person could do what he did. He had no right to scare those women in the bank nor shoot at him. Excuse the cliché, but now it was personal.

By the time he got out of the walkway into a car park, perhaps a dozen people had come out to see what was going on.

'Which way's he gone?' Jim asked.

They pointed across the car park.

'Ring the police and tell them where he is,' Jim said, as he followed their pointed fingers down a hill towards Wharf Street. When he got to the street, the robber came back into view, perhaps only twenty metres in front, crossing a vacant lot on the other side of the road. The only way Jim could explain how he was so close to the guy again was that maybe he had waited in ambush but then been spooked by the gathering crowd.

He followed across the vacant lot, going as fast as his body would allow, while the perpetrator just trotted along, still not seeming to care. At the bottom end of the vacant lot, on Marsden Parade now, Jim had reached a big old Moreton Bay fig tree when the robber turned again, lifted the gun and aimed at him from about 25 metres away.

Jim heard the whoosh of the bullet flying overhead a split second before the crack of the gun. Next thing, the guy was running at him flat out. Really moving. *Well, this is it.*

Jim tightened his muscles and waited for the next bullet to hit. In those seconds that went on forever, waiting to die by the fig tree, he knew that if he'd had a gun he would shoot to kill. The question within himself – 'could I kill a man?' – had been answered.

But the guy didn't fire. Jim didn't understand why, but he knew he had to make a break for it up the hill. The pursuer became the pursued. Jim didn't have the speed to get away, but he had to try. So he ran up the hill with his early-70s army training coming back to mind: *I'm going to be silhouetted against the horizon. I'll be an easy shot.*

He went towards three parked cars nearby and got behind a white Ford Laser, KA model, 1981. (The details would stick with him.) He got down behind it and was looking at the guy through the little quarter window at the back. The robber walked over to the back of the car.

He's going to shoot me like a mongrel dog. Jim crouched, ready to launch himself at the guy and do the best he could, even though the guy was bigger and obviously stronger.

The bandit came to the rear of the car. He stopped and looked up, took in the surroundings, then jogged away.

When Jim stood up, he saw that there were people – witnesses – all over the place now, standing on the road watching. 'I must be a slow learner I suppose,' Jim would recall, 'because I continued the chase again. I was also joined by an onlooker – an off-duty security guard who'd witnessed part of the chase. I managed to tell him that the guy had robbed the First Provincial Building Society. Then I started to slow up. I couldn't keep up.'

The security guard continued the chase through a video store and into St Andrew's private hospital.

*

Orderly Dean Hepburn was talking to a nurse when a man came into the ward and started opening doors and looking around. Dean and the nurse stopped talking and just watched the guy. When he walked outside, they followed to ask what he wanted.

'I'm looking for Brad,' he said.

A Brad did work there, so it made a bit of sense. But just then a security guard appeared.

'Grab him! He just robbed a bank,' the guard yelled.

The guy took off down the street and Dean chased. It seemed like the right thing to do.

About 150 metres later, having run through a private house, the guy stopped, took a bag off his shoulder and slowly started pulling out a gun. It seemed to Dean that the barrel just kept on coming. It was huge. As it was almost out of the bag, the sight got caught on the zipper and the guy had to wrestle it free. *Fuck, that's a gun. That's big.*

Dean hid behind a house about 100 metres away and the security guard caught up to him. They peered around the corner and saw the guy running across a vacant lot behind the hospital. Despite having seen the enormous weapon, the two men set off after him again.

The guy was on the other side of the street from the two pursuers. He looked at them, pulled the gun out and showed it to them again. Just his luck to run into a suburb full of fucking heroes. Didn't say a word. The gun was going to do the talking now.

The first shot landed right between Dean and the guard. The next bullet went into the trees overhead.

Just then a police car came squealing down the street, and the two men ran out, waving their arms. They explained to the police what had happened as they watched the guy hopping fences. The police car raced ahead to cut him off, and Dean and the guard resumed the chase, hopping fences behind him. They ran through backyards. Kids played on trampolines.

People watered plants. Dean felt a profound sense that he had to see this through. Nothing was going to stop him, short of a bullet.

The dog squad appeared with their big slobbering Alsatians. And suddenly the robber, who hadn't been able to shake a man on a walking stick, just disappeared.

But the thing was, Dean had recognised him. He'd seen him at the hospital before. His colleague Brad had pointed him out as a member of the local footy team, the Ipswich Jets. He just couldn't remember the guy's name.

Later on, down at the police station Dean went through hundreds of photos until he came to one that looked a bit like the guy. But it wasn't quite right. He took a few minutes to compose himself and suddenly the name came to him: 'Peter Potts' (not his real name).

In the rugby league heartland of Ipswich, Potts was a somebody.

He was a somebody to the police, too. They had a photo of him and when they brought it out, Dean knew he'd got it right. 'That's him. That's him.'

Potts was arrested a few days after the robbery.

*

Jim Runham remembers walking back up the hill after he'd finished his role in the chase, thinking, 'Well, I've done my civic duty.' By the time he got back to his son, maybe twenty minutes after it all began, the boy thought his dad had been shot. The bangs of the gun had scared him. 'Nah, mate, I'm fine. Bad man can't hurt Daddy.'

It was only later that night when Jim took off his boots that he saw blood and realised that he had actually been shot.

Sam had a nightmare that night – bad men coming through the window – and Jim had to sleep on the floor in his room.

Over coming days and weeks, Sam would see things on telly that affected him, so Jim had to constantly reassure him that the bad man wasn't going to get him.

Soon after the incident, the family had just returned from a special-education camp when police rang to say they had a suspect. Jim was shown an ID board and he picked out the man he was sure had done it. It was Peter Potts.

That's when the trouble really began for Jim. 'One of our very close friends who was in the same ethnic group as the perpetrator told us we'd better leave town. "You're marked for payback if you testify."' The friend wasn't saying it as a threat, he was just trying to help. As it turned out, Potts's cousin lived over Jim's back fence. Soon after the arrest, piles of rubbish started coming over the fence along with reams of invective. 'You're a liar. You're scum. You hate blacks. White supremacist. You're only doing this because we're black.' Jim couldn't let the kids play in the backyard – not that they wanted to go out there anyway with all the abuse flying over.

The legal process took its time, winding its way up to the Supreme Court because Potts was charged with bank robbery and attempted murder. The longer it went, the more the abuse escalated. Jim reported it to the police, but what could they do? No crime had been committed. One senior policeman, a friendly chap, advised him to get a gun in case the guy came around. 'Put the first round into his chest, the second round into the ceiling and when we get there tell us you fired a warning shot.'

Jim was scared enough to get himself a shotgun and put it by the front door. Ever since the fig tree, he knew he had the capacity to do as the friendly policeman suggested. That scared him.

One afternoon, Jim got a call from his other son Richard's school. Richard had been bashed up and was taken to hospital unconscious. Jim arrived at the hospital to find Richard's face a swollen mess. His eyes were sunk between fleshy black bruises. His nose was blue. It was days before they got the full story from Richard. He'd been jumped by three strangers outside the gate. They punched him and rammed his head into a brick wall. Before he'd lost consciousness they'd told him, 'Your dad testifies, there'll be more of this.'

Richard missed seven weeks of school in his final year. His marks suffered so he had to go back and do it all again the next year to get into the teaching course he wanted.

*

The court case didn't go well for Dean Hepburn. In his initial statement to police, the hospital orderly had said the perpetrator was clean shaven but when Potts was arrested a week or so later, he had a lengthy beard.

'How do you explain that?' the defence lawyer asked.

'Maybe I was wrong.'

'So you might have been wrong.' The lawyer fed the confusion, and Dean, years later, is still down on himself for coming across as unreliable. He blames himself for the failure of the prosecution.

But for Jim Runham, the legal system was to blame. His take on it was, 'The judge in his wisdom ruled out all the other ID witnesses because they'd been in the same huge operations room at the police station and they might have somehow influenced each other.' Jim wasn't part of that group identification. He'd made his ID separately, so he was the only other identification witness the judge let the jury hear. When the defence lawyer asked Jim how he could be certain it was his client who'd shot at him, since the gunman wore a wig and glasses, Jim replied that he could identify him clearly, 'as I wanted to see the face of the man who was going to kill me'. The judge instructed the jury to bring down a verdict of not guilty.

'Mate, I just couldn't believe it,' he says. 'It shattered me. After all I'd been through. My son being bashed up, the young fellow seeing bad men coming through the window every night of the week, living like a prisoner in my own home. It just ripped my guts out.' He walked up to Potts's barrister and asked, 'What's it like to prostitute yourself? What's it like to get paid money to tell lies?'

'The hardest thing I've ever had to do in my life,' Jim says, 'was not being shot at, it was coming home from court. I couldn't talk about it in the house with the disabled boy. He was still having bad men coming through the window in his dreams. We'd told him, "Bad man's in jail." I took my older boy for a walk down the street to tell him what had happened and to say that everything we believed in, the system, everything that I thought was true and right, the moral fibre I was trying to instil in my son, had broken down. I was prepared to stand up and be shot for truth, justice and all the Superman crap. It was very difficult for him to understand. We sat in a park and I cried and he couldn't believe it. "Dad, how can it be?" Remember, he'd been put in hospital over all this.

'Not long after that, that's when the demons started to come for me.'

Jim started reliving it every night. Cold sweats. Nightmares. The cancer of his soul, he'd call it. There'd be people coming to get him. He'd feel that concussion hitting his sternum and pushing him back into a wall. Trying to get free, fighting, fighting. By day he was hyper-vigilant, overreacting to squealing tyres and loud noises. He was cranky and irritable with the family. Sleep deprived, he withdrew. He didn't want to go out, couldn't be bothered socialising, couldn't be bothered showering and brushing his teeth. But it wasn't until he woke up one night strangling his wife, Jan – or rather, Jan woke up with him strangling her – that he realised he had lost it.

He sought medical help. He got a little therapy and a lot of medication. He took the pills for years.

He couldn't teach any more. How could he stand in front of a class full of kids when he could hardly leave the house? But he found another full-time job and persevered with that. He kept up his volunteer work for people with disabilities. 'I strove on, saying it's important to help these kids. It became meaningful. I got to see the smiles on their faces.'

It was in the middle of all the nightmares and trauma that a letter arrived from Government House. He opened it in the front yard. They wanted to give him a medal – the Star of Courage. He sat on the lawn and cried. *I don't want your medal. Forget about it. Look at what all this has done to my family.* He felt affronted that the system that had screwed him, screwed justice, was now trying to reward him. He couldn't cop that paradox. But Jan talked to him over the coming days. 'Take a step back. This'll mean something to the kids.' He came around and realised that even though the bad guys had won, even though his life had fallen apart, he knew that he'd stood up for what counted, and at last someone, somewhere, was saying he'd done the right thing. It helped restore his belief system. 'I thought it had been stolen from me. But they were saying I still had it – what I did was good.'

*

Dean Hepburn didn't suffer any psychological trauma, but he felt the need to get out of Ipswich. At his bravery award investiture he met a National Party politician who he thought was a total goose. He realised politics was a game that anyone could play, so he might as well try it himself and do some good for the world. He moved to the Gold Coast and became a candidate for the Greens – a bit like going to a State of Origin game at Brisbane's Lang Park wearing a New South Wales jumper. He has run unsuccessfully for parliament five times. 'I never had any inkling I would be successful. I just want to make a difference. Do the right thing.

'I found out two or three years ago that [Peter Potts] was in jail for armed robbery so I figured it's all square in the end. But there will be people out there suffering and if I had done a better job in court they wouldn't be. That's the way it is. The court case still pisses me off today. I wasn't a strong witness.'

*

The day I first meet Jim Runham in person, I note that there's a flag on a pole on the front lawn of his home, still in the Ipswich area. He is wearing a naval cadets uniform and is running late for the cadet meeting, but he lingers to talk. We sit for a cuppa and the conversation turns to the time in 1997 – right in the midst of his battle with post-traumatic stress disorder – when he'd been out fighting a fire for days with the volunteer bush-fire brigade and his truck got into trouble, trapped on a ridge with a wall of flame approaching. They had nowhere to go so he got his crew to use the fuel in their burning-off cans to light a little fire around the truck. It almost got out of hand but when they had it under control, they got back in the truck and got the blankets ready just like in their burnover drills. As they waited for the flames to engulf them, they got out their phones and called their loved ones.

Jim called Jan. 'Darling, we're in a bit of bother. I'm just ringing to say goodbye. I love you.'

'What the hell are you telling me for? I'd rather not know. And I love you, too.'

Jan has a good laugh about it now, sitting around the dining table with us.

As it turned out, the breeze changed for a few moments, Jim saw a gap in the flames, revved the truck and rammed it through the opening, safely down into a gully – and out of mobile range for hours – while Jan sat thinking her husband was dead.

It was around this time that Jim wrote a lot of letters to politicians and anyone he could think of about the legal system and how it had to be changed so that smart lawyers couldn't go around excluding crucial evidence from trials. But soon after this second near-death experience, he realised he didn't have a hope of changing centuries of legal sophistry.

He redirected his energy towards seeking out others who'd been through the same experience as him. He figured there must be others out there. Before he was given his award he'd read a booklet which outlined the story of Darrell Tree and his Cross of Valour. Reading what Darrell had done in rescuing the boy from the powerlines, he was awe-struck. *I've got to talk to him.* He found Darrell's phone number and rang it.

They talked about their awards and what had transpired since, and it wasn't like they bared their souls to each other, but there was a spark of understanding. Jim was struck by how much worse Darrell's situation was than his own. Interestingly, both men were volunteer firefighters.

After that, Jim found Victor Boscoe's number and rang it. Again there was that common thread. They were each suffering in their own way.

He was contacted by the ABC's *Australian Story* and the three men appeared on it, squeezing their three stories into fifteen minutes. During the show, Jim floated an idea to form an association of bravery award winners and soon after he got cracking to try and organise something.

Government House was very accommodating. They didn't have all their bravery award recipients on a database – just a sheet of paper per recipient with the citation and address at the time of the award. They allowed him in to photocopy them all. It took a week on his first visit to Canberra, then four more visits, to get it all together. Then he had to find current addresses for all these names – 1800 of them. He spent a year scouring electoral rolls on microfiche with a mate, John Bowles. His plan was to organise a big gathering of award recipients in Queensland and perhaps get an association off the ground – what he was already calling the Australian Bravery Association, Queensland. But unbeknown to him, someone else was trying to do the exact same thing in Canberra.

SIX

John Thurgar

John Thurgar looked across the United Nations buffer zone
to his left. The Turkish army had brought an artillery battery up to the ridge so that everyone knew what was there.
They towed the big guns along the horizon then disappeared.
Radio messages followed. 'Stop the illegal activity,' the Turks
demanded. There were more radio messages. More threats.
John knew from experience that the Turks kept their word on
such things. Then the message came through that the 'illegal
activity' had to stop by 1200 hours or they would start shooting.

A squadron of Turkish M60 tanks rumbled up to the ridge,
revved their engines so no one could mistake their intentions,
and disappeared back behind Turkish lines. John radioed it all
through to his United Nations commanders but they insisted
he push on.

John was on a small track that ran down the middle of the
no-man's-land separating the Greek and Turkish armies on
Cyprus. The Turks had invaded five years earlier, in 1974, but
tensions were still high between the opposing trenches filled

with well-trained young men with a rigid hatred for the well-trained young men on the other side. John's job as officer in charge of the unarmed United Nations police contingent in a sector on the edge of the capital, Nicosia, was a constant diplomatic challenge.

In this area, the no-man's-land was a wide valley of valuable agricultural land going to waste between the barrels of the opposing guns. The Greeks occupied the edge of the city on one side, heavily dug into backyards and houses, with trenches and strong points behind a barrier minefield. Across the fertile valley, the Turks occupied a slight ridge about a kilometre away.

The United Nations economics branch had determined that, as part of its job of returning life to normal, Greek farmer Yani Mousarous would be allowed to plough his field in an area of the buffer zone where it had been determined there were no landmines. And so Yani had turned up at the designated hour, 0600, and begun ploughing his field despite the protests from the Turkish side. The United Nations had anticipated trouble so Yani on his little tractor had an escort of Royal Irish Hussars in Ferret scout cars with 50-calibre machine guns mounted on top. Lying back out of sight behind the Greek lines was a contingent of Canadian Lynx armoured personnel carriers with 50 cals on top, ready to charge in and rescue those in no-man's-land if there was trouble. And then there was John Thurgar, an unarmed Australian Federal Police officer, and his driver Sergeant Stan Wilson in their Land Rover.

As the 1200 hours deadline approached, John readied himself for battle — a state of being with which he was familiar. Nine years earlier, he had been with the Special Air Service (SAS) in Vietnam, going out on two-week long-range patrols, always close to the enemy, watching and waiting. There'd only be five of them out there, and so there was a constant possibility of bumping into much larger enemy contingents. When they found a Vietcong camp, they would reconnoitre, always scanning for booby traps or the triple prongs of M16 Jumping Jack mines sticking through the leaf litter. He'd hear his heart beating in the silence. The SAS's main job was intelligence gathering, but sometimes they were allowed to attack. In the moments before, his heart would pound through his sweaty shirt so bad that when the bullets at last started flying, there was an enormous release. There was clarity and purpose.

John was wounded by an improvised landmine ten months into his Vietnam tour. After Australia withdrew from that war and the armed forces retreated into a peacetime shell, he left the army, but learned that you couldn't just walk away from those days. They stayed with him just as surely as the shrapnel that the surgeons couldn't reach remained in his shoulder. The adrenaline had taken him up, and nobody had brought him down.

The Commonwealth Police offered his best chance of getting another active posting overseas so he joined and worked diligently to make sure he got promoted. In 1977, as a chief inspector, John was selected on the twenty-man Cyprus contingent for his first tour and now, in 1979, he was on his second stint in the blue beret.

So, as the midday deadline loomed, he readied himself to be back in a battlefield, only this time he had no gun. The Canadian officer in charge of the sector was determined to press on and the Turkish officer over the ridge was equally determined that the ploughing would stop. John had warned the lieutenant colonel the night before in the planning meeting that the Turks wouldn't back down, and that they would clearly signal their intentions before doing anything.

They'd already done the signalling with the radio messages, artillery and tanks. The Ferrets were ready, the Lynxes were ready. Now, with just minutes to go, it was a matter of waiting for the shells to start falling.

Then, as all eyes focused on the tractor ploughing the field, a second tractor burst through the Greek front line about 800 metres away. John watched as the man on board this blue tractor lowered a harrow and began carving up the land, right in the middle of what was thought to be a minefield. The Greeks wouldn't tell anybody exactly where the mines were. The United Nations knew that the small area that had been designated for ploughing was clear, but somewhere between that area and where the second tractor was ploughing, the minefield probably restarted. John got Stan to drive across the cleared part of the paddock as far as they dared, in the hope that they'd be able to wave the man down. He could see by the desperate waves of the Greek soldiers that they, too, had been taken by surprise and that they knew the danger the farmer was in. And so everybody watched, expecting a blast at any moment as the seven tines of the harrow cut through the baited soil. But no blast came. The tractor finished its first run of about 100 metres, then turned to the left to begin the next row.

The two Australians were still driving towards it when a great flash of red, then blackness, burst in front of them. John saw one of the large tractor tyres fly ten metres into the air – along with the driver's rag-doll body, thrusting up like a misfired rocket. It was an image that would stay with him. Then came the sound of the blast, followed by a shock wave that rattled the old four-wheel-drive.

When the dust settled, John saw the tractor had been cut in two. Way off to the left, he saw Turkish troops stand and wave and cheer. They'd got their way. There would be no more ploughing this day.

John figured from the strength of the blast that the tractor had hit a Teller antitank mine. Stan had, meanwhile, continued to drive towards the scene through an area that they hoped – but were by no means certain – was clear of mines. They pulled up perhaps 150 metres from the tractor when they knew it would be foolish to drive further. John got Stan to call in the incident and request a helicopter dust-off for the farmer.

He got out to assess the situation. The man was all black, covered in diesel and oil and probably seared as well. It was impossible to tell if he was alive at first. Then his head rolled, revealing red eyes looking out from the blackened face. Even at that distance, John was sure he could see a pleading in those eyes, like a dog that's been hit by a car.

John looked up and saw powerlines. It was windy, so a helicopter wouldn't be able to winch him out. If he waited for the sappers to clear a safe lane, the farmer would be dead. The other United Nations vehicles had all pulled up behind his now, and all the men had got out, looking at him for direction. He had the three pips on his shoulder. He had to make the call. The only option he saw was for someone to walk across the minefield to get the man. It was way too dangerous a task for him to ask for volunteers. Therefore it was him.

But first he had to focus, plan, give orders. He nominated a landing zone and asked a sergeant from a scout car to mark it out and direct the landing. He ordered Stan to not let anyone else follow him in. And then he set out towards the broken man.

John knew that there were large antitank mines in there, buried deep under the soil. They usually required more than 100 kilograms of pressure to set them off. He weighed 95 kilograms. He also knew the Greeks had used M16 Jumping Jack mines which, when triggered, leapt out of the ground on a two-second delay and exploded at about crotch height, sending out a 360-degree spray of shrapnel. A single M16 had killed eight Australians and wounded 29 the month after he'd arrived in Vietnam. John also knew there were M14s out there, designed to blow off a man's foot and leave him wounded in the field, a burden on his platoon. He would only learn later that there was another mine out there, too – a South African model designed to take out an unarmoured vehicle. It was triggered by a much lighter weight than the antitank mines.

In the latter years of the Vietnam war, mines and booby traps were responsible for a third of all Australian casualties. No soldier left there without a certain 'mine neurosis', and certainly not the ones like John who'd been one of the casualties. For the rest of his life, he couldn't go for a walk in the bush without subconsciously searching for the telltale spikes.

So ignorance was not on his side as he took his first tentative steps into the minefield. His army training would have had him prodding a bayonet into the ground at 45 degrees to clear a path but he had no such tool with him, and no time, besides. He took a step on jelly legs, looked, took another. Shitting himself with each short stride. He is not religious but he said a few Hail Marys. He was about halfway in when he heard someone yell from the Greek lines: 'Go back! Go back! There are more mines near the tractor.' *Hail Mary mother of God. Pray for us now in our hour of need.* His eyes fell on a disc-shaped Teller antitank mine exposed by eroded soil. He knew that antipersonnel mines were usually laid around the antitank mines. He saw prongs. An M16 Jumping Jack. And he saw another exposed Teller mine. More prongs. His legs weakened further. He was shaking. *Is it worth it?* About 50 metres from the tractor, he entered an area that had obviously been ploughed at some time in the past. The ground became more disturbed and he knew the mines would be much harder to see.

But he was close now. He could see the man's left leg was a lump of raw flesh from knee to ankle. The man tried to crawl towards him and said something, holding his hand out. And always those pleading eyes.

John took more ginger steps until he arrived at the stricken man whose name he would later learn was Chrysos Seas.

Chrysos's clothes had been blown off his blackened, seared flesh. The left leg was hanging by a flap of skin. His naked body was peppered with shrapnel wounds. It appeared that while his rear tyre had hit the antitank mine, his front wheel had hit a Jumping Jack whose shrapnel had added their insult to his already considerable injuries. This man was going to die soon. There was no time to wait for the engineers to clear a proper lane.

John knew there'd be a delay before the helicopter got there. The crew would have to be alerted and briefed, the chopper started and warmed up. He could see the injuries needed immediate tending. But he didn't want to be moving around the body in the middle of the minefield and risk disturbing any more mines. He decided he had to take Chrysos back to the vehicles.

Chrysos was lying on his back now, so John got one arm under his crotch and one under his head and lifted him into a fireman's carry. He estimated the farmer weighed about 70 kilos — light to John who was pumping a lot of weights, benching 100 kilos, full of post-Vietnam anger and energy. Their combined weights put them well over the trigger point for the antitank mines. So the walk back out was even more dangerous than the walk in. He wanted to follow his own footsteps back but he couldn't see them on the hard earth. And he knew he just had to hurry. This man needed his wounds dressed. He was losing a lot of blood. John saw the lip of an antitank mine and headed for that, knowing the antipersonnel mines would be laid about two metres from it. But he didn't see any more prongs on the way out and soon he was back with the United Nations vehicles.

Chrysos was bandaged up and the Whirlwind helicopter arrived exactly fifteen minutes after the blast. John jumped in with the farmer to hold the stretcher steady and apply pressure to the femoral artery.

They flew to Nicosia and landed on the Canadians' baseball field. The small truck for the officer's mess was nearby, it was conscripted into the drama and the Canadian operations officer came with them to the general hospital. Arriving at the front, the Canadian went in while John continued applying pressure to the femoral artery, but then the Canadian came back out alone. Nobody would pay him any attention in there. They weren't allowed to treat United Nations personnel and the hospital staff thought it was a United Nations soldier in the back of the truck. John got the Canadian to hold the artery while he marched inside, channelling that anger and aggression. Again, the doctor refused to come out: 'No, no. No UN.' John grabbed him in a bear hug and carried him out through the waiting room and put him down at the back of the truck.

'He's yours.'

The doctor saw it was a civilian and started yelling. People turned up and grabbed the stretcher and Chrysos Seas was away.

Emergency doctors talk about the 'golden hour' – essentially, if you can get to an injured person quickly, you're much more likely to save them. From blast to hospital, John had got Chrysos there in just twenty minutes.

*

John Thurgar says he felt no euphoria in the hours and days afterwards. 'It was just so darn serious. When I was advised he had survived and they'd been able to dress all the wounds and debride them, but that they'd had to take the leg off, I was very pleased. I went to see him after a couple of days. He was just thrilled at being alive. During the actual confrontation, he'd been an engineer and laid mines so he knew what they could do. He'd laid mines in a different area to the south. He'd been conned by a wealthy landowner to come up from the south and plough this land. After I left Cyprus in early 1980, I found I wasn't able to physically or psychologically revisit him.'

John was awarded the Star of Courage for his efforts, but back home, he found the honour was a hindrance to his career in the federal police. 'It made many people jealous. You tend to be pushed aside . . . My time in the police afterwards was very non-rewarding and that's why I left in 1987. Life moves on,' he says, with an obvious sadness.

I ask him what he has done since. 'Oh, this and that,' and moves the subject along. He has remarried for a start and, approaching 60, has just become a father again with his wife Hedonna. He is sitting on a hospital bed, his arms covered in old tattoos – Neptune on the right and a young woman in a tutu on the left. His legs are covered in sores, and that gives the first hint of what 'this and that' might entail. He explains that he was bitten by insects and the bites got infected. But I later learn that he was leading a tour group to Papua New Guinea when he was bitten. And thanks to the internet I could probe some more.

One telling detail which he'd omitted from his original interview with me was the fact that the injury that had sent him home from Vietnam was caused by 'chicom' or what we'd now call an 'improvised explosive device'. It was a somewhat pertinent detail to omit in the telling of a story about walking across a minefield. I had asked what his experience had been of the effects of mines and he'd answered only that he'd seen people who had been hit. 'Why didn't you tell me you'd been hit by a mine?' I later asked.

'People think you're big-noting or full of shit, you know,' he said.

The internet also revealed he won an MBE from the Queen in 1995 for his work setting up homes for children with disabilities in Port Moresby and an Order of Australia for the Port Moresby work plus similar efforts in India. 'I did volunteer work for the Ryder-Cheshire Foundation established by Sue Ryder and Group Captain Leonard Cheshire.' Englishman Leonard Cheshire was a World War II bomber pilot and Victoria Cross winner. He suffered deep depression and was discharged from the Royal Air Force, with a pension, for psychoneurosis. He went on to perform many heroic acts of charity but 'his postwar career was punctuated by long intervals of nervous collapse'. John got to know Sue and Leonard well. 'I was the Australian international voluntary projects officer, which meant I paid my own way and did all the work myself.'

John was also the deputy chairman of the company that lobbied for a welcome home parade for Vietnam veterans and then acted as parade marshal when the lobbying was successful. That two-dollar company morphed into the Australian Vietnam Forces National Memorial Committee which lobbied for and bought a Vietnam memorial in Canberra. They raised $1.2 million with 'chook raffles, plus a very small donation from the Federal Government'.

After leaving the federal police in 1987, John started a retreat for veterans, the Mountview Foundation. 'A number of Vietnam veterans were committing suicide. The Vietnam Veterans Counselling Service had a lot of people they couldn't deal with. They turned up for appointments drugged or drunk or violent. They wouldn't talk to them so some of the better counsellors referred them to me. I'd get a cohort together and take them to the Snowy Mountains. We'd share an intensive experience for seven days and build networks, then these people would help themselves get better. The counselling service sent two psychologists to assess the programme and worked out it was terribly beneficial and they took it over as an in-patient one-month course at St John of God Hospital out near Windsor [on the outskirts of Sydney]. I have heard the programme is run in other states now, too. I did myself out of a job which was what I wanted. I just had to do something for these blokes so severely affected by post-traumatic stress disorder.'

And his own life was affected, too. He attributes the failure of his first marriage to post-traumatic stress disorder. In his mind he wrapped the Cyprus incident up with the traumas of Vietnam to form one big parcel of anguish. He won't talk about the details, just that he went through 'all the classic symptoms'. 'I was able to seek help. I never made a claim for it. I just wanted counselling and guidance to get through it. It's not like you've got a headache and you take a tablet and it fixes it. It's more about putting things in perspective . . . When you've been in that unreal world then you come back to the real world, your perception of the real world is different. That's all I'd like to say on that.'

The incident had affected him so deeply he couldn't drive a diesel car because the smell reminded him too much of the diesel-smeared body of Chrysos Seas. For the same reason, he'd avoided trying to meet the farmer again. It would be too distressing. They confined themselves to annual Christmas cards. At first, Chrysos's cards would just say, 'To Jack, Merry Christmas from Chrysos', but as his children learned a little English they extended the message to usually say something along the lines of, 'We are fine. How are you?' But in his 2008 card Chrysos wrote that he had a problem with his 'heard'. John didn't know if it was his heart or his head, but realised it might be life threatening so he decided to face his demons and return.

He arrived at the Seas family's front gate in June 2009 to find Chrysos waiting for him. He had done well in life as a farm contractor. He showed off his new prosthetic leg which he could even cross over his other leg. His wounded arm was working, but his heart was no good. He suffered shortness of breath and carried a pacemaker. They looked at the photos of the two of them when they were young and strong. Chrysos told the *Cyprus Weekly*:

> I took Jack out to see the minefield he rescued me from and we were both in tears. Jack is one of the community's better individuals and I will never forget the fact that, although Jack has children and a family of his own, he still risked his life to enter the minefield to rescue me. I hope Jack will come back soon and spend more time here next time.

Chrysos died later that year.

*

John had heard about the associations they had in Britain for Victoria Cross and George Cross awardees. The United Kingdom government looked after them. They were reimbursed to attend public functions. Wealthy donors had set up a sizeable trust fund. So back in the mid 1990s, he thought Australia needed something similar. He'd noticed that civilian awardees received their medal, wore it on the day it was given, then put it away in a cupboard, never to bring it out again. And he also knew that there would be awardees out there who would need help, just like him, so he set about the idea of forming an association.

'I knew from what I'd done with Vietnam veterans that they could help each other, and by helping somebody else you can help yourself. By sharing experiences where there is no jealousy, people can openly express how they feel and get on with their life. And so I wrote to Government House, but they wouldn't give me the names of the award recipients. I'd worked at Government House in the VIP protection squadron. I'd worked with the governor-general. I knew some of the people there and I was able to say "Come on, you know me. I'm not going to misuse this list." They knew I wasn't going to go away so in the end the official secretary agreed to me writing a letter to all the award recipients and Government House would post the letters and if people chose to respond they could. And that's what I did.'

It was some time after the letters went out that someone from Government House told John that Jim Runham from Brisbane was proposing something similar. Jim had a huge and more comprehensive database of up-to-date addresses.

They got in touch and Jim threw his hat in with John's Canberra plans – that there'd be a gathering and a meeting with a call for the formation of an association.

John had to pull every string he could to put on a weekend of functions that included a reception on the lawns of Parliament House, a service of remembrance, a barbecue lunch and dinner at the yacht club, all for 50 dollars per head. About 200 people turned up.

Jim Runham remembers having a great time. It was a catharsis. 'There were so many wonderful people – everyday people who had done extraordinary things.' He and his wife Jan had read all their citations while putting the database together and now he was meeting them. He cried a lot. It was validation for him. These people knew he had done the right thing when he chased that robber; that it was okay that he'd suffered because so many of them had suffered, too. At last he felt like the events that started in the Ipswich building society seven years earlier were leading somewhere positive. He had control and purpose back. Maybe he hadn't quite elucidated these thoughts so clearly on that night back in 2000, but they would firm in his mind in the years after.

The night was tinged with sadness, too, because family members of many posthumous award winners were there.

People like Coralee Lever from Mildura, Victoria, whose husband had pushed her to the floor in Port Arthur's Broad Arrow Cafe as gunman Martin Bryant was running amok.

At the end of the night, Jim was in the car park walking to his car. He'd told Jan to go on ahead because he'd come down with a headache. All the tension was unwinding up there in his cranium. He was dawdling along on his bad leg when he felt a tap on the shoulder. He turned to see a woman, much shorter than himself, pretty, but maybe a lot younger than she seemed. 'I finally have someone who understands,' she said, squeezing his hand. He looked down at her name tag: Carolyn Loughton.

He immediately remembered how her citation had moved him, but it had just been words on a piece of paper. Here she was, the real person, with tears streaking her cheeks. It was clear life had been difficult since her incident. They spoke for maybe ten minutes. Jan came back looking for him and they agreed to talk again.

Next day, at the yacht club, Carolyn told him how she had been in the Broad Arrow Café and had thrown herself across her only child, Sarah, aged fifteen, trying to protect her as the gunman walked the aisle, aiming and shooting.

As Carolyn spoke of her situation – the guilt of being alive, the failure to save her daughter – Jim couldn't believe how little hate she expressed towards the man who had caused all this to her. It was as though the despair had crowded out any room for hate.

That day, a meeting voted to form what they would call the Australian Bravery Association (Jim's choice of name), forged from this collection of people who had been to places that most of us can only hope we never have to visit. John Thurgar was elected the inaugural national president, and Jim Runham became Queensland president.

SEVEN

Bob Jeppesen

Bob Jeppesen was a major in the Australian Army Reserve – the highest ranking military policeman in the Queensland reserve. In September 1990, he was sent to reconnoitre possible staging posts to house large numbers of soldiers moving across western Queensland on their way to the Kangaroo 91 military exercises.

After three days on the road, Bob and fellow army reserve officer Peter Hanlon had inspected twelve sites and covered more than 1000 kilometres in a small rental car. The plan had been to stay the night at the central-western Queensland town of Ilfracombe, but Bob suggested they push on to Longreach. 'I know a family who have a pub there,' he said.

'Yeah, all right,' Peter said. Didn't matter to him one way or the other. It was only 27 kilometres down the road.

They got to the Commercial Hotel not long before dark and booked rooms. They went to the bar, played some pool and threw some darts, before retiring to the dining room about 7 pm. After dinner, they drank some more, talked to the bloke who drove the septic truck, and Bob excused himself about 9.30 pm. He took his bags up to his first-floor room, then went back to the lounge bar where he had a few more drinks with a group of people. They all went to bed about 11.30 pm.

It was little more than half an hour later that Peter was woken by a deep and controlled voice. 'Fire!' Pause. 'Fire!' Pause. 'Fire! . . . Fire! . . . Fire!'

At first, Peter didn't smell smoke or see flames, he just heard the thunderous crackle of a bonfire and knew he had to get out. He went straight through the door leading onto the big old verandah. Looking left, he saw the room next to his ablaze. He picked up his bag, threw it over the balcony and climbed down the drainpipe.

All along the corridor, guests were being woken by the deep, controlled voice. Those who looked out into the corridor, where the voice was coming from, found the smoke and flames too thick to get through. Most then went out via the verandah.

Further down the hall, another man, Telecom technician Ross Kerle, heard someone in the hallway yelling 'Fire! Fire!' But this voice was more drawn out, weaker. By the time Ross got out of bed, the flames in the hallway were licking the window above his door. Ross got some gear together and went out onto the now flaming balcony. He noticed the voice that had been yelling had stopped. So he yelled 'Fire!' a few times, before throwing his bag over the balcony. He lobbed his belt over the 240-volt drop-off cable and slid down it like it was a flying fox, landing on a car bonnet.

Truck driver Stan Hartley was woken by the sound of two men's voices calling out 'fire' – probably Ross Kerle and the voice in the hallway. He opened his door into the corridor and saw it filling with smoke. He grabbed his television and as he made his way down the smoke-filled corridor he heard 'Help!

Help!' being shouted from the area of the lounge room behind him. The voice became fainter as Stan felt his way in the opposite direction towards the fire escape, through smoke so thick he couldn't see.

Police officer Paul Keightley saw Stan moving slowly down the external stairs like he was drunk or dazed, carrying the television while the ceiling above his head burnt fiercely. 'Forget the TV. Run!' the policeman yelled but the old guy didn't respond, so he ran up the stairs and dragged them both down.

Paul McKerlie from Alice Springs was woken by someone on the verandah yelling 'Fire!' – perhaps Ross Kerle. Paul grabbed a fire hose but found it useless against the inferno. There was no pressure and he could barely get it to squirt three metres. He kept trying anyway. A minute or two later he saw a skinny bloke in flames at the top of the stairwell. 'I put the hose on the bloke to try and put him out, but I couldn't get near him,' he later told police. 'The ceiling collapsed on him.' Paul retreated to the street.

Already, cars parked outside were going up in flames. The old wooden pub had been destroyed in five minutes but would continue to blaze for hours, so hot it welded shut the post office boxes across the street.

*

Outside, Jeppesen's army reserve colleague Peter Hanlon had been preoccupied with getting the publican's wife, Anne Dale, and her two sons over the balcony. They'd ended up jumping and Anne, being a big woman, landed hard, breaking her hip. She needed to be carried away from the flaming awning. Peter had then helped the septic-truck driver Bob Carthew push his truck away from the hotel. Septic trucks are full of methane and they could have been looking at a serious problem if it had got too hot. The driver had also been woken by the man calling 'fire'. Just in time, too. His hair was singed running through flames in a now-or-never dash to safety.

After helping Bob Carthew, there was nothing left for Peter to do. Dressed in tracksuit pants, T-shirt and no shoes, he gathered with the other hotel guests in a glum little pyjama-clad group. It was only then that they started accounting for everybody. Paul McKerlie piped up that he'd seen a man trapped inside. Peter looked around and knew in his heart that it was Bob Jeppesen.

Peter hadn't twigged that it was Bob waking everybody up. It wasn't until the next day when somebody mentioned it that he realised, 'Of course, it was Bob.' Aside from the fact no one else had come forward to say it was them, it was exactly the sort of thing Bob would do.

*

It appeared that the fire had started around the lounge room at the top of the main stairs to the first floor. The corridor ran off it in two directions. Round a dogleg in one direction, and in the other direction it went straight to Bob Jeppesen's room at the far end. Bob – a light and alert sleeper – must have left his room and gone towards the fire in the lounge room, alerting everybody on the way. He'd then continued past the fire into the next part of the corridor, around the dogleg, alerting all those up the far end. 'By the time he got back to the stairs near the seat of the fire, that's where he came to grief,' Peter recalled. 'I always wondered why Bob hadn't tried to get through to somebody's room, get to the verandah and go over the side.' The coroner found that a lack of properly lit exit signs may have contributed to his death.

There were fifteen people including Bob Jeppesen sleeping at the Commercial Hotel that night. Seven of them were woken by the voice in the corridor. Two were woken by general yelling, and one by a voice on the verandah which was probably Ross Kerle who himself had been woken by the voice in the hall. Another was woken by a siren and Anne Dale was woken by her son Daniel saying he smelt smoke. Anne couldn't help but think Bob had died trying to get to her, because she and her boys had been the last to get out.

'I think he saved most of them,' says Peter. 'I think I would have still been asleep, too. We'd had a few beers in the afternoon, had a glass of wine with dinner. I was pretty sleepy by the time I went to bed.'

The fire was so fast, so brutal, Bob's actions clearly saved a good portion of the fourteen others in the hotel that night. It was a few quick minutes of great courage, then his life was over. But back in Brisbane, a wife and two children at primary school were about to embark on a new life of slow pain, with futures thrust onto unforeseen trajectories.

*

In mid 2010, I telephoned Fay Jeppesen but the Telstra 101 message I left dropped out of her message bank before she got around to responding. Twenty years after Bob's death, she was busy organising her retirement, I would later learn. She was exhausted.

A few weeks later I wrote her a letter and received a long email response. In it, she wrote:

> My son Cameron, who was eight at the time – his dad's best mate – sat on the front steps for two years after school, waiting for his dad to come home from work. Cameron locked himself away from everyone, wouldn't communicate . . . My father, who passed away last year, was very close to Cameron and they spent a lot of time together, with him teaching him a lot of life skills. He has grown up

into a nice young man (now 28) and is a truck driver, lives near his grandmother Elva at Ipswich and keeps close to her.

My daughter Kelly, now 31, still feels quite bitter and angry about what happened . . . Kelly was a Queensland aged swimming champion at the time and also won some Australian school championship events. She struggled with the impact of me now being a sole parent taking on all the extra things that both she and her brother had enjoyed together previously . . . No more camping holidays, no more family dinners. Christmas and birthday celebrations were morbid, when their dad was such a fun, make-everything-happen type of guy for them. I believe both Kelly and Cameron never saw us as a 'family unit' again. They both leant very heavily on my parents for support with their grief, to protect me.

Me – have never gone into another relationship, remarried, etc. I have devoted my life to my children and my parents, in advancing myself through study and work to change my role from mother and supporting parent to being everything, and have been a Regional Facilities Manager in the Department of Education for the past nine years and more recently as Project Director of the BER (the Rudd Government's Building the Education Revolution stimulus spending project) delivery team. I have worked extremely hard to provide the best that we always dreamed of for our children, to give them the opportunities in life that we wanted for them. I have been a swimming mum, a rugby league jersey washer and canteen worker, a scout treasurer, a swimming referee, attended all the parent working bees at schools, and bought a small boat for fishing with my son and also attended many motor racing meets to give the gender balance of opportunities for them.

But there is a cost . . . I am very exhausted and during the past four weeks have made the decision to retire. I am 57 years old, but believe my health is suffering and I need some time for me. Both my parents have passed away during the past 18 months and I have nursed and supported them extensively during the past five years as well.

*

A few weeks later, Fay and I talk on the phone. When I mention how so many of the people featured in this book seem to be strongly community minded, she tells me how, aside from being in the army reserve, Bob was a Queen's Scout, a Freemason, an environmentalist and a keen volunteer in a local bush regeneration project. He'd go off weeding some tract of scrub while his own backyard lay in disrepair. He was Brisbane City Council's counter disaster officer and just two weeks before his death had done a counter disaster course in Victoria.

I ask her if Kelly had been able to keep up her swimming after the fire. 'Yes, we got up every morning at five o'clock to go to training. Scot Volkers was the coach. She was in the same squad as Sam Riley. I had to get Cameron up as well. He was eight. I'd carry him downstairs and put him in the back seat of the car, then go to the pool, a thirty-minute drive, then bring Cameron home, do the normal housework stuff, leave home at seven, go back to the pool, pick up Kelly, feed her breakfast in the car, take her and Cameron to school, and be at work by eight myself. Then work to four-thirty, pick up my son and take him to swimming or football. My mum would take Kelly to swimming in the afternoon. At six-thirty, I'd leave to go back to pick her up at seven.'

All this while battling to find out what had actually happened in that pub. She made a number of trips to Longreach and hired a barrister for the inquest. She'd remember Paul

McKerlie, the guy who had seen her husband die on the stairs, telling her that he had been unable to sleep indoors ever since. The effects of the fire kept rippling outwards.

Money was tight and she knew she now had to create a career for herself. Being a school secretary was no longer going to be good enough. She also felt people perceived her differently now she was a single mother. 'I never shopped at the same shops again. Bob and I used to do our shopping together. You had to start doing things differently with your life that didn't remind you of what you used to do together.' And the impact that Bob Jeppesen's life and death had on others made it that much harder for his wife to put it behind her.

Fay estimates she must have been to ten tree plantings put on by the various community groups wanting to honour and remember him. The military police created an award in his name. The gestures were lovely, but each one was hard – getting the kids dressed up, then going through what was like a funeral all over again.

One night four months after the fire, she got home from work late. (Her parents were minding the kids.) She opened the mail box and found a letter from Government House. She opened it and read that they wanted to award her late husband a Star of Courage. The letter said she had to let them know if she accepted the award or not. She didn't want any award. She wanted her husband back. She collapsed on the front lawn and lay there for an hour until a neighbour saw her and came out to help.

EIGHT

Sharon O'Leary, Rob Rodgers, Glenn Kelk and Jim Birmingham

I tell you this not as aimless revelation but because I want you to know, as you read me, precisely who I am and where I am and what is on my mind. I want you to understand exactly what you are getting: you are getting a woman who for some time now has felt radically separated from most of the ideas that seem to interest other people.
Joan Didion, *The White Album*

I am at Jim Runham's house in Brisbane's western suburbs, paying him a social call. Jim is in his naval cadets uniform and I am holding him up, making him late for the meeting, exactly as I had done the last time I'd visited him two years earlier. He, of course, is too polite to make a fuss.

My phone rings and it is Sharon O'Leary, a woman who, for the last several weeks, I had been hoping would call me after I'd sent a letter to an address I'd hoped might be hers. She tells me she can't go through with an interview. It would be too hard. She says goodbye. But five minutes later she calls back and says she's changed her mind. She'll talk to me at a friend's place which, by coincidence, is just a few suburbs away. She'll be waiting for me there in twenty minutes.

I say hurried goodbyes to Jim and his family and speed to the rendezvous – a big house on a big block. I'm greeted at the garage by an attractive blonde in her early 50s who manages to make an orange polar fleece appear somehow elegant. Her face is not nearly as aged as the story she is about to tell suggests it should be, but her voice is . . . slowed by two decades of sedatives.

Sharon grabs herself a XXXX from the fridge and sits me down to talk about 'the day when the sunshine turned to darkness'.

*

Sharon had been the director of a childcare centre, but always being on the go, meeting people, solving their problems, had left her burnt out. Her marriage was suddenly kaput and there she was: a single mother at 32, unemployed and living in a housing commission flat. It wasn't quite what she'd expected in life, but she had two beautiful kids aged six and nine, and they were happy. In mid 1989, they moved to a townhouse flat in Carmichael Court, Wynnum West, in Brisbane's eastern suburbs. It seemed like a good move. It was a nice place and next door were two lovely neighbours, Tony and Jeannie, with two kids a few years younger than hers.

She bonded straight away with Tony and Jeannie. They seemed like great parents, happy and laughing. She remembers sitting in the sun with the photo albums out, drinking coffee and catching up on each other's lives. New best friends. Their daughter Krystal, two, was always running around with a rag doll and chasing after Sharon's six-year-old boy, Luke.

Maybe Sharon heard her neighbours arguing once or twice but nothing remarkable. One morning Jeannie hosted a lingerie party at her place, everyone sipping tea and having a laugh like there was nothing wrong. But the next day Jeannie announced she was leaving Tony for another bloke and that was it. She was gone.

A few days later, 29 June 1989, Jeannie was due to come back and pick up some of her gear. It was the school holidays so Sharon had her kids with her when she walked past Tony's place on their way to the shops. He opened the door, agitated: 'Has she called you?'

'No, not yet Tony.'

'Are you sure she hasn't called?'

'Yes, Tony.'

An hour or so later, as she returned with the shopping, he opened the door again. His face had changed somehow. She saw that he'd been drinking wine. 'Have you heard from her?'

'Tony, I've just come from the shopping centre. How could I talk to her?'

He slammed the door shut, but then came to her flat a few more times – more drunk with each visit – asking if she was there yet.

Jeannie eventually did turn up at Sharon's just after lunch, with Krystal and the baby, Jonathan. Sharon felt she had to try to warn her that Tony wasn't right. 'Don't you think it's better you get the police or your mum and dad or someone to go in with you?'

'No. No. He wouldn't hurt me.'

'I don't know. He's not himself.'

They chatted some more before Jeannie decided it was time to go in.

'Krystal's playing with Luke,' Sharon said. 'Why don't you leave Jonathan with me?'

'He'll be fine in there.' And with that, Jeannie left, carrying the baby in her arms.

Sharon got stuck into the lunchtime dishes. Her daughter, Sophia, nine, was playing outside while Luke and Krystal scurried about the townhouse.

*

Up to this point in her storytelling, Sharon has been a bit disorganised, bringing disparate elements together, but something happens around about here. Her focus sharpens. Her body stiffens. 'Five, ten minutes later I heard Jeannie screaming, "Sharon! Sharon! Help me! Help me!" Funny enough, silly me, I just thought he was punching her. I ran in there. No, he was in the kitchen standing over her, stabbing her.' Sharon's voice trails off, almost dreamlike. 'Stabbing her . . . and stabbing her . . .'

At the time, I am struck by Sharon's eloquence and her pained body language. Later, listening to the recording, I realise that she is back there, channelling the moment.

'I said, "Tony, Tony, stop! It's not worth it. Don't do it." He seemed to snap out of it, and he stopped. He said, "I love you Jeannie. I love you." And then he went back to trying to stab her again. Jeannie was hysterical. Frightened and in a lot of pain. She kept saying, "Tony, don't! Tony, no!" I had to get her out. And he was *stabbing*. He was *crazed*. His whole face was different. I don't know how to explain what he was like. No one was home. So I wrestled Tony from there to the lounge and Jonathan was sitting on the lounge. I had to fight him. I had to punch him and fight him. He was crazed with that knife. I knew if I didn't get her out, she would be dead. She was in shock. Blood was everywhere. Everywhere. So I fought with strength I didn't know I had. Look at me, I'm a little person. I had to get her out the front door and maybe I could get help. Through the lounge he kept stabbing and stabbing at her and all of a sudden I pushed him away. He turned on me, pointed the knife at me. Before that he never turned on me. He went back to being Tony for some reason. His face changed. He went, "SHAAAAAROOOOOON!" I yelled "Tony! Stop it!" Next thing he went back to a crazy man again. And started stabbing her. I was so close to the front door. I had her by the legs, trying to get her out. He had her by the hair and was going for her throat. I thought, if he stabs her there, she's gone. So I pushed him with everything I had and he fell over the stairs near the door and I dragged her out. She couldn't walk. Then he slammed the door in our faces.

'She was bleeding everywhere. It was all over me, all over her. I can't remember. People said they were yelling, but I don't remember. All I remember is taking her to the car park and that her new boyfriend was there. I said . . .' Sharon pauses for almost a minute until she fills the silence with a sigh. 'I said, "You have to get her to a hospital because she is . . ."' Sharon is crying now, during another long pause, looking hard left like she's talking to someone over her shoulder. '". . . in a really bad way." And I think it's just our motherly instincts. She said, "Sharon . . . Don't worry about me . . . go and get my kids." So I ran all the way back . . . to get Krystal and Jonathan . . . I grabbed Krystal . . .' Sharon sobs, still looking hard left. '. . . I didn't even see my own son standing out there, and I started to run. That's when I heard the first gunshot. I didn't even know he had a gun. I picked Krystal up and put her on my hip to run faster. I ran for the tree close to the road because I knew by then somebody must be coming. Nobody was coming yet. The next gunshot went through my arm into Krystal's back and I fell over not far from that tree. I knew she'd been shot.

Her whole back just fell onto me and I stumbled on with her. I hoped she wasn't dead. I hoped like anything she wasn't dead. I didn't care about my arm being shot. I just hoped.'

Sharon put Krystal down near the tree and turned back to try and get Jeannie's other child, eight-month-old Jonathan. Tony was standing in the doorway, looking at her with that other face. 'Do not even try,' he said, slamming the door. She saw her own son right outside Tony's window. 'Luke! Run!' she called. And she thanks God every day that he listened.

'I didn't know where my daughter was. With all that happening, I was yelling out to everyone, screaming, "Get your children! Take them inside! Just get your children!" I ran to one lady's house. I knocked on her door and told her to ring the police. I told her how serious it was. She slammed the door in my face and told me to leave.'

Sharon pulls another cigarette and, with emotion wafting thick in the air, my eyes fixate on the pack of Horizon 50s – 'Smoking: a leading cause of death' – while I ponder that I've never before had the urge to hug someone mid-interview.

'Then the police turned up. By then I'd done everything I could and warned everybody and I had to find my own son and daughter. The police walked straight down the path in the line of fire and by then he was a *crazy* man.'

*

The first shot fired had hit Jeannie's new boyfriend, Brian Pottinger, in the shoulder while he was in the driver's seat of his car. He was able to drive to a medical centre a few hundred metres away before he reportedly passed out.

A neighbour, Barbara Clarke, had seen Krystal lying near the big tree where Sharon had left her. Barbara ran to the girl and picked her up, but she mustn't have known where the shooting was coming from because she ran straight towards the unit where Tony was. He shot her in the hip and she fell, leaving her and the child wounded in the no-man's-land outside his window.

The first police officers on the scene were plain-clothes constables from the Juvenile Aid branch. They got out of their unmarked car and were asking neighbours what was happening when more shots rang out. Constable Brett Handran was shot in the head and Constable Stephen Clarey was shot in the gut.

*

Constable Rob Rodgers was in the sergeant's office at Wynnum police station when the call came through at 1.13 pm that a man had gone berserk with a gun at Carmichael Court. The 26-year-old had the keys to the patrol car in his pocket. A whole lot of police ran out of the station and piled into the car. Rob drove, fast, with lights and siren. But these sorts of calls usually fizzled. They'd arrive to a quiet house and the shooter long gone, if there'd even been a shooter.

He saw Brett Handran and Stephen Clarey's vehicle and a Traffic Branch vehicle drive into Carmichael Court, but he pulled up on the main thoroughfare, Wynnum Road, at the side of the Carmichael Court public housing complex. A couple of shots echoed about and all the police drew their guns and took cover, some behind the police car, others behind trees. Rob could see commotion behind the Traffic Branch vehicle inside Carmichael Court, but he had no idea that two officers were lying seriously wounded on the ground in there. He called out to the Traffic Branch guys to see if they knew where the gunman was, but got no answer.

He called to two women on the second storey of the nearest block of units: 'Where is he?' They motioned to the next set of units.

Rob looked and saw what he thought was the next block of units. *If somebody's pinned down or under fire, I'm absolutely useless here. I need to get closer.* So he sprinted to a tree, then the next tree, zigzagging forwards, keeping his eyes fixed on the units so that if the gunman poked his head out, he could bolt for cover. Seeing no one in the units, he broke cover to run the last 25 metres to a power box surrounded by a picket fence. He dived in behind the fence where a worker from the power company was hiding.

'Do you have any idea where he is?' Rob asked.

'He's there.' The worker pointed to a completely different set of units recessed in behind the first set and Rob realised he'd just run all that way completely exposed to the gunman. *Oh great.* He dropped from his haunches into a sitting position where he stayed, realising he was pinned down.

'Somebody had better do something about those two others or they'll die,' the worker said.

'What two others?' Rob asked, ignorant of the carnage that had preceded his arrival.

'There's a lady there and a baby been shot.'

'Where?'

'On the path right in front of the unit where he's firing from.'

They were only about 25 metres away, but Rob felt useless. He needed to do something. Those people could bleed to death. He decided that the only way to help was to start talking.

'Can you hear me?' he called out in the direction of the gunman. 'I want to talk to you. There's some people hurt and they'll die if they don't get attention. Will you let me help them? Can I do it?'

'Yes, do it,' a voice came back from the unit, perhaps 35 metres away.

Rob wasn't sure if he could believe the gunman. 'I'm a

family man,' he called back. 'I want to survive this. I don't want to stand up and get shot. Will you let me do it?'

'Yes, do it.'

If he was going to help, he had to accept the guy's word.

*

Rob had wanted to be a copper since he was a kid. He applied when he left school and passed all the tests, but he just wasn't heavy enough. The police force of old required height and weight. So he embarked on an eat-a-thon and applied again, but after three months of stuffing his face he'd hardly put on a kilo. So he gave up on the dream and set about pursuing a new one – Bible college and a career as a pastor. But about a year after failing the weigh-in, the force contacted him and invited him to reapply. He was elated. The pastoral dream got overtaken by the childhood one. He'd married since his last application and there was something about wedded life that meant his weight had now looked after itself. His wife, Michelle, was in labour with their first child when he completed his last exam at the academy.

Unleashed on the streets of central Brisbane, he led his squad of graduates in their 'figures' – arrests and general police work. He was always eager to help. To be useful. But he was transferred to a quiet suburban backwater and no matter how hard he tried to get senior colleagues out there churning their figures, he couldn't fight the inertia and promptly fell to the bottom of his class.

After a few years working around the traps, including a stint in plain clothes, he'd landed at Wynnum police and was happy there – good people and good work. He'd been a copper now for five years and he aspired to be a detective. He was a happily married father of a young son. And here he was about to step into the sights of a berserk man with a powerful rifle.

He's not quite sure why he did what he did next. The adrenaline was pumping, all systems were powering. *If I'm going to carry two people out, the car's gunna come in handy.* So he sprinted back across the open space to Wynnum Road and jumped in the police car. He swung it left into Carmichael Court, then left into the car park. Past where the two policemen were lying wounded. He thinks they were being tended to, but he wouldn't remember much about them. He can't say with certainty if he even knew they were there. He honked the horn to move people out of the way. All his attention was on the woman and the child in no-man's-land and what he had to do next.

Rob parked the car behind the block of units he'd originally set out for then walked the path towards the gunman. 'I'm coming,' he called. 'Don't shoot. It's me. You know who I am. For God's sake, don't shoot. The child is injured. Will you let me get it? Will you let me get it?'

'Yes, do it.'

His gun was in his hand but he realised it wasn't going to do him much good. If the guy wanted to shoot him, he would. And besides, he'd need the hand to carry the victims. So he slipped the weapon back into the fancy quick-release, spring-loaded holster he'd just had specially made up. The idea had been that every second counted in such an emergency but now he was in one, he knew that it wasn't going to matter how quick he was. 'I'm putting my gun away. Don't shoot. It's me. I'm coming to help these people.'

He reached the girl first. Her pupils were dilated and she was still. He didn't see blood. Or his mind didn't register blood. Alive or dead? He didn't know. He just picked her up and ran back towards his car.

*

Concreter Glenn Kelk was no cop lover, but as he watched Rob Rodgers bring the girl to safety he thought the guy should have got four bravery medals for what he'd just done. Glenn had been working on a building site next door. He'd heard shots and come running over. He saw the two officers who'd been shot then he found two policemen hiding behind some trees or maybe posts – he only knows for sure that they were hiding.

'What the hell's going on?' he asked them.

'Get down for Christ's sake,' one of them said.

'They're not after me, mate. They're after youse blokes,' said Glenn, confident that his rubber gumboots would set him apart.

They watched as Rob picked up the girl and came over near them. There were two ambulances back on Wynnum Road but they weren't moving, and the other coppers just seemed interested in shooting the bastard rather than helping the victims so Glenn thought it might as well be him. *There's a kid involved, for Christ's sake.* He stood and walked to Rob who handed the child over.

Glenn saw blood everywhere. But the girl was alive, he was sure. She was moving. There was a neat hole in her front and her back had been blasted out. Glenn looked towards the stationary ambulances again. 'Get the bloody hell over here,' he shouted.

'Nah. We can't.'

So Glenn carried the child back across the open ground past the gunman to the ambulances, calling them every effing name that sprang to mind. He passed the woman lying on the edge of the garden bed and he didn't think she'd survive. He got to the ambos and served them up some more expletives.

'We couldn't go across there. We might get shot.'

'You get fucking shot, you get shot, you dickhead.'

He told them not to put the girl in the ambulance, that they could just carry her over the road to the medical centre, but the ambos insisted on putting her in the vehicle and it seemed like twenty minutes before they finally rolled off.

*

Rob Rodgers had gone back to get Barbara Clarke who was lying on the edge of a garden bed. She looked too big to lift so he tried dragging her by the arm, but her screams put a stop to that after about a metre. 'No, no, don't move me,' she said. 'I'm in terrible pain. Don't move me.'

I can't listen to that. I can't leave her here.

He got down with one hand around her shoulders and under her armpit and the other under the back of her knees, and he lifted. 'No, no, don't move me,' she screamed. He probably wasn't being as attentive to her needs as he might have been, but under the gaze of the gunman just metres away he was bent on getting her away. He struggled under her weight. He couldn't quite straighten. His knees wobbled like a weightlifter about to falter but he staggered off, vaguely aware that it would be comical if it weren't so dire.

He got Barbara to the car where there seemed to be plenty of willing hands to look after her. He yelled in the direction of the Traffic Branch vehicle, saying he needed an ambulance urgently and that the woman might bleed to death. 'I don't think he'll shoot at an ambulance. He let me in right in front of him.'

But Rob was unaware of the drama unfolding with the two shot policemen near the Traffic Branch vehicle.

*

Sergeant Jim Birmingham had heard the call over the police radio. He and his partner in the scenes-of-crime car, Detective

Senior Constable Terry Ryan, put the siren on and hightailed it to Wynnum West, about 25 kilometres away. There'd been a long stand-off by the time they got there. They could see the wounded officers on the ground with nobody able to get to them. The ambulances weren't allowed in; it was too dangerous. Terry turned to Jim: 'Jim, can you grab one of those ambulances and I'll grab the other and we'll get these blokes out of here.'

And that's what they did. They had no idea about what Rob Rodgers was doing just as Rob had no idea about them. So it is difficult to know when exactly they did this, but they went over to Wynnum Road, commandeered the two ambulances and drove into no-man's-land where the wounded officers were lying close to each other next to their unmarked car. With the possibility that the gunman could open fire on them at any moment, they got out of their ambulances and collected the wounded men. Jim got Brett Handran into his ambulance and Terry got Stephen Clarey into his.

Jim wouldn't remember if he was alone or had someone with him. He thinks someone must have been there because he can't see how he could have lifted Brett into the ambulance alone.

'We knew Brett was in a bad way, he was bleeding to death. He was still alive when I put him in the ambulance, but he didn't have much life left in him when we got him out.' Brett Handran was pronounced dead soon after.

*

With Barbara Clarke being attended to by onlookers, Rob Rodgers thought that since he'd built a rapport with the gunman — in that at least he hadn't been shot — maybe he could go back and talk him into surrender.

He went into the end unit of the block closest to the gunman's block. He knocked on the door and the people inside allowed him through to the rear bedroom. He opened the window and called out, 'It's me again. I want to talk to you. Will you talk to me?'

He heard the guy say something but he couldn't make out what it was. By now media helicopters were hovering overhead.

'I don't know your name. Can you tell me your name?' Rob asked.

'You know my name.'

'I can't hear you properly with all the noise. Do you have the phone on?'

'No.'

Rob kept trying to talk and at one point the gunman did call out a phone number but Rob couldn't hear it. He realised he was useless where he was. *If I can't hear him, I'm no help to anybody.* So he decided to go down the path to the unit next to the gunman's. He didn't feel in danger. They had a rapport.

On the way, he passed a man hiding and asked him if he knew the guy's name.

'Tony.'

'Tony who?'

'I can't remember his last name.'

'Do you know what he looks like?'

'He's got red hair.'

Rob went into the neighbouring unit through the back door and made his way to the open front door. Just then, he heard footsteps at the back door and he swung his revolver around. He heard a shot fired. And as it echoed about, a policeman appeared at the back door. At first, Rob thought the gunman had shot at the other officer, but then realised the shot had sounded muffled.

Rob called out through the brick wall. 'It's me again, Tony. I'm next door.' No answer. 'This is a terrible mess, mate, but it doesn't have to end up a tragedy. Nobody else has to die and you don't have to die.'

Still no answer.

Rob wanted Tony to live. He had no idea of the carnage he'd wrought. Even though he'd picked up Krystal with her back blown out, he didn't know for sure she'd even been injured. It was like his brain had blocked it out. And he only knew that Barbara Clarke was hurt because she'd told him so emphatically.

Rob and the other policeman called out some more to this man they'd never laid eyes on. A baby was crying inside Tony's unit. Rob dialled triple-0 and informed the duty inspector of his suspicion that the gunman was dead. He went upstairs and saw that a ledge ran under the window. He could walk along it and get into the unit . . . *But what would I do then?* Caution got the better of him and he stayed put.

*

Night was approaching when heavily armed police stormed the unit and found Tony Dolerud, 25, dead on the floor. Shot in the head. The baby, Jonathan, was safe and well.

Constable Rob Rodgers was told by an inspector to go back to the station, dictate everything he remembered into a tape recorder, then go home.

Glenn Kelk had already gone back to work. He had concrete going off.

Sharon O'Leary had found her son, Luke, and she'd been told that her daughter, Sophia, was safe with a neighbour, saying her prayers. Sharon had bunkered down in another unit until word came through that it was safe to come out. But it was not over for her.

*

'The night was dark,' she tells me. 'Ambulance people came to see me. Then the detectives got me and said they wanted to do a video, to maybe help them in the future. Yeah, well, great. Might help them in the future, but don't worry about poor old me. I hadn't even seen my daughter. So you go, "Yep, okay." And there's your unit and you have nice memories of what it was like in there. And there's Krystal's little doll on the footpath, her favourite bird in the cage, gone. You look down and you see nothing but blood and brain matter and you look up and there you see Tony's body, not covered, nothing.' Sharon has been sniffing then sobbing through this monologue. Now she pauses a long time. 'Not even covered.' She stops again. A long, angry and sad silence. 'You see the hole in the wall. Behind the upstairs where they said he blew his brains out. They ask you to start from the beginning and you see the blood, you see everything, and it's hard. Then they take you outside. And it's dark. And you just see a million people. Right over the road to Kentucky Fried. All cordoned off. You see the news media. You see everybody and they hide you around a corner. And while they're asking you more things, they say, "Do you want a smoke?" I only just gave up. I had a thing in my ear. Ripped that out. Then you stand there with 'em and you see Tony's body going out in a black bag and all the guns and everything he had. And I started crying. Might sound stupid. It's the weak . . . I think it's the weak that can't handle things in life. I don't hate him. I never hated him. I probably hate them [the detectives] more than anything. They had no right to take me in there with his body not covered, his head blown off. All the time I was with them, I kept asking, "Is Krystal alive?" And they kept saying, "Yeah, she's in hospital." I was so happy. *I've done it! I've saved Jeannie. Jonathan's safe. Krystal isn't well, but she's fighting.* You go to the same doctor Krystal saw because you need to be treated for shock and the bullet wound in your arm and the doctor has to tell you, "I never made it with her. She died." She is out in the back room, waiting for the coroner to pick her up. How cruel can the detectives be? They knew all along she was dead but they made me believe for hours and hours. That destroys you. I tried so hard. I thought I was so close. The night was dark. Nobody told me.

'I went back into my unit. It was ransacked. Upstairs in my boy's bedroom, the window was smashed. You've got two kids frightened to death and you've got to find somewhere that night. It's freezing cold and raining. The media's gone. You don't know where you're going to go and you've got nobody. You've got no family, you've got no husband. My ex lived in Melbourne. You see others, they have a partner come and give them a cuddle and you're just alone and after that you're totally alone. You are *so* alone. From then on we were always alone. You do your best to bring your kids up. I had some good friends from my kids' karate. We moved in with them – all together in a bed. Didn't matter. We felt safe.

'I went to see Jeannie in the hospital and her whole family was there. Jonathan in his pram. They greeted me with hugs and kisses and lots of love. Jeannie could hardly breathe. She was stabbed everywhere. And I felt like a failure. I failed her. We hugged and cried, and we hugged and we cried. She could hardly talk and she said to me, "You tried." But I knew I'd let her down. I didn't make it with her little precious.'

*

Sharon later moved back into her unit. Somebody organised some people to cleanse the evil from next door. She didn't believe in all that hoodoo-voodoo but the gesture was nice. Neighbours gave her flowers and said if it wasn't for her screaming out they might have lost their kids.

105

With no family support, Sharon had to keep getting up in the morning to take the kids to school. That didn't last long. She couldn't do it. She couldn't go out the front door. She couldn't even go out the back to hang the washing because she saw Krystal playing there. A lovely social worker tried to help. Sharon booked into Belmont psychiatric hospital. She should have stayed for a fortnight, a month, but there was nobody to look after the kids. She knew she just had to get strong again. She checked out after two days.

The housing commission was slow finding her a new place so she tried her mum's. 'She kicked us out. She said I was stupid to get involved. So since then it's been me and the kids, three musketeers, going through everything, trying to be strong. I've let them down a few times, but I still get back on top of things.

'And the media were all over me. I just told them I didn't want to speak to them, so I didn't. The only reason I spoke to *New Idea* was that everybody thought we were all unmarried mothers living in housing commission and because you lived there you deserved it. So I got all dressed up, make-up, the works, to lay it all straight. I'm actually a very intelligent woman. Always have been. Always *was*. A company director. But I can't even leave my home any more. And a newspaper reporter tracked me down. He told me that the incident had turned him into an alcoholic and his wife and kids had left him. I felt sorry for him. He asked me then, "Would you do it again?" I said, "Yes, I would." And if you asked me now, I'd still say, "Yes, I would help somebody". Why wouldn't I?'

*

Two years after the incident, it was announced that Sharon O'Leary, Rob Rodgers and Barbara Clarke were to be awarded Stars of Courage. Concreter Glenn Kelk and the two officers who requisitioned the ambulances, Jim Birmingham and Terry Ryan, were each awarded Commendations for Brave Conduct.

The *Courier-Mail* focused on Sharon in its story: 'When it comes to fearless courage, Sharon is a star.' She told the reporter:

> I feel so special. Apparently it allows me to have the letters 'SC' after my name. Imagine that – I feel like I've been knighted. This is the first good thing to come out of the incident. For two years I've lived with that day – with the blood everywhere when he was stabbing Jeannie and the shock I felt when I got shot and didn't realise that the bullet had killed Krystal . . . It's all still there with me. I'm still taking grief counselling and have the sleepless nights. And when I'm in the shower and have nothing else to concentrate on, the tears come. Yes, nothing good has come out of that day – until now.

*

Sharon started to cry during the newspaper interview and her daughter Sophia – eleven-years-old but wise beyond her years – told her: 'You've got us, Mum – and me and Luke have got you. Imagine that, we've got a hero for a mum.'

At the awards ceremony the next month, Sharon was seated next to a woman whose husband had been killed in a hotel fire at Longreach. It was Fay Jeppesen, and even though Sharon has long since forgotten her name she has never forgotten her good grace, turning to Sharon and saying words to the effect of, 'You deserve this so much more than my husband.'

'No, you've got to be proud of what your husband did.'

But Fay Jeppesen wouldn't remember any of this. She was lost in her own daze of sadness, needing help just to get out of her seat to accept Bob's award.

They retired to the Government House grounds where wine and canapés were served – last thing in the world Sharon wanted, she was wound up so tight. The other award recipients from the shooting were there, too, including Barbara Clarke and Rob Rodgers. And then the media flocked. Here they all went, again.

*

The hoo-ha over, Sharon packed the medal back into its little case and went home. She'd love to use the letters SC after her name but never would because it might cause somebody to ask her what it meant. *Who's Who* put her in, then hit her up for 270 dollars for a copy. She paid it the first year and every year they ask her again. They had to be kidding.

She was filled with anger. Anger that you wouldn't believe. It ate away at her. 'Why me?' 'Why that day?' 'Why didn't I do this?' 'Why did those detectives do that?' So angry she just wanted to punch someone or something. She was a different person. A beast. She did the round of psychiatrists. Took their drugs. Walked out more crazy than when she walked in.

About six years after the incident, she found a psychologist who taught her to walk again. She was all bent over, clutching her bag tight to her chest, protecting herself. Weird ways of walking were one of the first things doctors noted about shell-shock victims in World War I. 'You never dreamt of such gaits – the craziest, un-text book things,' noted Canadian doctor Sir William Osler. 'One fellow was just like Blondin [a trapeze artist] on a tightrope . . . with his feet far apart, the arms out, the man balancing himself and making several attempts with his hind foot before taking a step.'

Sharon had to learn to stand up, breathe, relax, shoulders back. The psychologist didn't believe in all the drugs but she still needed the sleeping pills . . . and the pills to get her through the day. She needed tablets for her blood pressure. The stress was shutting down her kidneys. Her immune system was shot. Nothing works well with all that adrenaline pulsing through your veins.

*

The workings of the brain continue to be a mystery to medicine, but it is thought that the high levels of adrenaline, noradrenaline and cortisol might physically damage vital areas. Certainly, people with post-traumatic stress disorder do have differences in their brains from the broader population. There is a part near the temple called the hippocampus which is important for memory. It is smaller in sufferers of post-traumatic stress disorder, but it is not known if it was smaller before the trauma or if the brain chemicals have shrunk it. Near the hippocampus is an almond-shaped region called the amygdala which stores fear memories. That is, memory of the fear itself. The memories of the actual events are stored elsewhere. The amygdala doesn't distinguish between the fear you have for bikes because you once fell off one, or your fear of sausages because you once almost choked on one. It just remembers the fear. And if something triggers the amygdala – the smell of sausages, say, or the ringing of a bicycle bell – it can set the body off on full flight-or-fight mode, releasing all the adrenaline and noradrenaline of the original event, effectively hijacking the brain. Recall John Thurgar's unwillingness to smell diesel fuel (see Chapter Six). His amygdala has stored the fear memory with the smell memory and forever linked the two.

Balancing this should be another part of the brain called the cingulate cortex, which works to dampen down strong emotions. A person anxious about having to make a speech will have their cingulate cortex working to counter the anxiety so that they can still function. In sufferers of post-traumatic stress disorder, the cingulate cortex has been found to be both smaller and less active, but again it is not known if this was pre-existing or if the trauma caused it.

*

'My doctor says I'm one in a million,' Sharon continues. 'He says he doesn't know how I could go through what I've been through, plus many other things I'm not going to talk about, and survive. But it did destroy my life. I won't catch a plane. I won't go in a bus. It's all closed in. I won't go in a lift. I don't like people close to me. I need space. If I have to leave the house, it's a big deal. Plus the clinical depression. But having said all that, at least I'm still here. I'm strong, I think. I have wonderful grandchildren. Don't tell everyone the doom and gloom. Give 'em some hope.'

She says she'd like to write a book about her life. She's had so many people tell her she should. 'I just need to find a really good author. I could give people some hope. Taking your own life is not the answer.'

I tell her I think she needs a happy ending.

'I don't think it will ever come in my life. You ask Mr Bob [Rob Rodgers, who she knows I am going to interview a few days later]. I really hope he's coping but I feel so sorry for him.'

She hasn't seen Jeannie since Jeannie turned up to Krystal's funeral in a wheelchair. She spoke to her many years ago on the phone. Jeannie didn't remember anything. Sharon is starting to think she'd like to contact her again, but she's not sure if she's ready. 'She told me after that day that she'd keep everything and as Jonathan grew up she'd tell him he must come and visit me. I'm still waiting for that day. He must be twenty-two or something by now.'

Her daughter, Sophia, has become interested in the events that so radically changed her mother. She wants to research everything she can and meet Jeannie. And Sharon only discovered a few weeks earlier that her son, Luke, can remember seeing a blue flash from the gun when she and Krystal were shot and then he saw Tony point the gun at him, but didn't fire. Luke declines to be interviewed for this book.

We say our goodbyes and I head for the car. The emotion of such an encounter has left me . . . Buzzing? Spinning? I'm not sure of the word for it. Sharon calls out: 'You talk to Bob and tell him from me, I hope he has let that anger go because if he hasn't, anger is just going to eat him up and up and up. And if he's seeing a psychiatrist, tell him from me, don't bother. They only screw your head up.'

I tell her to keep working on that happy ending for her book.

'The happy ending is that I'm still alive. I'm still here.'

*

The day after the awards ceremony, the *Courier-Mail* came out with the headline 'Shooting hero braves the unemployment queue'. It said Rob Rodgers had hardly worked as a policeman again after the incident and retired from the force on medical grounds six months later.

Rob (he was called Bob in the police force but prefers Rob now) had been reluctant to be interviewed. We had talked on the phone and he told me he recently knocked back a television interview request, 'because hardly anybody around me knows about this. I'm not really interested in chasing fame or notoriety on the back of it. It happened. It fuels me for my mission in life, but I'm not really riding on the back of it in any way.'

He asks to read some chapters I've already written, 'so I can see where it's heading'. I send a few off and a week or so later he agrees to talk when I'm in Queensland on my research trip.

He greets me at the door of his two-storey Sunshine Coast home wearing a black sloppy joe: 'I heart Bli Bli Community Baptist Church'.

He makes me a coffee and we sit down to talk.

Having read the article – 'Shooting hero braves the unemployment queue' – I'd expected to find somebody as badly affected as Sharon O'Leary, but Rob assures me that he hardly ever thinks about it. He tells of the events as a story, not like Sharon who told them as if she was back in the moment. He sees the humour in him dashing from tree to tree, only to realise he'd been exposed to the gunman the whole time. The slapstick in him stumbling under the weight of Barbara Clarke. But it was not so simple at the start.

He fronted up for work the next day and continued to work as rostered for the next couple of weeks, but he was running on adrenaline, couldn't get it out of his mind, couldn't sleep. His wife, Michelle, remembers him being a bit depressed – maybe because he couldn't save the girl.

He thinks the depression was more a product of not being able to sleep and having the events looping in his brain.

'I remember doing some real thinking after the incident. See, I wasn't a policeman when I got married. My wife hadn't married a policeman as part of the deal. I don't think she was very happy with me being a policeman and less so after that day. I was wondering whether to stay in the police force or not. I remember an inspector saying to me within a couple of weeks, "I think you're going to get a medal for this. And basically wherever you want to transfer to, you're pretty much assured of it." Wow. I could've gone and been a detective or got in the water police. Nobody gets in the water police. But then, was this really good for us as a married couple? I had this real yearning to get away from everything. To buy a boat and go. I'd made some friends who owned a yacht at the Manly marina. These guys were cruisers. They'd work somewhere for a while, then up anchor and go. I'd love that life. I had an obsession with that.'

With all this going on in his head, somebody recognised post-traumatic stress and recommended he see the police psychiatrist. He doesn't remember talking to the psychiatrist at any length. It was more a matter of 'take these twice a day and off you go'. Rob was prescribed the antidepressant lithium.

'I really can't tell you much about the next six months. I was so drugged up that I don't remember. My wife, Shelly, tells me I walked around the house like a zombie. Got out of bed, flopped on the lounge. When it was time for bed, I got up and went to bed. It was a nothing kind of existence. The only thing I do remember is shortly after, I talked to people who claimed to be on heavy doses of lithium and I'd say, "How much are you on?" And it turned out I was on three times their dose.

'I was on indefinite sick leave due to being zombified by this psychiatrist. So I was no use to them. I guess they thought, "Let's superannuate him out before it gets too expensive." They retired me just weeks before I was due to get a stripe and the payout would have been larger. I'd never seen anyone superannuated out so quickly. It wasn't against my will, but I didn't have a clear head to make good judgements at that point.

'I made a decision near the end of that six months to get off the medication. My head cleared up and I was fine. We ended up buying that yacht and we went off in it for a while, but my wife hated the yacht even more than she hated the police force. We sold it. I'd already got my life right with God. We settled on the Sunshine Coast.

'After the award ceremony, I was so cheesed off when I read that article. The unemployed hero thing sounded pitiful. The journalist just said at the end, "What are you doing these days?" I wasn't doing anything. "I'm looking for a job." Then to see these headlines. I didn't say I couldn't get a job, I said I was looking for work. It sounded like the next port of call was me hitting the streets as a wino. It had a pathetic ring to it. It wasn't how it was at all.'

He got involved in a church and did three years Bible college plus an extra two-and-a-half years part-time to get a graduate diploma of ministry. Then Rob and Michelle spent five years in Indonesia doing mission work and teaching English as a second language, but the funding dried up. Rob's mum died of cancer and his dad was living on his own, not coping so well. 'It was time to come back.'

Rob did a bit of security work for a while. 'What else does an ex-police officer do?' In 2005 he took on an interim ministry as a caretaker pastor, before starting the church in Bli Bli in 2006. 'We had to jump through a lot of hoops, presenting a strategy to Queensland Baptists, gathering demographic information on Bli Bli. What's the benefit of planting a church here?'

'How do you get yourself a congregation?' I ask.

'What we don't do is what they call in pastoral circles "sheep stealing". We don't convince people to leave a church to come to ours. Most of the people who come to ours have never been to church or have not been to church in a long time. They've been burnt somewhere along the line and given up on church. In almost four years we've built the congregation up to about fifty, including a dozen kids. We're an odd bunch. We're very loose and informal and rough around the edges. It's a great community of people who really care about one another. It's maybe not like other churches, but it seems more like the churches in the Bible to me.

'Carmichael Court did shape my life, in leaving the police force and changing my philosophy on life. I just really see life as a journey but a very unpredictable one. The only thing I'm convinced of is that this unpredictable life starts with God and ends with God. The only thing that's of critical importance is to be right with God. That's my task now – to help people find their way to be right with God. I think I'm still in the business of saving souls. It's not flash, it's not dramatic. It'll never make it into a book, but to me it's more important than what I did back then.'

NINE

Len Williams

Whether or not the guard compartment on the all-stations from Gosford to Newcastle is at the back of the train or the front is determined purely by the whim of shunting staff. As it happens, on 10 January 1983, when train guard Len Williams starts work he finds he'll be at the front of the little two-carriage diesel railcar plying the New South Wales central coast.

Early in the journey, after departing Narara Station, he pokes his head in next door to say g'day to the driver. They exchange pleasantries and both men are looking out the front when an object comes into view on the opposite track. Maybe it's a dog, they aren't sure. But then, when they are about 200 metres away, the object stands up and it suddenly becomes clear that it is a toddler dressed all in white.

The train, travelling about 80 kilometres an hour, jerks hard, sliding on locked wheels. 'Has the express passed yet?' Len yells over the squealing of the wheels to the driver.

'No.'

The Newcastle-to-Sydney express service is due through at any moment on the track where the baby is standing.

'Blow the whistle. It might scare him off.'

With the wheels still squealing, Len opens the external door and climbs down the ladder, thinking he'll jump off and grab the kid, but the train is moving too fast. Sparks fly off the wheels.

He climbs back up to get a clearer picture of what's going on. 'Keep blowing the whistle!' Len climbs back down, ready for the train to slow. He is four rungs down the ladder when he sees the express, maybe 300 metres on the other side of the baby, gliding through the bend at Niagara Park Station, doing about 100 kilometres an hour. At that rate it covers 100 metres in 3.6 seconds. At 300 metres distance, the child has 10.8 seconds to live.

Shit! The kid's dead. I can't get to him. And Len knows he'll be dead, too, if he stays where he is. The suction of the passing train will surely rip him off the ladder. He feels he doesn't have time to clamber back up. The express driver blows his whistle for the level crossing at the station, still oblivious to the drama unfolding out of the curve.

The little diesel railcar has slowed to maybe twenty kilometres an hour now and Len takes his chance, jumping with the intention of rolling clear to save himself. The kid is as good as dead. His feet hit the ground running. He stumbles as he sprints with the train's momentum. But he regains his balance and looks up. The baby is suddenly a lot closer — maybe fifteen metres away — and so is the blue-faced express.

There is no time to weigh options and distances and risk, but as he runs beside the train some primitive part of his brain is doing just that. And that's when the impulse shoots into his head. *I can do this.* He figures he might just be able to grab the kid's arm and dive clear. *If I miss he's dead. If I don't have a go he's dead. If I don't throw myself clear in time, we're both dead.* At the instant he makes the decision to have a go, the little fella in the white singlet and cloth nappy looks at him and screams a scream of utter terror. With the squealing steel wheels, the diesel railcar whistle still blowing, the child screaming, Len's world goes inexplicably quiet. There is total silence as he floats along the tracks.

Shit, I'm dead. I didn't get to him and the train's hit me and this is what it's like being dead. I'm in some sort of afterlife instant replay . . .

Research on perceptual distortions in combat has found that 85 per cent of police officers involved in a lethal gunfight experienced diminished sound perception – they couldn't hear their own gun firing, for example. Seventy-four per cent reported a feeling of being on automatic pilot; 72 per cent reported heightened visual clarity; and 65 per cent reported feeling that they were in slow motion time.

Len Williams is experiencing all these distortions. He can feel his legs moving, but not touching the ground. He can feel an intense awareness of every metre that the express bores down on him for the few measly centimetres he covers. He can see the face of the express driver who is hanging on the whistle with no time to stop.

For all that, he feels he still has a chance in this game of chicken: Man versus Train.

It's close, so close. Now he thinks he won't have time. Won't be able to bend over to pick up the child. But the baby, still looking at Len and not the looming train behind him, puts his hands up as if to be lifted. The simple act gives Len a chance. He grabs one wrist and dives – feeling the hot air pressure from the passing train push him down the embankment. If he'd had to bend, he wouldn't have made it, but now, as he tumbles down the bank he feels no weight in his hand.

Shit, I've ripped his arm off. Coming to rest in the ditch he takes stock. *Where's the kid?* He can hear him but he can't see him. His head is fuzzy. He cannot breathe. *There he is*. He's clinging to Len – two arms, two legs, a head. He is all there, screaming a scream that pierces the guard's head.

'For Christ's sake little fella, shut up and give me a go,' says Len who wants to cry, too. He tries to stand but can't. His legs just won't work. His arms don't work either. He is dizzy. He thinks he's been hurt, but he just has to wait a few moments to start breathing and for the oxygen to get back to his brain.

The driver of the diesel railcar comes back towards them, tentatively, hoping to God he isn't going to find two bodies minced along the tracks. 'Are you okay?'

'I think so.'

'That was bloody close. I thought you were both gone.'

When he's regained the energy to climb back into the guard's compartment, Len puts the baby – with muck and grease smeared over his face and through his hair – on his seat, he rings the bell and the diesel railcar rolls into Niagara Park Station. Len recognises the blue trousers and black shoes of an off-duty policeman getting off a train and he tries to get him to take custody of the child, but the copper doesn't want to know.

At Ourimbah Station he unlocks the signal box and calls through to Sydney and arranges for police to meet the train at Wyong, two stops further on.

The police wait there and he hands the child over. Len and the driver give their names and details and get back on the train. Len rings the bell and the driver eases the train out of the station. They are running six minutes late. Len Williams is the sort of train guard who will remember details like that and he'll also remember that they make up the six minutes and the train rolls into Newcastle spot on time.

*

When Len got home that night, his wife Carmen blew up at him. 'How dare you risk your life like that?' she'd remember saying. 'You could have left me a widow and the kids without a father.' But then she told him she was proud of him.

The parents of the boy, Ray and Vicki Armstrong, came to their house. Vicki threw her arms around Len and thanked him profusely.

'What can we do for you?' Ray asked.

'Nothing.'

'You just saved my son's life. We've got to do something.'

'Okay, when he grows up, tell him he can buy me a beer.'

*

Even before this incident, Len was getting to the point where he'd turn up for work in the morning wondering if they were going to kill some poor bugger today. After almost 30 years on the railways, he'd seen a few things he wished he hadn't. There was the little immigrant boy who'd hopped on the wrong train and, afraid of copping a hiding from his dad for being late, promptly hopped off it again – at 100 kilometres an hour.

Len saw him floating in the air outside his guard's compartment window. It felt like the kid was out there for three or four seconds, so close he could have reached out and grabbed him, before he hit a stanchion and promptly disappeared from view.

There was the woman who'd jumped under his train at Strathfield and gone under the power car. He'd got out onto the track to see where she was, hoping that he'd find her dead because then he could walk away and leave it to the emergency services. But she was moving, and just centimetres from a live 15,000-volt motor. He had to get down and calm her and keep her still then get her to crawl along underneath the car while hot metal burnt into his back. Her hand was missing and she had a great hole in her head that he shoved his hanky into. He dragged her onto the track while empty trains thundered past him on the next track and 200 people stared down from the platform above.

Then, not long before he saved the toddler, a woman pedestrian at the Woy Woy level crossing had stopped for a train to pass, then walked out behind it, not waiting for the boom gate to lift. She was cleaned up by Len's train coming in the opposite direction.

Len got out to investigate the body jammed into the cowcatcher at the front. He saw the rings on her fingers and her shopping bags strewn about – it seemed so personal – but her head was missing. He found it 50 metres further on.

A policeman came over to look at the body. The copper could hardly talk. 'Where's the um . . .'

'You want to see the head?'

'Yes.'

Len took him to it. 'There it is.' The policeman started to vomit. Uncontrollable, heaving vomit. Len turned away and by now the ambulance guys were there, starting to put the body into plastic sheets. He refused to look as he walked past to rejoin his train.

He still had to get his passengers to Gosford, but the impact with the woman had broken the small pipe that controlled the dead-man relay valve. The only way they could move the train was for the driver to go to the driver's cabin in the middle of the train. He applied the power from there while Len sat up front, relaying signals to him with the bells. The body fluids on the train had left a nauseating odour so he tied his handkerchief around his face like he was about to hold up a stage coach as he signalled the train forward through the next four stops to Gosford, trying not to breathe the foul acidic air.

'I put that out of my mind for many years,' he would recall

when we meet in early 2010. 'It's been coming back over the last few years. My wife says I've got to have some help. She's the one who suffers when I wake up thrashing around the bed and screaming out.'

After the incident with the kid on the tracks, his nightmares started out featuring two kids on the tracks with a train bearing down on them and Len having to save them both. Then there were three kids, and he could only save one. Then there were five, fifty, hundreds. They were in cots, in bassinettes and strollers. The train would be ploughing into the babies with body parts flying everywhere while Len screamed at the driver to stop.

*

There is a common perception that post-traumatic stress disorder – a term first recognised in 1980 – is a modern phenomenon with roots dating back perhaps as far as the shell-shock victims of World War I. But 'nervous disturbances' had been noted decades earlier, with the rise of the railways and train collisions. A Manchester surgeon, William Thorburn, gave a paper in 1913 on 'traumatic neuroses' based on his experience with 5000 patients, including hundreds thrown into the sea when a seaside resort pier had collapsed in 1885. Thorburn found:

> Railway collisions, their sudden occurrence, their dramatic setting, association of large numbers of injured, the social prominence of many victims, the wide publication of newspaper reports, and the growing importance of financial claim had all created a lurid mental picture in the injured, and indirectly affected the general public in such a way as to prepare a fertile soil for nervous disturbance, while, owing to the nature of the railway collision, there appeared also many cases characterised by great pain in the back.

For Len, the nightmares never had a chance to affect his performance as a railway guard. Just six weeks after he saved the baby, a car came at him on the wrong side of the road and he and Carmen were both seriously injured. A year later he was retired from the railways on health grounds and he hasn't worked since.

In October 2000, at Len's 60th birthday party, Carmen had invited a friend who worked for a local radio station. She was interviewing Len about his life when she asked him about the rescue on the tracks. He didn't want to talk about it.

'Do you ever wonder what that boy is doing now?' she asked.

'Yeah, I hope he's all grown up into a nice young man. I hope it was worth it.'

'We've got somebody here who wants to meet you.' A young bloke walked in holding a sixpack of Crown Lager and looking nervous. 'Do you know who this is?'

'I wouldn't have a bloody clue.'

'It's Gavin.'

'You've got to be joking.'

They hugged and shared an emotional moment.

Since then they've re-created that meeting for two television shows which made out they were being reunited for the first time.

Anyway, Len was proud of the Bravery Medal he was awarded for his rescue, but he gets annoyed when – as an ex–army reservist – he wears it to something like Anzac Day and has some Vietnam veteran look at it with great curiosity: 'It's a buy-your-own is it, mate?'

He might tell them he used to work on the railways and he picked it up in lost property, but when he tells them it is in fact a civilian bravery medal they'll offer to buy him a beer. Then he walks around the other side of the gathering and someone else will start staring.

'What's that, mate? A buy-your-own?'

TEN

Jeff Brackenrig and Sally Gregory

Sales rep Sally Gregory was entertaining clients – taking a bunch of scuba instructors and dive masters for a dive at Julian Rocks, off Byron Bay on the New South Wales far north coast. The ocean was still, the sun shining. Her friend Thilo sat on the bow playing his violin, sending gentle notes across the water away to the ragged ranges in the distant west.

The boat's skipper, Jeff Brackenrig, was struck by the beauty of it all. He was in charge of the two boats Sally's company had chartered to show off the new dive gear it was importing. At the end of the dive, as the divers slowly made their way to the surface to be greeted by the violin's strains, a weird shape suddenly broke the millpond water – flesh-coloured and conical. It was Sally wearing a prop from the new film *Coneheads*. She'd put a hole in the top so it wouldn't float off, then hidden it in her pocket to put it on underwater. Everyone laughed. That was Sal.

With all the divers safely back in the boat, Thilo was playing 'Ode to Joy', building to the crescendo. Jeff was at the stern pulling up the mermaid line – still marvelling at how wonderful the moment was – when he heard a call on the radio. He couldn't make out what was being said over the violin and people chatting. But he recognised the voice as Roger, the captain of a rival Sundive boat out at the rocks this morning. And he recognised stress in the voice.

'What was that about?' Jeff asked nobody in particular. 'What's wrong with Roger?'

'He's had a shark attack,' one of the blokes answered.

'Don't muck around. You don't joke about that sorta crap.'

'No, no, that's what he said.'

Jeff saw the other boat working with him for Byron Bay Dive Centre take off for Roger's boat at Kendricks Reef, about 800 metres away, and he swung his vessel around in pursuit. Thilo was still out on the bow. 'Sit there and hang on,' Jeff called out. 'You'll be right.' He ran at three-quarter speed so Thilo wouldn't get thrown off.

Approaching Kendricks Reef, he saw two of the divers on the other Byron Bay Dive Centre boat gearing up to go in.

'What are you doing?' he asked the skipper of the other boat.

'I'm going to put 'em in to see if they can find him. They reckon a bloke's been taken by a shark.'

'Nah, nah, you can't let them go in. Even if they're dive masters, they're still paying customers. But somebody does have to go looking for him. It's either you or me. Do you want to go?'

'I'm not goin'.'

'All right, it's me.'

Jeff turned to his diving peers on the boat. 'Somebody's got to go. I believe it should be me. Does anybody disagree with that?'

No one opposed him.

He motored over to Roger's boat, *Blue Groper*. All its divers were still in the water. The only people on board were Roger and a distraught woman huddled on the deck screaming. Roger was clearly distressed, too. Jeff recognised the woman immediately. Her name was Debbie Ford and she'd come into the shop the day before with her husband, John. They were both keen divers and they'd wanted to go out early this morning before heading back to Sydney. The earliest Jeff could book them in was 11.30 am because he already had Sally's charter to do. They took that timeslot reluctantly and the three of them chatted for 45 minutes about all things diving. They'd laughed and joked, said they hoped to see a grey nurse.

But they returned to the shop a little later and apologised that they were cancelling the booking. They'd been able to get on an 8.30 am boat with Sundive.

*

Earlier this morning, while Sally and her crew were in the water, the Sundive boat had come past, close to Julian Rocks, to check the current. Jeff waved to Debbie and John and they'd both waved back in high spirits.

Now as he manoeuvred his boat next to the Sundive boat, trying to get a direction on where the attack occurred and what the currents were doing, Debbie looked him straight in the eye from the other boat, desperate, pleading. 'Bring back John,' she said. 'Bring my husband back to me.'

He was in the crucible now. He had to find this bloke.

Sally offered to put her gear on and go down. 'Nah, I'll do that,' said Jeff. 'You go over there and do the girlie thing.'

He put a qualified skipper in charge of his boat. 'I want you to drive Sally over and put her on that boat and then follow my air bubbles.'

Jeff would remember Sally helping him to gear up. She doesn't remember that. As soon as he could, he was leaning over the side, ready to step into the deep. But before he did, something red and flesh-like caught his eye. He fished it out and had a look. It was probably lung, he thought, maybe a thigh muscle. He was no anatomist, just a country boy who knew his way around a carcass. The outlook appeared bad for John Ford, but Jeff felt that even if there was a smidgen of a chance he was alive, he had to try to bring him back. He put the flesh into a white 22-litre pail he carried under the deck and put the lid on. Now he had his bearings on where to get in.

He felt calm and in control, but his left arm wouldn't stop shaking. He couldn't understand why. Everything felt so clear.

'If I don't come back,' he said to Sally, 'tell Mum that I said you can have my 900 [Yamaha].'

'Don't talk like that, Jeff. You'll be coming back.'

'You never know.'

And with that, he grabbed his face mask and jumped into the ocean.

*

Sally could see the woman in the stern, greatly distressed, alone. All the other divers from that boat were still in the water, oblivious to the drama. Sal doesn't know why the boats didn't just bump gunwales for her to step across from boat to boat, as per Jeff's instruction. Perhaps it was impatience. The anguish on that poor woman's face demanded help, so Sally dived in to swim across. And somebody called out, 'Aren't you going to put your fins on?'

'It's not that far. I can swim it.'

'Yeah, but they said there was a shark.'

Oh, maybe I should.

But Sal doesn't remember seeing the chunk of flesh and she had convinced herself that this was all just a big misunderstanding. They'd probably seen a harmless grey nurse and been spooked. The husband was probably just hiding on the bottom.

So Sal swam the twenty metres across deep, dark water. She pulled herself up onto the other boat and introduced herself to the distraught woman. 'Hi, my name's Sal. I'm a dive instructor. I'm here to help you. If you tell me what's happened, we'll know what to do and how to help you.'

'A grey nurse took John, my husband,' the woman said.

Sally thought it seemed odd. Grey nurses didn't do that sort of thing.

'Tell me what happened,' she said.

'We came up from the dive. Then we went down to do a safety stop and this great big grey nurse shark came up to me. It circled us then swam away. Then it came back again really fast, heading for me. John grabbed me and put himself in front. It took him and went to the bottom.'

'A grey nurse? Are you sure it's a grey nurse?' It didn't sound right to Sally because grey nurses don't swim near the surface, they're not that big and they're placid.

'It was huge and it was grey with white underneath.'

That sounds like a great white. The sensation in Sally's body at that moment, she'd later say, was like when the cartoon character Sylvester the Cat gets a fright and turns into ice cubes, crumbling with a tinkle, tinkle to the floor. She realised the huge danger Jeff was in and that the woman's husband was probably gone.

'Oh no,' she heard herself saying.

'We're on our honeymoon,' the woman added. Both of them were crying now.

*

At a depth of ten metres, Jeff Brackenrig neutralised his buoyancy so he didn't float up or down, allowing him to have a look around and get a feel for the current. He couldn't see any divers from the Sundive boat.

He looked east and slowly worked his way around to the landward side and suddenly there it was – a fish the size of a submarine, swimming about seven metres behind him – a great white. And it looked interested, like it was searching for more food. And, since great whites attack upwards, he made a rush to the bottom, seventeen metres further down. He got in amongst some rocks he knew, backed himself into a crevice, and sat there figuring out what to do next.

He waited a few nervous minutes but didn't see the shark again. So he figured he might as well start a grid search for the missing diver. He went out a short distance, covered a patch then returned to the crevice. All seemed okay, so he went out a different way, covered more ground and returned to his nook. He backed himself snugly in to plan his next search. It had been perhaps fifteen minutes now since he'd seen the shark. His fears were subsiding. There was a job to do. He had put one hand down on the floor to lift himself off and was just kicking away when, suddenly, there it was, just a metre or two from his eyes, sliding by, filling his world for the seconds it took to pass.

It couldn't be a coincidence, he thought. This thing hadn't just passed him at ten metres down, then again so close at 27 metres depth. It had known where he was the whole time. It was stalking him.

I've gotta get out of here.

He watched it until it was almost out of sight, but he didn't want to wait too long. He wanted to be able to see it still going away. He kicked like buggery for the surface, twisting and looking to see where it was, but he lost sight of it. He didn't slow for a safety stop. The bends were the least of his worries.

His head broke the surface and spun, swivelling, desperate to lock his eyes onto the boat that was meant to be following his bubbles. There it was, hundreds of metres off, heading further away. He flapped his arms and cursed to himself, mighty pissed off about people not following instructions. No point yelling. They were too far away. But soon he saw the boat swing around towards him.

He later learned that one of the girls on board had kept watch for him on the stern, knowing the others were going against instructions.

He doesn't know how long it took for the boat to return. It might have only been a minute but the world had slowed to geological time and at the end of that long dark aeon – looking down between his legs, waiting to play matador without a cape – the boat pulled alongside. He kicked so hard he lifted out of the water up the side of the boat. He would have made it aboard with the full 25 kilos of kit hanging off him except the weight belt got caught on the lip of the gunwale.

'Did you see anything?' they all wanted to know. 'What was down there?'

'Just get me in the boat,' Jeff said, his legs still dangling in the water while visions ran through his head of one of them about to be torn off.

'Yeah, but did you see anything?'

'Get me in the fucking boat. Now!' He was ready to kill, furious that they hadn't followed his bubbles.

'We saw something over there,' someone explained. 'Some debris.'

*

Sally went with Debbie to the police station. 'She thought John was still coming back,' Sally says, 'because she hadn't seen any proof of his death. She said, "I'm all alone." And I said, "No, you're not. I'm going to stay with you as long as it takes for them to track your parents down and get them up here." So we did. We stayed together and talked about all sorts of things.

We got to know each other pretty well because we weren't just going to talk about the attack and we weren't going to talk about the weather. I was in the ambulance, telling her, "Oh, I'm just coming out of stuff. My husband ran off with my best friend, blah, blah." And she said, "Oh, you poor thing. That must be terrible." I thought, How ironic is this? I was just telling her this to take her mind off it and she was amazing. She was so kind and supportive and so stoic. Just a very classy beautiful young lady. We went back to the cabin to clean up the stuff and John's gear was still there, of course. It was a loss of innocence for sure.'

*

Out on the water, a flotilla of boats had come out to search. Jeff watched local fishermen Gavin Dwyer and Ronnie Boggis bait up an enormous hook with a mackerel. *That's not gunna work. He'll be long gone.* But in quick time something huge had snapped the thick line.

They baited up again, but Jeff was certain it was game-over now.

'That's gunna be a waste of effort, isn't it?' he said to Gavin.

'Nup. You watch.'

They hooked the shark again and this time the line held. It towed their boat six kilometres out to sea. They reeled the shark in close a few times and it was bigger than their 5.8-metre boat. 'That thing was as big as a truck,' Ronnie later told the media. 'We had it so close to the boat a couple of times we could have had a picnic on its back.'

Jeff went into the surf zone to pick up a powerhead – an underwater firearm that uses a bullet to kill sharks and crocodiles up close. When he got back to the fishing boat to deliver the death blow, the shark was gone. It had rolled and snapped the trace, disgorging a headless human torso as it did so.

'I didn't see the roll, but I helped pick up the bits and pieces and I have never smelt anything like it in my life. The acidity from its stomach. I remember picking up a piece of weight belt webbing floating on the water and it was probably two-and-bit inches wide and three or four inches long. Normally you wouldn't have even seen it, but the smell led me to it. It was just putrid. I was picking these things up with my fingers. Having grown up on farms I'm not squeamish about using my bare hands, but I couldn't get the smell off my hands for days. I washed and washed and washed. Horrible.'

Later that afternoon, Debbie Ford asked him if he'd found her husband.

'John won't be coming back,' he told her, but he wasn't sure if she accepted that answer. It was difficult to read what was going on in his own mind at a time like that, let alone someone else's.

Jeff had earlier got all the blokes from Byron Bay Dive Centre together, told them that what had happened had happened. 'Go home to your loved ones, give 'em a hug and get on with life.'

Instead, people gathered at the pub. Jeff remembers a quiet night of reflection over a few beers. Sally remembers, 'We got drunk and cried and cried.'

*

Next day, the local council put on a debriefing session. Everybody who'd been involved in any way was told they had to be there. Jeff wouldn't have gone otherwise. They all sat around in a big circle and Sally remembers wondering why there were so many people there. Acting police inspector Kevin Jones got the ball rolling, saying his name and position, what he did on the day and expressing his feelings about what a terrible tragedy it had been. The speaker's hat passed around.

Jeff takes up the story: 'It got to Dave Martin, who was driving our other boat, and he had a few tears when he was saying his bit. When it got to Billy Smedley – an old instructor who'd come out with the second lot of boats – Bill jumped up, because Bill was a nervy sort of character who suffered from depression, and he goes, "I'm a dive instructor, a big bronzed Aussie and all that, but right now I'm afraid to go to my office. What's it matter to you fuckin' blokes anyway? It doesn't matter. I'm the silly fuckin' bastard that's got to tell all these kids and everybody that it's okay to get in the water and fuck me dead look what's fuckin' happened . . ." He went right off and I'm sitting on the other side of the circle trying not to laugh because it was so explosive and out there. *Are you for fucking real?* I just got up and said my bit and that I did what I did because I believed that was the right thing to do. A lot frowned at me.'

The guy from the morgue got up, and the counsellor asked why he was there: 'You see death all the time.'

'I can't get the smell off my hands. I cannot get rid of the smell.'

Others described doing what they could, bringing fuel or sandwiches to the beach to help the rescuers, and Sally could see how wide the ripple effect was in an incident like this.

The last part of a debriefing session is called the 'teaching phase' where the counsellor – often the graduate of a two-day debriefing course – runs through a list of symptoms everybody might suffer in coming days, such as sleeplessness, flashbacks, loss of appetite, short temper, nausea, nightmares, the shivers. They were told it was all normal. Don't feel bad about it. Get help.

Sure enough, Sally went home and acquired a portion of those symptoms. 'I shut down and couldn't eat. I was having all the shivers and chills and goosebumps. Friends would say, "Come on, Sal, we're going out to dinner," and we'd go out somewhere and the food looked great but I had absolutely no appetite. I'd just have a cup of tea. It all closed down. I was getting goosebumps and stomach cramps and headaches and flashbacks and pictures of everything.'

After ten days, her boss said, 'Don't you think you should be coming back to work now?'

'I don't know. I feel so different on the inside.'

*

The dive shops in Byron Bay had agreed that nobody would dive the day after the attack in honour of John Ford, but the wind and weather blew in and nobody dived for a week anyway. Jeff wanted to do a thorough search of the area before paying customers came back in. He didn't want any punter finding an arm or a leg.

So, a week after the attack, all the town's instructors gathered for a search. The shark was still out there somewhere. Participation was voluntary, but they all turned up. It was a tense time. Billy Smedley, who'd had the rant at the debrief, was adamant he had to be involved. As they were gearing the boats up, he approached Jeff. 'If you feel anything nudging you in the arse when we're out there, don't worry, it'll only be me trying to crawl in.'

They went out and found the tank, the regulator, the buoyancy compensator with large comma-shaped bite marks. The blokes from Sundive found John Ford's head. And when everything was clear, they returned to shore.

*

Jeff didn't hesitate. 'I started diving again no worries. It didn't affect me. Bill Antico, whose family owned the dive shop, he said he believed I had suicidal tendencies. I gave him a fair spray over that. I rang Cape Byron imports looking for Sally and a girl there said, "Oh no, Sally hasn't been at work for a week." I rang her at home and she was all upset about it. I remember saying to her, "If I'd known it was going to affect you like this, I would never have asked you to do it." She just sort of sobbed and mumbled. And I said, "I want you to get your act together and get back to work. We have to move on." With that she started back at work a few days later.'

But Sally struggled. 'I called my sister up and said, "I have to go back to work but I feel so different. I don't know why I feel so different." She did some kinesiology and some hypnosis on me. I didn't know what my issues were, but she worked out that I felt I couldn't do enough, that I couldn't fix it. And that happens a lot with rescuers, particularly if there are fatalities involved, even if they saved one person, the mind focuses on the failure to save another. Once I realised what the problem was, I was then able to talk about it being an unfixable situation and that John was already gone before I got there. I could focus on the upside: that I was able to help Debbie and she wasn't alone for the seven hours it took for her parents to get there. So I was able to make a difference.

'When I dived again a few weeks later, it was like coming home. It got me eating again. But the nightmares, rolling around and waking up and yelling out, they lasted for about six months and then started dissipating. The shivers, and recalls on a daily basis, they went on for many years. I'd see a picture of a shark and my skin would crawl. But that passed.'

*

Jeff got out of the dive business about six months later. 'It had nothing to do with the attack whatsoever. I just decided I'd gone as far as I could. I don't dive much any more. Not because of the incident. I just don't have time. Having grown up in road transport, I went into trucks. I was going to buy one truck and work three or four days a week, and make a simple living, but that grew into a fleet of seven trucks and three loaders and eleven employees. It got a bit out of hand. I suffered a kidney disease in 2000 or 2001 and didn't work for a couple of years. I sold the trucks. I got involved in the tractor business and then came back to the farm in 2008, growing organic Russian garlic and jap pumpkins, when I was diagnosed with bone cancer, multiple myeloma. Nothing's happening with the farm at present. I want to get some garlic in for seed stock for next year. I don't want to walk away completely. We'll make it. You've just got to be practical about these things.

'They found a tumour, seven and a half centimetres by five and a half centimetres, that had eaten out through the pelvis and was pushing on my sciatic nerve. It turned out I had five other tumours. One on my skull, one on my C4 vertebra, three on my ribs. It's just how it all turns out. You can be lucky. Eventually it'll kill me, but I'll make sure it's a long time from now. The death rate from multiple myeloma is around twenty-five per cent, per year.

'At this stage I'm handling the chemo better than what the average person does. It makes me a bit tired and crook but I'm still better off than a lot of others. I think I'll be around for a long time.'

The interview has been conducted bedside at Lismore Base Hospital with Jeff — bald head and wearing bright red and blue boardies — hooked up to the chemo drip while his ward mates throw in questions and comments. He's bright and cheerful, antagonistic to his disease and contemptuous — yet patient — towards the annoying guy with the grey ponytail in the bed opposite. He's full of fight.

We get talking about Sally, and it is clear that he thinks the world of her, but there is an underlying tension. 'She says she wasn't affected but then the other day she said to me, "I've never had my closure to it", and I thought, okay, it did affect you.'

I say that Sally admitted to me that she had been badly affected by the incident.

'Probably doesn't want to admit it to me because I'll get cranky about it.'

*

I ask Sally about Jeff's idea that she hadn't admitted her own shocked state after the attack. 'Oh no. I give public lectures on it.' Sally now runs the Australian Bravery Association's Queensland branch. 'He never wanted to talk about it. I say, "Jeff, your health went to shit after that shark attack." He says, "Nup, nothing to do with it."' Sally says this making her voice deep and very Australian, and still managing to convey a great affection for Jeff.

'You know what? He only told me in December, sixteen years after, that he holds himself responsible for not doing a better job. He felt he failed. I said to him, "You're kidding, aren't you?" He said, "No, I should've been able to fix it."

'His whole life turned around after that. He left the dive industry, he started getting sick. He never talked about it. He just internalised the whole thing and look at him now, booooone cancer. If there's any chink in your armour, stress will bring it on.'

I point out that Jeff denies he got out of the dive industry because of the incident (and he also made a point of not blaming anyone or anything for his cancer).

'That's the whole thing,' says Sally. 'Denial. God, I hope he gets through this because he's such a good bloke, but he's a stupid Australian male. Your body and mind are so intimately connected. You don't have two separate entities. I chose to redefine my life with it. To spend the rest of my years helping those that come behind me so that they don't feel like the weakest link.'

ELEVEN

James Long

*I gloss over anything in a man decorated for gallantry –
just as sins were forgiven in the Middle Ages by buying a
pardon – to me Courage is a Man's Pardoner.*
Donald Featherstone, military historian and war gamer

James Long, a 44-year-old local councillor and tramways
inspector, is stopped at a traffic light on Bourke Street in
Melbourne's CBD at 10.30 pm, on his way home from his girlfriend's place at Southbank. There is a commotion up ahead in
the distance. Someone is being attacked at a tram stop – a short
person with long hair. He hears a scream. A man is running
now with something held close to his chest like a football. The
short person is chasing. *This is a bag snatch. This isn't right.* He
drives his Toyota Seca after the guy who sprints down an alley.
James turns in behind him and pushes on until the lane grows
so narrow the car can't go any further. He jumps out and chases
on foot, leaving the keys in the ignition and the door wide open.
This guy has to be caught. He is a bully. James can't stand bullies.

He follows for about 200 metres, pacing himself so as not to blow out, until he rounds a corner and there is the guy trapped in a dead end, facing him. Flannelette shirt. A bit of a bogan. The guy reaches into his jacket and pulls something out. *A knife?* But he is holding it funnily. James realises it is a syringe.

'What have you got there?' he asks, mustering all his bravado.

'A syringe. HIV positive, mate.'

James is scared, but he knows he must show no weakness. *How am I going to deal with this?* The answer comes in a flash — a brilliant lie: 'Mate, that'll do you no good. Guess what, I've got HIV.' He opens his white shirt, bares his chest. 'I've got nothing to lose.'

He sees the syringe shake in the guy's hand, the shoulders droop and the mouth falls.

James knows he has control. His confidence grows. His officer training from the army reserve comes into play. There are two parts to giving a command: the thinking part and the execution part. 'Drop it. Drop it now.'

The guy drops the bag. James watches it fall to the ground and, as he does, the guy bolts past him. The victim is there now, too. An Asian student. She comes down the alley and James looks back to see her picking up the bag as he scoots off again in pursuit of the thief. If James doesn't catch him, he'll just go and do it to someone else, and eventually someone will get hurt.

And so he runs. Down the street and around a few corners. They reach a crowd milling outside a nightclub. James sees the guy take some keys from a young woman and jump into a panel van. *Now he's stealing a defenceless woman's car.*

James sprints past the woman and hurls himself onto the bonnet and grabs the windscreen wipers ready for whatever the driver might throw at him. He's not going to let this bloke get away.

'Don't worry about it, mate,' says the woman. 'It's only a car.'

But it is much more than a car. It is a principle.

*

I first meet James Long at a bravery association gathering at the Canberra RSL Club. By this time he is the deputy mayor of Melbourne's Bayside Council. The 54-year-old tells me that he's a good chance of being elected mayor. We sit down and I ask if he'd care to tell me his story. But he doesn't give an immediate yes or no. Instead, he alludes to having been smeared by political opponents. Politics is a brutal game, he says, and when he started getting good publicity out of the bag snatch incident, it prompted his opponents to dig dirt on him. 'Everybody has made mistakes. I certainly have,' he says, measuring each word. I can see him gauging me, wondering how much he should tell. 'Well, I'd rather you hear it from me than them.'

He has my full attention.

'I grew up in North Melbourne,' he begins. 'My neighbours were car yards and petrol stations. It was a time when the working-class dream was to move to the outer suburbs. Their empty houses were converted to offices. It was the big decline of the inner city. There was a stigma to living where I lived in the fifties and sixties. It was the slums.'

James's family lived just around the corner from a pub so it was common to have drunks asleep on the doorstep, even occasionally in the outdoor dunny. He remembers one night as he entered his bedroom to go to sleep, he got a strong whiff of stale booze and urine. He didn't turn on the light because his father didn't allow lights. A waste of electricity. The street lamp outside provided a little illumination and as young James's eyes adjusted, there, on his bed, he saw an old wino fast asleep.

That was the backdrop, but there was a lot of hard growing

up to be done. His mother left his elderly father for someone more her own age. His dad was often sick. His brother was killed by a person known to the family and James felt that justice was not done.

Despite the scenery, James says he grew up naive. While many neighbouring kids succumbed to temptation – robbing warehouses, stealing cars – he stuck to his books and studied hard at his Catholic school. 'I learned a lot of very interesting lessons in life there, and values. That can really decide how you act in future matters of conscience and strength. I also learned Latin.'

He was studying at teachers college when he did a stint working on the trams during the holidays. He realised that tram drivers got paid more than teachers, so he dropped out of the college and became a full-time tram driver.

He'd only been in the job a short time when he picked up some young drunks on the corner of Melrose Street and Flemington Road, North Melbourne, during the afternoon peak. The conductor pulled the bell cord and off he drove. A few stops later, the conductor knocked on the driver's door. 'I've got a problem with the passengers,' he said. 'They won't pay their fare.'

James stopped the tram and came out of his cabin. He sized up the troublemakers – young blokes about the same age as him, except their leader who was older. 'Come on, lads, you've really got to pay the fare.' The young toughs paid up and James told the conductor to stay down the end of the carriage away from them. He got back in his cabin and rolled on. But soon a passenger knocked at the door. The conductor was being belted. James picked up a point bar, the heavy metal rod that he used to manually change tracks. At tram-driver school, the instructors had taught him to always carry it in an altercation with passengers, just never use it.

The conductor was copping a hiding and James went around and tapped the thugs on their shoulders, showing them the bar. 'Now stop it,' he said. 'Let's have a talk outside.' His gambit worked and the hooligans alighted onto a traffic island.

James followed them out. 'I've got to report this incident,' he told them. 'I'll need a couple of names and addresses.'

The punch got him in the face and he went down. 'The guy who hit me was a big tall guy,' James remembers. 'I was a little guy but my father had taught me some wrestling moves. I jumped up, got him by the neck and dropped him onto Flemington Road in a headlock. The conductor got onto another guy, but the leader was free, so it wasn't a fair fight. Not that it was a fight. I was just trying to restrain the guy.'

James remembers the leader putting his hand in his jacket pocket. 'Don't mess with us. I've got a brass in my pocket.'

James wasn't overly concerned. *Brass knuckles, oh well.* But then the leader produced a pistol and he realised 'brass' must have been criminal slang for a gun. The leader cracked him on the head with the butt and another of the gang picked up a metal pipe from a Cyclone fence and whacked him over the head with it. 'I've still got a lump on my head from it,' he tells me, pointing. 'It's just there. I won't be so bold as to ask you to feel it. It came up and never went down. It was a very hard blow.'

But James still wouldn't let go of his guy.

Tram driver Peter Lancaster was driving in the other direction and saw the melee. He called out to James, 'Let them go! Let them go! He's got a gun to your head.' James felt the cold metal at the back of his skull. He released his grip and saw the gun wrapped in a handkerchief – later surmising that this was so the shooter wouldn't get powder burns on his hands.

He knew they were hard-core crooks, but there was a principle involved. They had belted his conductor, caused a great disruption to the service, and distressed the passengers who were in his care. If he didn't stop these blokes, they'd go do it to someone else. So when they took off, he followed them – groggy and filled with fearless righteousness.

At school, he had been bullied and never retaliated. The school rule was that since it took two to fight, you both got punished. So he never fought. But this was different; he was in the right.

When the leader of the gang saw James following, he turned, raised the pistol in two hands, aimed and fired. James heard a whizzing noise. The windscreen shattered on a car parked next to him. A second shot was fired and he remembers having the thought: 'If I'm wounded or killed, imagine the bureaucracy. Struth, there's a lot of paper work here already.' He worried that people might think he caused the problem. He stopped and walked back to the tram, feeling guilty now that he'd let the toughs get away.

*

The next day, he fronted at work, on time, feeling sore, but keen to shrug it off. Colleagues bagged him. He should have been at home on compo, they said. The conductor, who was less injured than James, wasn't seen again for a month.

James received no official recognition for his act, but the tramways bosses suddenly knew who he was. Shortly after the incident he put in for a promotion that drivers twenty years his senior were applying for. He got the job and suddenly he was a boss and his former work mates didn't respect him for it.

The bosses obviously thought he had guts, but here he was, unpopular with the drivers, beating himself up for not having caught the thugs, and wondering why he was waking at night re-enacting this thing in his head. In his rare moments of sleep, his dreams were filled with driving trams into a nether world with no tracks, no lights, no electricity. His brain grew fuzzy with the sleep deprivation. When he was putting figures in columns, he would think one number but his hand would write another. Then he'd be belittled for his mistakes. The drivers he beat for promotion showed the faulty work around the yard, spreading the joke.

One of his main jobs was to get the trams on the road on time, but malingering was rife. He didn't have the staff to cover all the sickies. He felt responsible to the passengers standing on the streets waiting for services that never showed.

Depression was weakness, so he could never let on that he was suffering. He had a reputation to live up to. So he pushed on and, in the next couple of years, he got himself his first girlfriend. He went back to uni to do a Bachelor of Arts part-time. He saved hard, lived frugally and paid off his house, aged 22 – then bought another. Life went on. He became a union rep, joined the army reserve, got involved in local politics, rose to be a deputy mayor. He found a lovely wife. Had an ugly divorce. That low gave him an insight into how homelessness could creep up on a man. But he picked himself up and felt stronger for it. Which brings us back to that car bonnet on the night of 9 November 1998.

*

It was a Holden Kingswood and he knew the windscreen wipers would hold him. No plastic in those babies. But the thief didn't drive off. He opened the window and leant out, trying to prod James with the syringe. Like trying to get a parking ticket off the windscreen without leaving the car, he couldn't reach. So he put the car in gear and sped off. James braced his rubber-soled shoes against the roo bar on the front as the guy swerved then braked, accelerated, swerved and braked. But James wasn't budging as the car raced off again. He saw a parked car looming. He gripped harder and braced. Crash! But James was still there as the car reversed then lunged forwards. Crash! He counted four parked cars that they hit as he clung on, barnacle tight.

They went around the block and James could see he was back outside the nightclub. The driver shouted to the girl from whom James thought he'd stolen the Holden. 'Get in! Get in!' He realised they were in cahoots and this was the getaway car. She got in and they sped off again, accelerating, braking, swerving and running red lights. At one point they stopped and she yelled at James, 'Get off! Get off!'

'I'll never get off,' he said.

He figured if he stayed there long enough, a police car would come by eventually. But then they turned into the Spencer Street Station car park where the wheels squealed on the concrete floor. James thought they were about to smash him into a brick wall. *Nah, they wouldn't do that. This is their getaway car.* The driver accelerated again and James saw speed bumps approaching. He braced, but didn't factor the force of the lift. He lost his grip and flew off the front, landing hard. The car's bumper hit him on the chin and opened a gash. Lying on the concrete, dazed and beaten, he saw out of the corner of his eye a police car cruising Spencer Street. He lifted himself with the bumper, ran and leapt a fence to wave the cops down. He was covered in blood, mouthing gibberish: 'Car . . . Robbery . . . Syringe.' He pointed at the Holden now exiting the car park and the police car moved to block its path.

James thinks he lost consciousness with the sense of relief that flooded his body.

*

It is our second interview and we're driving through the streets of Melbourne looking for a Lebanese restaurant in Richmond where we are to meet his Masonic friends. He's telling me about the police sergeant who came in while he waited to get stitches in his chin. 'He said he wanted to shake my hand but couldn't because I had all this blood on my hand. He said the media were already calling me "Mel" – as in Gibson and Melbourne. It was the era of those *Lethal Weapon* movies where he'd done something like me.'

After his release from hospital the next morning, James spoke to the cameras outside, then when he got home there was a tangle of tripods, spiral notepads and fluffy boom microphones waiting at his front gate. 'I'm not a hero. I'm just an ordinary person, but sometimes you have just got to do what is right to make up for what you have done wrong in your life,' he told the media.

'I was stressed and in pain,' he recalls. 'I had bloody knees, stitches in my chin, bloodshot eyes. I couldn't think clearly but I think I gave a good account of myself, answering the questions and recalling events. I needed a bit of counselling, debriefing, you know what I mean.

'Radio station 3AW offered to send me to Hamilton Island for three weeks all expenses paid. I said thank you but I didn't accept. They sent me flowers, wanting interviews. I said, "Thanks. Can you give them to the victim?" I didn't want to be seen to be profiting from my action because it really denigrates the act. It didn't seem right.

'I was in the front room of my place and they all came in. There was Naomi Robson from *Today Tonight* and her producer. The phone was ringing and the producer kept hanging up, making sure I wouldn't answer the phone because it was the rival station. I couldn't believe it. I said, "Wait till I change my shirt." It was a white shirt with red drops of blood down the front. They said, "No, no. Leave the blood on it." Channel Seven said, "We'll take you out to lunch at Donovans.

You'll only speak to us, won't you?" "Oh yeah." I was hungry. I thought I'd need something to eat. Then Ray Martin wanted to speak to me on *The Midday Show*. I told the producer I'd already given my word to Channel Seven that I'd only speak to them. "The only way I'll do it is if I get the okay from Channel Seven." So she rang a phone number and said, "Look, I've got such and such from Channel Seven for you, James." She put her on and she said, "That's okay, James. Just do the interview and we'll see you in the afternoon." So I did the interview. Before going to lunch, Channel Ten got me to re-create the scene. I hadn't had a shower. They're taking me around re-creating the scenes. By this time, I'm a bit stressed out. Part of what they shot ended up on the Comedy Channel. They used it out of context: "Get a load of this guy. Don't you reckon he needs his medication." I hadn't slept or had a shower. My hair was dishevelled. I'd just come from a life-threatening situation. I was so fatigued.

'I did *Midday*. I remember, Ray Martin asked me, "Why?" and I said, "No one's perfect, but sometimes you've just got to right some wrongs." Then Channel Nine arranged the taxi for me to go to the Channel Seven lunch. I got there a bit late. They said, "James, where were you?" "I was over at Channel Nine." "But, James, you gave your word you'd only speak to us." "Yeah, I did, but they cleared it with you guys first . . . Remember?" The penny dropped. I had trusted, naively, their honesty. It's cut throat but I didn't understand that. I'd only ever dealt with local newspapers.'

*

It took days for the media attention to fall away. After it all, some people thought James had HIV, others thought he was unhinged. A lot of blokes got on talkback radio and said he was an idiot for intervening. And the Comedy Channel had their little dig. Some blokes in North Melbourne recognised him and called him a rat and told him if he jumped on their car they'd smash his head in. It was all demoralising. And just like after the tram incident, he was reliving the event and having sleepless nights.

Political rivals started calling him 'Loony Long', but he continued to run for public office, first attempting to get a Labor Party endorsement for a council election, before running as an independent for lord mayor of Melbourne. He opened his lord mayoral campaign riding a white horse and handing out tea and honey – promising a sweet, clean fight.

But that's not what he got.

Two of his opponents contacted the media with the dirt on James Long. Did they know he used to be called Tony and that he once faced certain charges?

The *Herald-Sun* pursued the story and James explained that it all happened after his marriage break-up. He met a girl in a shop in Moonee Ponds. 'She looked twenty-one and had stars in her eyes.' She was managing the shop alone so he had no reason to question her age. 'I fell in love with her and she with me,' he explained to the paper. 'It was a normal boyfriend–girlfriend relationship.' They went out as a couple for a year but when he found out she was actually fifteen years old, he ended it. Her parents called the police. The jury found him not guilty in May 1993 and after that he adopted the Christian name James – in honour of his father.

He explains to me that he'd been on medication after his divorce, suffering depression. He'd attempted suicide. His judgement was clouded. But the nuances rarely come across in a twenty-paragraph news story with headlines like 'Hero's haunting past' and 'Sex smear claim'.

'I've got to accept that these things will be brought up,' he says, switching to an almost Churchillian conviction, 'but it will certainly *never* get in my way of doing what needs to be done. I always say, if you think a person has done something wrong and you want to background their character, ask, "What person would put their life in danger for the sake of a stranger?" You can understand it if it's your loved one. But for the sake of a stranger? Doesn't it tell you that the person is a good person who has got the right values? Why do I, James Long, go and, for a few measly pennies, put myself up for public scrutiny in local government when I could be making heaps of money? I get involved in Rotary for so many hours. I've got to go this weekend to mentor people. It's a discipline I've set myself. You've got to give something back. We're on a limited time on earth.'

He says he was surprised to learn that there are actually people in the back rooms of politics who really do set out to destroy others. They're not psychotic. They're cool and calculated. And his past has exposed him to them. 'I hide nothing. I could have been very guarded with you when I spoke to you. I pointed you in the right direction because I've got nothing to hide. I'm putting my confidence in you because Jim Runham has said to me, and I don't know Jim well, but a person of his ilk says you're a good guy. I'm going to appeal to your better nature to say, "Yes, he is a good guy and he believes in what he does and he's not a person to harm anybody", but some people could lead you to believe I'm not all that I seem. The nature of politics is that they always find an Achilles heel. Everyone's got one. We're not perfect beings . . . You're getting tired,' he says, looking at me.

I am, yes. It is almost midnight and the waiter has failed to come and take our orders for coffee.

We leave. In the car, James brings up his fears about how I'm going to portray him. I say I am going to mention the charges. I'm interested in why he keeps going in the face of such attacks. Such a thing would send me scurrying into a hole. Every time he is mentioned in the papers, the reporter mentions the charges – more often than they mention the bravery award. 'They keep hitting me over the head with it but every time I just keep sticking my head up and keep going on. I have a whole lot of people who believe in me.'

He goes on to tell me how he doesn't accept political donations from anyone. It would taint the process. I get out of his car wondering how I can portray him as a good guy, which I think he is, and still tell the whole story. For I believe in Tom Wolfe's dictum that a writer's loyalty lies not with the subject – no matter how much you like them or how much time you've spent with them – it lies with the reader.

Earlier that night, I'd asked James if his post-traumatic stress disorder problems after the second incident were worse than the first. He said the second was much harder because, long before then, during one of his sleepless nights, he'd had a premonition that he'd experience three such incidents in his life. And that in the third incident, he would be killed.

'I keep asking myself, "Why did I survive each time?" I'm not indestructible. But in a way I've come to accept it'll be the next time I do it. I'm not sure how it'll come about but I'll probably die in the aid of someone . . . Not intentionally. I'll try to survive, but I won't survive it.'

TWELVE

Colin Brooks

Colin Brooks was living his dream. Here he was at 30, sailing from Melbourne to Darwin with his girlfriend, Melina, in a yacht he'd built with his own hands. They were entered in the Darwin to Ambon yacht race which came with a fifteen-week cruising permit for Indonesia, a hard thing to come by. After Indonesia, maybe they'd keep sailing right up through South-East Asia. It was a world of possibilities and endless horizons, but first they had to dock in Cairns to wait out the cyclone season and build up the bank.

For a law school dropout, Colin was pretty good with his hands. He was a qualified shipwright and so got a job as a boilermaker, doing twelve-hour shifts, pulling in the dough, and Melina walked into a good job as an administrator at Falcon Airlines, a local outfit that flew to Cape York and the Torres Strait Islands.

One night she gave him a call as he headed home from another long day. 'I'm at the pub with the people from my work,' she said. 'Why don't you come by?'

He dropped into the Irish pub on the north side of town and met the airline crowd. With long blond hair down to his belt, he felt uncomfortable with all the clean-cut types, but got talking to one bloke, David Kilin. While they were yacking, Colin admitted that he'd never actually been in a light plane before.

'Melina has to fly to Horn Island to look at the booking system in a couple of weekends time,' David said. 'Why don't you fly up with her and spend the weekend in the airline's house?'

Sweet. A free flight up over the Great Barrier Reef.

So a few weeks later, Colin got on the twin-engined Piper Aztec and loved it, bouncing up through the clouds, looking out over the waters. He made the decision right there that he was going to become a pilot.

The following day, while Melina worked in the office, he hooked up with the pilot and his wife and toured Horn Island. The World War II plane wrecks scattered around the place were fascinating. 'Look at that piece of motor embedded in the side of the hill!' When those babies came down they really came down. It was all good fun.

*

The flight back to Cairns departed about 3 pm on the Sunday, 3 November 1996. When it came to the seating arrangements, Colin was right up front. 'Maaaate,' he said to the pilot, 'I'm a big bloke. Those seats down the back are really small.'

He was upgraded to the cockpit and handed the second set of headphones.

'Cool. Copilot.'

A Thursday Islander had rung up desperate to get down south for his brother's funeral so they'd diverted to Bamaga, the strip that services the communities near the tip of Cape

York Peninsula. Colin was full of questions as they took off for the short hop. He heard the pilot discussing with the chief pilot over the radio whether he had enough hours in this craft to be allowed to fly a commercial passenger, but the chief pilot talked him into it. And so a big fella got on at Bamaga and stooped his way to the back seat of the six-seater plane.

When they came to leave, the first engine ticked over fine but the second took a long time to start. Eventually the pilot got it going and they motored off into the afternoon sky for the almost 800-kilometre flight to Cairns. This time it was even better. The future pilot in Colin could watch all the dials and figure out what they meant. The master mariner in him could study the reefs and channels below.

About halfway to Cairns, he started to notice dials edging into the red. He peered sideways at the pilot and saw stress on his face. Colin was still full of questions, but the pilot stopped answering. He had a pen and paper out, doing calculations.

Suddenly, the door next to Colin flew open for no apparent reason. *Faaaaaaarrrrrrk!* A latch was holding it so that it didn't open all the way. The pilot descended, and Colin had to lean out into the ferocious slipstream and use all his strength to wrestle the door back in and latch it up. This light aeroplane caper was certainly full of adventures.

The pilot regained his cruising altitude and they continued south over the reef in the fading light. But soon after, Melina tapped Colin on the shoulder and pointed out the window. A plume of thick smoke trailed out the right-hand engine.

Colin elbowed the pilot and pointed. The pilot looked at Colin then out the window but it didn't seem to worry him. (Colin would later learn that this craft was called Old Smokey.) The pilot made an 'okay' signal with his fingers.

Colin wasn't convinced. Those redlining gauges didn't look right.

'Mate, what happens if one engine stops?' he asked.

'We've got another one. We'd get back easy,' the pilot answered.

By the time they got to about Cow Bay near the Daintree, 85 kilometres north of Cairns, Colin could see the pilot was rattled.

He heard him radio Cairns tower, announcing a change of course. And just then the right-hand engine started running rough. The whole thing was getting creepy now. Over Port Douglas, 60 kilometres from Cairns, the pilot called in that he was having trouble. He gave the tower a couple of codes and was given priority landing. Colin took his headset off. He didn't want to hear any more negative shit.

Colin knew these waters well and was happy to see Palm Cove below. They were just 30 kilometres from home now.

The right-hand engine promptly coughed . . . and died.

That's cool. We've got another one.

The pilot turned to his passengers, 'I'm sorry, I'm going to have to try to land on the beach.'

What about the second engine? There was no opportunity to ask. The pilot was busy grappling with a bunch of levers – which Colin later learned were fuel levers that he was trying to use to feed fuel from one tank to another. Colin looked out for sand. He saw that the beach was a thin white line. Straight down. The descent required seemed way too steep. Yeah right, he was thinking, when at that exact moment the second engine cut out.

This isn't real. This isn't real.

The pilot turned to his passengers. 'I'm sorry. We're going to have to ditch. I want you all to brace yourselves and I want you,' he said, looking at Colin, 'to hold the door open.'

'Why, mate?'

'When we hit the water, you might never get it open again.'

The pilot was already on the radio. 'Mayday! Mayday! Mayday!' He gave the flight number.

'See that light down there,' said Colin, 'that's Wangetti school.'

'We've got Wangetti school on our starboard wing,' the pilot said into the radio.

'We've got you in radar,' a controller said.

It was 6.40 pm. About 25 knots of breeze.

Colin – quite familiar with the workings of the door by now – cracked it open. The wind was pushing the door towards the closed position so he had to put his weight against it. He reached back and grabbed Melina's hand. She pushed him away.

That's a bit cold, he thought, not realising that she was making a statement: 'This is not the end. We're not saying goodbye.'

The pilot was fighting the controls as the plane went into a wobbly dive, turning from side to side, like it was walking itself down on its wing tips.

Colin looked at the instruments. They were at 3200 feet. Doing 86 knots. The pilot had managed to really slow the craft. He was wrestling it.

Colin meanwhile was alternating from second to second between thrill seeking and terror. The surfer in him came out. *Awesome. This is the biggest drop I'll ever take.* Then, *I'm not going to see my nieces and nephews grow up. That's a piss off.*

He adjusted his feet, trying to figure out what would be the best way to brace them for impact. He put them square on the floor. *That's no good.* He moved them up, crossed them, parted them. *What am I doing this for? We're all gunna die.*

And during the long two minutes they plummeted, he thought about his life. *I've had a decent go. I've really tried, I've never shirked it. I'm not a bad person. It's all right. I can go.*

I can die. Thank you for flying Springfield Airways. His imminent death seemed such a ridiculous idea, it felt like an episode of *The Simpsons*.

*

The plane was coming down at such an horrendous angle there was surely no chance for survival. But the pilot kept wrestling and as they neared the water, he started winding something up. It changed the angle of the nose cone, and he managed to flatten the wobbly trajectory of the Piper Aztec a little. Just a little.

Then . . . whack! They hit the water hard. There was no skimming across the top, just thud.

There was the sound of metal rending and breaking like a car crash, but there was no sound of breaking glass. And in an instant there was only darkness and silence.

What's going on? This is really weird.

Before there was any time to think about it, the plane suddenly bobbed up out of the sea, bursting into the fading twilight, still ploughing forwards, but quickly coming to a halt. Colin took stock. The Thursday Islander's face was in Colin's crotch.

'Am I alive?' the Islander asked.

Colin, looking straight down the leg of the guy's shorts, was trying to work it out. *What's going on?* The guy had hurtled from the back seat to the front. Colin scanned his own body looking for blood. He found a little on his knee where the Islander's teeth had ended their days. The Islander's face was bleeding, too.

Colin looked at the dash. The clock on the GPS said 6.42 pm. Then all the electrics started sparking, before promptly dying. Looking out, he saw the door was gone, as were the wings.

Colin picked up the Islander and threw him into the

water. He undid his own seatbelt and climbed out onto the stub of the wing. *I've survived a fucking plane crash. Thank God for water. I'm alive!* He threw both arms in the air and yelled 'Whooooooooooooooo'.

He could see land a couple of kilometres away. Car headlights snaked up the Port Douglas road. *That's not far to swim.* The sea held no fears for him. He'd grown up swimming in it, sailing on it, surfing its edge.

Then he looked back into the plane. Melina and the pilot's wife were both conscious but looked like they needed direction, sitting in the cabin that was fast filling with water. He reached in with his left arm, grabbed Melina with one of his big calloused hands and pulled her out by the scruff of the neck, throwing her into the water. He would not be able to explain the strength later, but he wasn't asking questions. Next girl, same thing.

The pilot was sitting there blank, mouth open. There was a hole the size of a twenty-cent piece in the middle of his forehead matching the disc from the middle of the steering wheel. The plane was sinking now. Quickly.

The pilot's head occupied the last pocket of air in the cockpit as the thing went down. And Colin, outside the window, had to decide what to do about it.

Should I or shouldn't I? Should I or shouldn't I?

He dived into the cockpit. The pilot was shaking. Underwater now, Colin grabbed the epaulets of the pilot's uniform and pulled him out and up.

As they surfaced, the pilot came good. 'We've got to stay with the wreckage,' he said. 'We've got to stay with the wreckage.'

Just then, the tail of the plane came towards them as the fuselage went down. Colin had to frog kick away, still holding the pilot, to avoid it hitting them. Then he turned the pilot around with his shoulders so he could see his wreckage disappear. No debris floated up.

About one minute had passed since impact.

And as the little group of five bobbed about in the tropical sea, the Thursday Islander threw his hands in the air. 'I die now.'

Colin, treading water like there was an outboard motor beneath him, pulled the guy up by the collar. 'What are you going to die now for, mate?'

'I can't swim.'

Ripper. 'What's your name?'

'BJ.'

'Hi, I'm Colin. I'm going to teach you to swim.' He knew the guy could swim a little because he'd seen him take a dozen or so strokes after he'd thrown him out of the plane. But as they paddled there now, the guy, sinking and desperate, tried to climb up on Colin, clawing at his clothes. Colin punched him in the face. 'Calm down, mate. If you want to live, calm down. Now lie on your back.'

Colin's board shorts had a long drawstring. So, with it still tied around his waist, he used an end to tie a slipknot around BJ's wrist to keep them connected. But BJ seemed to have given up. He became a dead weight.

The pilot kept repeating, 'We've got to stay with the wreckage.'

'Shut the fuck up. Haven't you done enough? Listen to me. I know about this stuff.'

Colin didn't see himself as an authoritarian type but he was finding the sergeant major within. Every ocean sailor has contemplated going overboard so he felt that he had a few ideas on the subject.

'This is what you'll do. If you want to live, listen to me. Get all your clothes off.' The water was warm and relatively calm. He knew they'd be drifting north, and that every minute they were in the water the search would widen its radius from the crash point. He'd been involved with searching for people who'd gone overboard before.

'We've got to swim south,' he said. 'At least try.'

He asked the pilot's wife, who had a large cut on the side of her face, how well she swam.

'Yeah, I swim pretty well,' she said.

He turned to the pilot. 'How well do you swim?'

'Not that good.'

'You're going to look after your husband,' he said to the pilot's wife.

Two factors were at work in that call. One was that Colin already had BJ tugging at his shorts, flopping and sinking. He couldn't take on another one. The other factor was that he wanted the two big bleeders together. No one mentioned sharks, but they were all thinking about them. There were plenty of tigers out there. And they fed at night.

Suddenly Colin's backpack floated up out of the depths, the only piece of debris from the whole wreck. He reached in and pulled out his mobile phone. It was alive. He punched in triple-0. *It's working! It's working!* Words flashed onto the screen – 'Battery Discharging' – and the thing promptly died. *Shit!* He hadn't bothered charging it because he was going to be out of range all weekend. He tossed it, then pulled out all his clothes, unfolded them and laid them out flat on the water in the hope a rescue helicopter might spot them.

Just then, something bumped his leg. He looked around. It wasn't BJ. *Shit! How bad can this get? You're in a plane crash, you've got all these drowning people around you and now a shark's gunna eat ya. Fuck it.*

His mind had to reason it away. Some people might have just hoped it was a turtle, but Colin decided that it was his dead cattle dog, Cactus, swimming around down there, looking after him from the afterlife, herding them all together. He's not a spiritual person, but his mind had to file that bump away as anything but a shark.

Part of him was being the sergeant major hero, part of him was getting spiritual, part was just a scared little kid thinking about *The Simpsons* episode where Homer attempts to jump Springfield Gorge on a skateboard. After plummeting to the bottom, a helicopter winches up Homer's broken body, slamming him against the cliff on the way, before he is loaded onto an ambulance. Seconds after driving off, the ambulance crashes into a tree, Homer rolls out on the gurney and falls back to the bottom of the gorge again, with a slight pause before the gurney lands on his head. There was someone there in Colin's head cacking himself.

Meanwhile the sergeant major knew there was a job to do, that these people needed him. It was pitch black now so after every eight strokes Colin took, he'd make everyone say their names. He dragged BJ along, talking to him, making him hold his breath. 'If you hold your breath you can't sink.'

But the guy just didn't seem interested in surviving. He was a dead weight. Colin couldn't get him to kick or even paddle his hands. A little flutter of the hands would have been a huge help. He couldn't think of any way to get inside his head so the only reference he had was to be like a footy coach inspiring ranting hatred in his charges.

'You black cunt,' he said. 'How weak are you? You want to die? That's why we're the master race.' These words and a lot more like them would haunt Colin's mind for years. He couldn't believe that he would say such things, but he just had to come up with something to mottivate the guy. It worked, BJ started to do some little paddles.

Off in the distance, Colin could see a light swaying on the

top of a yacht's mast. After a while he had a better look and realised it was a helicopter with a big light. It felt good that somebody was searching, but it was so far off across the wide black sea that it didn't seem like it had any chance of finding them.

And so they paddled on in the darkness, keeping the car headlights to their right. Sometimes the helicopter came closer, then drifted off again to another point in its grid. The time was punctuated by the roll call. Until, maybe an hour into the swim, the pilot's wife didn't call her name.

Shit, there's the first one gone.

All of a sudden a shape came floating back towards Colin. It was the pilot, moaning. Colin grabbed him and took the other end of the Quiksilver board shorts string and tied it to the pilot's wrist. His boardies were shredded from when BJ had been climbing up him, but they held it together enough to keep the two men connected to him.

Colin's mood was pretty black now. BJ was pulling him down. The pilot was helping a bit but it was getting harder and harder. It crossed his mind to just take off his boardies and swim to shore. He knew he could make it, no worries. Melina was dog paddling beside them, holding herself together. She was a country girl, not used to the ocean, not a strong swimmer, but stoic.

They'd been in the water maybe 90 minutes. Colin was doing three or four underwater breaststrokes before coming up for a huge breath. Cramps were starting to knot his muscles from his little toe to his little fingers. Every stroke he took he braced for the pain.

He was going under. He knew he couldn't keep going much longer. Then Melina put her hand on his shoulder.

'What are you doing?' he complained, pushing her off. 'I can't swim for three of us.'

'I just need to rest,' she said.

'I can't do it, Mel. I just can't . . .' He thought about it some more. 'I tell you what, Mel. If you can swim for yourself, I'll marry you.'

She paddled away, but something had clicked inside him. He'd had enough. He reached down to the string and untied BJ, then the pilot. It was over. *Sorry, fellas.* They were going to drown. He'd done his best. He would get Melina to the beach. That was all he could achieve now.

The two men floated off to their fate.

*

Right at that moment, a guy came swinging by on a wire with lights hanging off him and it suddenly became impossible to swim. They were in a helicopter downdraught and it was like swimming in foam.

The guy on the wire dropped into the water. The pilot perked up immediately. They all went towards the rescuer and he pushed them away. He grabbed Melina but she resisted. 'Take him,' she said, pointing at BJ.

The wire man got the strap over BJ and as the winch tightened the cable, it came up between Melina's legs, lifting her high into the air before she twisted and fell.

Down in the water, lit by the powerful Nightsun searchlight, they looked up and screamed, 'Throw us life jackets!' But nothing came down. When BJ was safely up in the chopper, it suddenly flew off and started hovering several hundred metres away. Floating there, they wondered what was going on, but then they saw in the powerful light that the pilot's wife was being winched up.

Soon, the chopper came hovering back. It picked up Melina next, leaving just Colin and the pilot who now seemed fully alert. It gave Colin the shits that he'd towed the pilot all this way and now suddenly he seemed so with it. Nevertheless, he was prepared to give him some leeway because of the way he'd battled that plane to bring them down alive. *He's done an all right job. We've got out okay.*

Colin turned to him. 'Is there anything you'd like me to say in the aftermath of all this?'

'You tell the truth,' the pilot answered.

They shook hands. 'I'll tell the truth if you tell the truth.'

The wire man descended again, this time holding an uninflated life jacket. He threw it off to the side and Colin swam for it – 'like a dog', he would later say – wondering why the guy did it like that. He pulled the cord to inflate it and put it under himself like a surfboard, thinking the ordeal was over. In minutes he would be on dry land. The pilot went up the wire with the rescuer, then all of a sudden the light faded.

Colin looked up and saw the helicopter lifting up and away, heading south towards Cairns.

In moments, the incredible noise, the blinding light, the rippling white-foam chaos were all gone – replaced by silence and blackness.

It was more than just being alone, it was the rejection. It was all the nightclubs he'd never been let into, it was every person who ever said no to him, all rolled into one giant ball of abandonment. *What the fuck have I done to deserve this?* A dozen years later he would still find it difficult to talk about that feeling. But less difficult to talk about what he did next.

*

He lost it. He was overwhelmed with white-hot hatred. *I'm going to live through this to kill the bastards. How dare they? You guys are done.* He broke into flat-out freestyle, gunning for the light at Wangetti school, with the jacket underneath him for buoyancy.

It felt great to be swimming without those dickheads dragging him down. He was in a state of pure delirium, stroking hard, breathing hard, churning the water with his kicks. *You are fucking dead. You are fucking dead.* He would find out who the pilot of that helicopter was, he would track him down and he would murder him. No question.

Periodically, Colin stopped swimming and dived down, leaving the life jacket on the surface, to see if he could touch the bottom, before resuming the churning swim.

Suddenly, a boat nearly ran him over as it sped past. He thrust his body up like a water polo defender, waved his arms, but the jokers just kept going. They were running some sort of pattern. He watched them come back and he went up again.

You'd think the fuckers would stop and turn the engine off and do the odd 'cooee'.

On the third pass they saw him, came over and pulled him into the inflatable rescue boat with its huge twin outboards on the back. They were airport firemen.

Colin was laughing hard. This was too much. Then he cried, then he laughed. He didn't know what he felt, except he was cold. Really cold now.

'Mate, you got something you could wrap me up in? I'm freezing.'

'No, mate, I haven't.'

'What?' Colin could see the fireman kitted out in his fancy wetsuit and all-weather gear.

'Sorry, mate. I'll give you these.' He took off his wetsuit booties and handed them over along with a dry life jacket.

'Thanks a lot,' Colin said with belligerent sarcasm. 'What's in that box?' he asked, pointing at a great big container, thinking it might have something useful in it.

'A two-hundred-man life raft.'

Colin wasn't feeling a lot of respect for authority figures at this point. They took him in close to the beach then steered around in circles. He got frustrated. Land was only 100 metres away. He had a primeval urge to feel it between his toes.

'Mate, what are you doing?'

'We're just trying to find a point to muster you on the coast.'

'Mate, why haven't you got a handheld GPS with all the mustering points logged in it? One button: "Go To". Easy.'

'That's a great idea. Tell the boss about that.'

'Mate, who's in charge here? What qualification you got?'

'A recreational shipmaster's licence,' one of them offered.

'Mate, I'm a master five. I'm in charge. Steer to that light, you'll come up on a nice white sandy beach. I'll get off.'

'Nah, mate, you're delirious.'

'No I'm not.'

They knew he was delirious, but when they steered towards the light they saw that he was right about the beach. There were three fire engines, ambulances, police, all waiting there. The boat hit the beach and two firemen came out to carry him in, but that urge to feel solid ground overcame him.

'Put me down. Fuck it.'

A press photographer came up to them and Colin was certain one of the firemen stopped to flex his muscles for the camera. He crow-pecked the guy. The fireman dropped him, and Colin bolted.

See ya.

He made it the Cook Highway, 500 metres inland, turned left and kept running. A mate of his lived at Palm Cove. He decided to run to his place, have twenty beers, 300 joints and try to come to grips with what he'd just been through. It was only sixteen kilometres away. He was wearing nothing but his shredded brown boardies that were more like a grass skirt the way BJ had torn them.

But he didn't get far before he started to tire, needed a rest. He crawled into some bushes by the side of the highway, laughing, crying, picking up the beautiful, beautiful dirt and rubbing it in his face. *This stuff is great. I never thought I'd see you again.* He ate it, scraped it through his hair.

Why is it so light? It can't be daytime yet.

It was a television news crew, filming him with a huge light on the camera.

He got up, pushed the cameraman aside and bolted back up the highway. The police were there. They had him surrounded.

'You've got to get in the ambulance, mate.'

'No. I don't want to get in the ambulance. Soon as I get in the ambulance, it's forty k's to Cairns hospital, you'll give me a bill. I'll go in a car.'

'No, mate, you've got to get in the ambulance.'

'I'll go in the car.'

They moved in and got him to the back of the ambulance. One of them grabbed his arms and spread them on the side of the ambulance like he was a villain.

It didn't make sense. He thought he'd done pretty good out there and now it was like he was under arrest. A boofheaded young copper put his knee into the back of Colin's knee, collapsing his leg beneath him. One of those tricks they learn at the academy.

Colin got back to his feet. 'I'm over this.' Still the guy had a little smirk.

So Colin gave him something they can't teach at the academy – a right that opened the copper's face from his mouth to his eye.

The next one came at him. Pow. He had that much adrenaline in his veins, as far as he was concerned he had them outnumbered. They were going to have to shoot him if they wanted him in that ambulance.

Suddenly . . . a moment of clarity. 'This is stupid,' he said. 'This is really fucking stupid. I'll get in the ambulance.'

He climbed in and laid down on the stretcher. They strapped him down across his chest and headed off down the highway. He could see a car following them with a guy hanging out the window filming. The lights were on in the back of the ambulance and he didn't like it one bit. It was really bugging him that these cameras could see him.

The next night's news showed him giving them the finger and mouthing 'Fuck off'. What it didn't show was him untying himself, making his way to the front of the ambulance, getting the ambulance driver in a headlock and telling her, 'Turn the light off or I'll kill ya.' It's another moment that will make him wince for the rest of his life.

But it worked. She turned the light off, he strapped himself back in and they continued on the drive to Cairns Base Hospital.

The doctors didn't find anything physically wrong with him, but then they didn't look very hard. No one seemed to want to get too close to the crazy dude with the dirt-smeared hair. He needed someone to jab him with elephant tranquilliser. Nightie night.

The social worker gave him a pack of cigarettes. He didn't smoke.

All of a sudden, it was 1.30 am. He'd smoked the entire packet and was standing on the street with Melina trying to hail a taxi with no wallet.

What just happened?

They were strangers from another planet.

*

There was a trauma debriefing session the next day. Colin and Melina turned up pissed. A part of the now-discredited debriefing process was what they called 'the fact phase', where each person sitting in the circle briefly describes what happened to them. As far as Colin was concerned, the pilot's wife just lied straight up. She said she never swam off on her husband.

'Well, how did I end up with him then?' Colin interjected. You're not meant to interrupt in these things. He didn't care. 'This is all bullshit. I can't deal with this unless she's going to tell the truth.' He stood up. 'See you later, I'm going to get drunk again.'

The day after was Melbourne Cup day. The papers were running stories about maintenance failures with Falcon Airlines. *Courier-Mail* journalist Paul Whittaker had found a former pilot, David Ingles, who made allegations of shoddy safety standards and claimed to have been sacked for raising his concerns. And it was revealed that the guy who'd invited Colin on the plane, David Kilin, was in fact a Civil Aviation Safety Authority safety inspector. He had been a part-owner of the airline, but had sold his interest in it earlier in the year to a woman, 'a close personal friend', Cheryl Bailey, who owned the house in which he lived but who denied being his de facto wife.

The Falcon crash was to become a weapon for the new Liberal Government in its pursuit of the Civil Aviation Safety Authority board. It would drag on for years and Colin felt the pressure of being a pawn in that larger game. He was interviewed by investigators the day after the accident and was just a gibbering madman. They gave him a tape of the interview and he'd find it embarrassing to listen to – his thoughts were so disorganised. He felt like it was their way of ensuring his evidence about the redlining gauges and the smoking motor could be discounted. The findings of the inquiry didn't bear any correlation to his memory of what actually happened.

But that Melbourne Cup day, while the media was trying to

get hold of them, he and Melina went to the Palm Cove Tavern for the cup celebrations. The publican gave Colin the whole hero bit, handing over schooners and B52 shooters – layers of Baileys, Kahlúa and Grand Marnier.

He was well gone, getting a bit emotional, when some bikie dude started in on him. He was later told that he picked this guy up and threw him five metres. He doesn't remember. But he knows that by being the angry guy, people didn't ask him questions.

Pains were starting to click in now. He had them over his chest, over his whole body. Two days after the incident his previously hairless chest started sprouting hair. It was all a symptom of the excessive adrenaline, he would later learn. The adrenaline causes an increase in testosterone which causes the body hair to grow and often causes head hair to fall out.

He went back to work a week after the incident but fell off a ladder and lost it. He stormed out. 'Nup, not doing this any more. Fuck yas.' He went reclusive. He just wanted to get on the boat and sail, but Melina wouldn't go. There was only the two of them. They had no family in town. It pushed them closer together. Lifted the intensity.

They got married as promised. But that incident, where he'd pushed her off, ate away at everything. She never felt safe with him. She'd only go sailing if there was no hint of a breeze. She couldn't handle the pitch of the boat because it reminded her of the aeroplane going down. This was a problem because they lived on the yacht. So they'd go out, find a snug little cove, stay there for weeks at a stretch, only pulling anchor on super fair days. He got Ross River fever. His immune system was shot because he was depressed. He ended up back in hospital.

Mel, complaining of constant pain in her neck, learned that she fractured a vertebrae, probably when BJ had flown through the cabin and hit her in the back of the head. They also learned that BJ had had a heart attack during the incident and that was why he acted the way he did. That gave Colin even more scope to beat himself up over the terrible words he'd said.

Colin was being hit for the cost of the rescue, the ambulance ride, and all his medical bills. He had full private health insurance but they wouldn't cover anything until the results of the inquiry were known. He fronted up to the counter at MBF: 'I think I'm crazy. I really need to see someone. My policy covers me for this.' But the girl behind the counter said it didn't. So he 'self-medicated', with liberal doses of booze and pot.

*

On the occasions when Colin could go back to work, it was night shift, where the only bastards he had to talk to were some crazy bikies. Life passed in an unhappy blur, dogged by an aching body and sad brain, until early one morning after finishing night shift at the shipyard, about a year after the incident, a bloke came up to him when he was walking to the shower at the yacht club. 'G'day, I'm from Channel Nine. Did you know you've won a bravery award?'

'What? Pardon? It's not me.'

'You've won a Commendation for Brave Conduct.' The guy convinced him that it was true and then said, 'You must be excited to get this award.'

Colin put two fingers on the reporter's chest and said, 'No I'm fucking not. For what? Because I'm being sued, I'm not happy about being left in the ocean . . .'

He spilled his heart out to the camera and to the other media that tracked him down that day. It was the first time he'd talked about it publicly. The headline in the *Cairns Post* the next day was something like 'Hero blasts rescue effort'.

The chopper pilot rang him. 'Mate, you have caused

Queensland Emergency Services irreparable damage,' the pilot said.

'Mate, well what do you think you've caused me by leaving me in the water?'

Colin hung up on him.

He and Mel went down to Government House in Brisbane for the award ceremony.

It should have been a recognition of all he'd been through, but there he was, in his borrowed suit with sleeves halfway up to his elbows, hair down to his belt, not feeling good about it at all. He knew he'd done something special, but it didn't sit right because of the things he'd said to BJ, leaving BJ and the pilot, punching the copper, threatening the ambulance driver. They didn't feel like the acts of a hero and he'd never been able to speak to any of these people again to say sorry.

He was ushered into a back room, standing next to some military bigwig whom he turned to: 'How, mate, did you get your shoes so shiny?' One of the military underlings ushered him away, keen to save the boss from the feral in the bad suit.

They went through the award ceremony where everybody clapped politely for the long list of people being recognised for lifetimes of service to the girl guides or the disabled or the beef industry. Colin's award was handed out last and everybody perked up when the citation was read out. He got two extra-loud rounds of applause.

Afterwards, he was standing by himself with a beer, delivered on a tray by the aide de camp, when the army officer with the shiny shoes came up and stuck out his hand: 'You're brilliant,' he said. It turned out to be Major General Peter Cosgrove, who would become famous the following year for leading international forces into East Timor. 'I try and train people to do the sort of thing you've done,' he said. 'Some people just can't do it.'

Colin will never forget that comment. It changed his life. Those few words made him feel good about himself for the first time in a long time. But Cosgrove never did explain how he got his shoes so shiny.

The comment didn't cure him, not by a long stretch, but it gave him a skerrick of an idea that he was all right – something he could cling to when he'd wake up, bolt upright, all senses firing, reliving the moment when he untied BJ and cast him adrift. He couldn't reconcile that and the racial abuse with the sort of person he knew himself to be. He'd beat himself up pretty bad and smoke more pot.

The marriage lasted less than a year. It was bitter, mental. They hate each other now. That hand on the shoulder got them married and it got them unmarried, he'd later say. He fell harder into the pot and the booze. Anything to blot out the thoughts. He'd load up the yacht with 1000 bucks of food and another 1000 of fuel and go and sit off Lizard Island where he didn't have to talk to anyone. He took risks, he went wild, did some things that are not for publication, but he got through.

He even joined the Australian Bravery Association and that's how I got on to him. Sally Gregory had suggested that he might have a story to tell.

*

Colin Brooks jumps in my car to guide me down to the car park of the Gold Coast high-rise where he now lives. Even though we're only going a few metres, he wants to drive and has to restrain himself from asking. He likes to be in control these days.

The plane crash has made him more assertive, he says. Whereas before he might have said to someone who owed him money not to worry, pay me when you've got it, now he just demands the money. He doesn't get screwed over any more.

He's employing six blokes, doing themed construction. He fits out nightclubs, Wiggles World, Movie World. Presently, he's working on a strip joint.

The blokes say he overbuilds everything. He says he's just preparing for any eventuality – 'bouncer proof', he calls it.

We talk over a few beers at a pub where the windows are flimsy. Wouldn't stop even a small airborne Samoan. His hair is short now, tousled, perhaps even fashionable. His new wife is a local hairdresser. He attributes much of his return to planet earth to her influence. She's lived through a few dark experiences herself, and he doesn't think he could be with anybody who hadn't.

Through the bravery association he picked up a mentor in Bill Hindson – a former SAS officer who served in Vietnam – who is straitlaced and very establishment. 'I never thought I'd be close to someone like that but he's a very post-traumatised guy . . . He helped me heaps. It's funny, a bloke like that, you know he's seen the bad side of the world. He's fought his way out of it and done what he's done honourably. I found a huge amount of respect for myself by him having respect for me . . . I can still get pretty dark on it. But I try not to. I've got two stepkids who are lovely. They're really proud of me. I give a talk once a year at their school. They have this heroes thing on their curriculum. They love it and I get a lot of respect for myself out of that.'

He's still got the board shorts, all tattered and stringy. 'You can still smell the adrenaline on them,' he says. He wonders if he should approach Quiksilver about getting some sort of advertising thing going.

I mention how so many of the people I've met for this book are strongly community minded. He said he never was before, but has become more so since the incident. 'I've always been a surfer but not a clubbie. I am now, though. I'll do patrols.

Do water safety with the Nippers. I designed a buoy. I patented a thing so that when that fellow came down the wire, he could have passed us a buoy – I call it the Brooks Buoy – it had a strobe and sea anchor and handles around it. They just laughed at me. "You're an idiot. What would you know?" I did a lot of things like that. I wrote a lot of letters. I got more community spirited.'

Towards the end of our long talk, he turns to me: 'I've got to tell you, bro, stranger things have happened to me since. The other day I'm driving home from work and I'm sitting at this set of lights, watching this chick do a U-turn. I'm thinking, you can't do a U-turn there. The poor guy on the motorbike didn't even have time to hit the brakes. Old matey boy has just ploughed straight into the side of her at sixty, seventy k's. I'm danger man. Say if this joint was on fire, I know I have the ability to save everyone. I can completely focus. I learned it in that crash. The guy on that motorbike, he's lying on the road with the motorbike on top of him, still running. The handlebars punctured the tank and fuel is just pissing out. He's lying in a puddle of fuel with his ankle right next to his head. He's broken his leg that bad. I'm first there. I've walked over. The battery is sitting in the puddle of fuel, connected to the terminals. It's twisted sideways. There's a guy standing there looking at it. I go, "Mate, we're gunna lift the bike off him. If it catches fire we're going to throw the motorbike and just drag him out – one shoulder each and just pull him out of the fire over to that paddock." I lifted the whole motorbike by myself, just walked it off him. Turned back around and went and held his hand. "Focus, mate, look at me." The coppers and ambulance rocked up and, "See ya." I didn't even give me name.

'A few years ago I was coming onto the freeway on-ramp at Smith Street. There was a mini-van upside down. I was about the third car to stop. It was a multiple car pile-up. There's this chick with her back to the concrete on the ramp. She's got her entrails just frickin' hanging out. I went and got a blanket and just pushed it all back in and tied it up. I just sat there talking to her. She died in the ambulance. I would have been the last one to talk to her. I don't go looking for it. This just happens to me.'

Except for the brief interviews at the time of the bravery award, Colin has never spoken publicly about the plane crash before. It might come up at a dinner party and his wife will say, 'Tell your story, Colin', but he gives the short version. He doesn't usually talk about what he really said to the ambo or to BJ. People aren't going to understand.

The thought of BJ continues to eat away at his sense of self. 'I've never talked to him since and that really affects me because I've never been able to say, "Sorry, I never meant any of that shit." Probably because I said all that shit he's never wanted to meet me. It's very hard. When I die I will go to my grave having regrets that I wasn't able to apologise about that. But at least it worked.'

*

I attempted to talk to the pilot who now flies for a big commercial airline but he didn't respond to my email. I rang Bamaga Council in the hope they might know BJ. The woman who answered the phone said, 'He's standing right here next to me.' In an extraordinary coincidence, he'd just walked into the council building to send a fax. We spoke briefly and he seemed friendly and articulate, but a little wary, especially when I mentioned I'd spoken to Colin Brooks. He gave me a number to call him in one hour's time but when I called it, it was disconnected. Subsequent calls and faxes failed to find him again.

THIRTEEN

Pam Davidson

Pam Davidson ran a business importing baskets, decorating them and on-selling them into department stores and homemaker shops. Business was good. She lived on a few hectares close to a beach near Coffs Harbour on the New South Wales north coast. The family had a little factory on the property so the youngest child, Nicky, four, was at home while she worked. The oldest, Jackie, six, was at school. Life should have been perfect, but Pam felt a deep underlying unhappiness with her marriage.

It was April 1988 and the weather was bad. She had appointments in Brisbane with a couple of big department stores. She'd normally drive up, but the highway north was flooded so she booked a flight.

At the airport, she was surprised when the passengers were directed towards a little eleven-seater Piper Navajo. She was expecting a big jet. Never mind. She flew to Brisbane in her hound's-tooth woollen suit, did her day of business and kicked a few goals. Returning to Brisbane airport in the afternoon, she ran into Gloria Dunne, a well-known Coffs Harbour retailer, but when they went to board, Gloria, a nervous flyer, got in the back because she said it was safer there. Pam sat right behind the pilot because she was interested in taking flying lessons and she wanted to see what he did.

The return flight stopped at Coolangatta and they picked up a guy who sat next to Pam. His name was John and they chatted on the 250-kilometre leg to Coffs Harbour. He was the manager of the Hibiscus Bakery, something of a landmark in town.

It was dark as they approached Coffs. Pam saw the runway lights through a break in the clouds, but the plane kept going south, and seemed to keep going for a long time. Eventually she had to ask, 'Where are we?'

'Over Nambucca Heads,' the pilot answered.

Pam wondered about that. It was almost 50 kilometres past Coffs Harbour. The pilot was checking charts and doing calculations. She felt uneasy because the weather was bad, but would have felt a lot worse had she known the pilot's landing beacon wasn't compatible with the one at the airport. He had nothing to guide him down but his own reckoning of how far they had flown in what direction and how long he'd flown back in the other.

They banked and he started descending through the haze illuminated by the plane's lights bouncing back at them. They dropped and dropped but still there was cloud all around. Suddenly it thinned and Pam could see the ground. It seemed too close. There were trees. *Where's the runway? I can't see the runway.*

The pilot continued descending. The trees were right in front now. She couldn't believe he was still taking it in. She heard herself screaming. 'Pull it up! Pull it up!'

The pilot did pull up. Hard. An alarm sounded in the cockpit. The plane lost speed, stalled and dropped again towards the trees. Pam felt utter dread, as her eyes fixed on the upcoming scrub.

They hit the first tree with a violent shudder. Then the second. The trunks were thin and bushy, maybe fifteen centimetres in diameter. Bang! Into the next. With each thud of a tree, the plane jerked hard, and with each blow Pam felt an increasing amazement that she wasn't dead. Other passengers would later report a woman in front yelling out, 'I'm alive! I'm alive!' She supposes it must have been her, but she doesn't remember giving voice to her thoughts as the plane continued crashing through the trees.

*

Pam's next memory was of being in total darkness. Everything was still. She became aware that someone was kicking something. She was completely disorientated in the blackness but it seemed like a good idea to follow the kicking noise. She undid her seatbelt and fell out of the seat, realising she had been hanging upside down.

She crawled forwards and followed the person out the pilot's window.

'Run, it's going to blow,' said a young man's voice heading off into the scrub.

She took a few steps in his wake. *Yeah, let's get the hell out of here.* But then she stopped. *What about Gloria? And what about John from the Hibiscus?*

There had been six passengers on board, plus the pilot. Only the two of them were out, so Pam turned around and went back to the hissing wreck that reeked of petrol.

'Is anybody in there?' she called through the window. 'Is anyone alive?'

There was silence . . . then a man's voice: 'How do I get out?'

'This way. Right . . . okay . . . undo your seatbelt. Come down to my voice.' She couldn't see anything through the darkness and the mangled metal. She leant in to help guide him to the tiny window and then she was aware of somebody else coming, too.

'Hurry! Hurry!'

Her own urgency mounted as the hissing noise and the avgas smell worsened. No sign of Gloria. No response from John. And just as the second man came through the window the whole thing went *whoomp*. A fireball engulfed her. She started running to get outside the flame. It was like there was a wall of fire and she just had to sprint through it. So she ran and ran across undulating sand but somehow just couldn't get through this flame.

Then she realised there was no wall of fire. It was her that was on fire. She was the fireball. She hit the ground and rolled.

The flames went out and she got to her feet, taking stock. *Wow, I've just survived a plane crash . . . I'm burnt . . . I got away, and I went back. That's okay. That's all right, Pam. Don't worry about it, you'll be okay. You're still alive. You're still alive.*

She had taken off her woollen jacket during the flight, leaving just a polyester business shirt covering her body. The shirt was extinguished now, but it had melted into her flesh. Her woollen hound's-tooth pants were intact, but they were holding a lot of intense heat that seared into the tender skin every time it came in contact. She had no idea how badly burnt she was. In the light of the flaming wreck, she could only see her hands. The skin was hanging off her nails, like it had melted.

God, I can't move my hands.

There was also a gold ingot around her neck that had heated up. It was chargrilling the skin it touched, as were the rings on her fingers and her belt buckle. They just wouldn't cool down and she couldn't do anything about it because her hands weren't working.

She asked someone, 'Can you take my belt off? It's burning me.' But they wouldn't touch her. She couldn't understand why. She'd later realise she must have looked horrific, but at the time it seemed all too strange.

The pain was bad, but would get much worse. For now she focused on survival, as the blank little group of four wondered what to do next.

Soon, they heard sirens and it seemed like they wouldn't have to wait long for help. But the sirens trundled on past them, getting further away. Then back again. It was clear nobody knew where they were. Including themselves.

One of the survivors wanted to head towards the noise through the bush. He was getting some support from the group but Pam insisted: 'We've got to stay here. They'll find us here. They'll follow the flames.'

They stayed put. But the flames gradually diminished as the plane was reduced to a black skeleton. A fellow passenger, who she would henceforth refer to as The Guru, wanted to get them all together to chant some mantras. He didn't get anyone interested, so he went off by himself. His Oms could be heard amid the distant sirens as the lights from the emergency vehicles bounced off the low cloud.

The guy who'd kicked his way out was unhurt. The first guy she'd helped out, an Indian vet, had some minor burns and The Guru had a badly burnt arm. They talked about the other people in the plane. They wondered where they were. Was there any drinking water nearby? And they waited. The drizzling rain felt lovely on Pam's burns but it further extinguished the fire. Soon the flames were gone and they waited some more in the darkness, lit up for brief moments by the moon breaking through cloud.

It felt like hours before a policeman came running down a railway track nearby and saw them. Then people came from everywhere, swarming up from the nearby beach.

She remembers one of the emergency workers put his coat on her. He reeked of bourbon. He went to put her in a four-wheel-drive but she wasn't going to survive a plane crash only to die in a drink-driving accident.

'No, get away from me, I'm going in the helicopter.'

'She's really badly injured,' someone said. 'She's not going to make it over the sand.'

'Please let me go in the chopper.'

An amateur pilot had heard about the plane crash on the news so he'd jumped in his little craft and come searching. Pam was taken out of the four-wheel-drive and put in his chopper with The Guru. She couldn't sit so she had to squat for the short flight to the Coffs Harbour hospital, but there was no chopper pad at the hospital. While they hovered above the car park, they could see people running out and moving cars to clear a space.

Pam was wheeled through the big doors into emergency. She begged for morphine and she got it. Things seemed a little better after that.

*

As is often the way with burns victims, Pam's injuries were far worse than she'd imagined. She was airlifted to the Royal North Shore hospital in Sydney that night. Years later, her daughter Jackie met the nurse on the flight who told her Pam wasn't expected to survive. Sixty-seven per cent of her body was burnt — the backs of her legs, her bottom, all over her chest and back where the shirt had been, her arms, her face, and especially the sides of her face. Pam presumed she must have put her hands up to save her eyes. 'My face was kind of burnt off, basically,' she would later recall. 'It blistered and just peeled off completely. Eyebrows, eyelashes, everything.' Her lips swelled into two thick tubers.

She remembers pain like no person should have to endure. Day after day of it. There was just nowhere to run from it. No way to lie or sit. Just unrelenting agony all merged into one long moment of wishing for death – but at the same time fighting against it. She'd suck on the nitrous oxide and wait for her next morphine shot. If it wasn't for the girls, she knows she would have just let herself die. Then, on day eleven, they took her morphine away. The pain had not eased up at all and now she was exhausted from a week and a half of fighting. She thought that her body was just waiting for permission to pack it all in. She asked her sister not to leave her because she knew death was nearby. It was going to be too easy to go to sleep and never wake.

She was still on pethidine so she'd lie there and watch the clock until her next dose. The time would come and there'd be that moment of bliss, of relief, before her eyes went back to the clock and the long four-hour wait for the next hit.

Her daughters hadn't been allowed to visit. At first it was because the doctors thought she was going to die, then it was because she looked so bad – with her head swollen out like a balloon and all the skin off her face – that the sight might be too much for them. But about two weeks after the accident they came. Because of the risk of infection, they could not kiss nor cuddle, the girls could not climb up on the bed and they were only allowed to touch her on the top of her head.

Every second day she would be wheeled into the big bathroom for burns patients where all the bandages would come off and she'd go onto a metal table that was raised up then lowered into a giant bath with various salts and potions in it. They'd debride the dead skin, and the physio would come in and make her move. She hated that physio for all the pain she inflicted. Really hated her. But as the days passed the physio ended up feeling like her best friend because, slowly, she started being able to move again without pain.

*

The doctors said Pam would be in hospital for three months; however, four weeks after the accident, she got herself transferred back to Coffs Harbour to be closer to the girls. But it felt to her like the Coffs Harbour hospital wasn't set up for the level of care she needed so she got herself discharged to go home. She had to promise to come back every day for a bath.

So, five weeks after the accident, Pam was back on the street, lathered in a cream and covered in plastic bags because her burns suit hadn't arrived from Ireland yet. She had been on pethidine up to her discharge, and no one told her about withdrawal. It was a good thing they hadn't, because if she'd known that the distress she was suddenly in was caused by an addiction to the drug, she probably would have gone searching for it.

She'd always try to get in early for her daily baths because The Guru was going in daily as well, and women from the maternity unit would use the thing and she'd get in there and it would have blood over the sides. She'd have to hose it out herself before getting in.

As far as life went, it seemed to Pam that everything should resume exactly as it was before the crash. The decorators still came to paint the baskets and she went out and joined them like she'd just had a few days off. But strange things were happening inside. It was like she had a motor running on full throttle. She'd be startled by anything, couldn't sleep, was always worried about the girls. If she walked down the street she'd suss out every single person, every car, within 500 metres, her eyes working relentlessly.

She went to a fireworks night at Woolgoolga, just north of Coffs Harbour, and absolutely freaked out at all the noise and light: she wasn't safe; there was going to be a fire; something awful was going to happen to the girls. She went on an overseas buying trip but the air travel knocked the stuffing out of her.

Something had to give and the first thing to go was her marriage. It wasn't that the trauma had created the problems in the marriage, more that it dictated the impulsive way she dealt with them. Three months after the accident, she put the girls in the car with a few clothes, a plate and spoon each, a toothbrush, a pillow and a blanket. She told them they were on an adventure. First night out they slept in the car. Maybe it was two nights – the girls would remember it differently from their mother. Then a friend gave them the use of a little shack by a beach. The kids thought it was awesome.

Pam tried to keep the business going but if she wanted to keep the orders coming in, she had to go out and sell, and the travel really took it out of her. Her products were becoming tired, her prices too high. The business needed invigoration but she wasn't the one to do it. She wound it up and tried casual teaching, but soon realised there had to be more to life than that thankless task. It was a low period, but out of the low came a decision to go back to university to study psychology.

The course involved regular flights to the campus at Bathurst in central New South Wales, but she was determined that her state of mind would not stop her doing anything. She graduated in 1996, became a school counsellor, then started in private practice in 2000.

*

Ambulance officers work on an injured child after a car crashed through a window and caught fire inside the Roundhouse Childcare Centre in Sydney. Dozens of strangers ran to rescue the bewildered children inside as the car's engine continued to rev furiously.

Darrell Tree survived a 19,000-volt jolt while freeing his friend from downed power lines. When he regained consciousness, he saw his friend's three-year-old son being electrocuted. He had to decide whether to save the boy and face electrocution himself or to leave him.

Detectives Gavin Dengate (*left*), and Allan Sparkes were making a cup of tea when they got a call that a child had been swept into a drain. Within minutes they were crawling up flooded pipes searching for Jai Galloway (*centre*).

Victor Boscoe thought a security guard had been shot when he decided to follow the masked gunmen. 'During the incident I backed myself to do whatever I could do. I could handle that. But the aftermath took away my life as I knew it.'

Jim Runham revisits the laneway in Ipswich where a bank robber in an afro wig shot
at him more than a decade ago. A school teacher who worked with disabled kids, Jim
endured threats and physical intimidation in the aftermath. He kept a shotgun by the door.

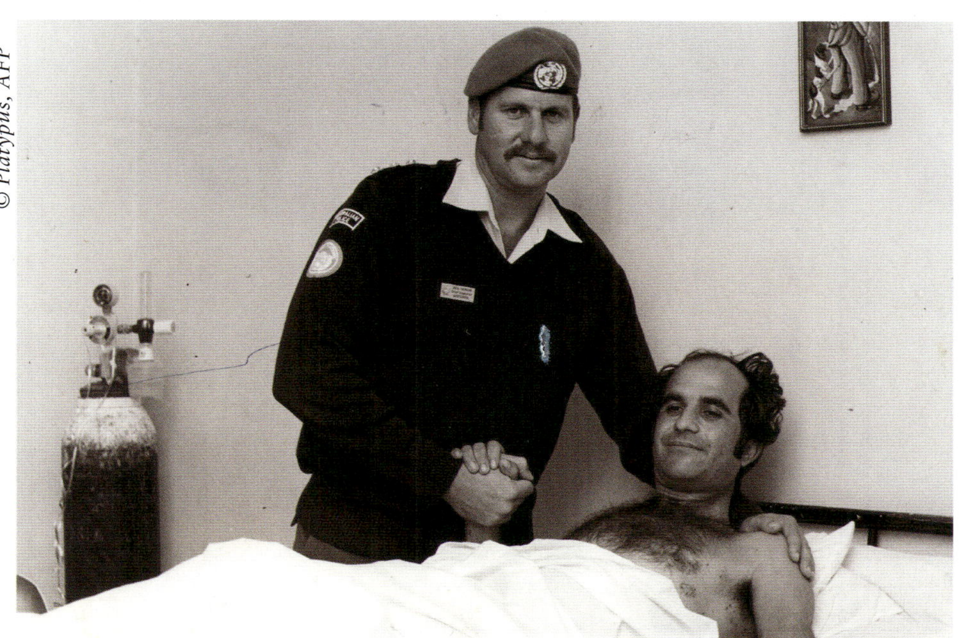

John Thurgar looks calm as he meets Chrysos Seas, days after carrying him across
an uncharted minefield in Cyprus, but John felt like a 100-kilogram bundle of
post-Vietnam anger and energy.

The Commercial Hotel in Longreach, western Queensland. Just minutes before the photo was taken, 14 people were asleep in the building but were woken by a strong, deliberate voice calling – 'Fire! Fire! Fire!' – until the voice grew weaker.

Jeff Brackenrig scooped a large chunk of flesh out of the water before diving in to look for a shark-attack victim off Byron Bay. Sally Gregory doesn't remember seeing any flesh before she too dived in to comfort the victim's new wife. Both their lives would change dramatically after the incident.

'Shit, I'm dead. I didn't get to him and the train's hit me and this is what it's like being dead,' thought Len Williams as he ran to pull a boy from in front of an approaching express train. His brain experienced a range of distortions common to soldiers in combat.

James Long promising a sweet clean fight in Melbourne's mayoral election. The former tram driver can't stand bullies and was prepared to put his life on the line to do something about it.

Joanne Lucas wasn't a strong swimmer. She usually came second last in the surf club swims. But when a man being circled by a giant fin called out for help, 80 metres off Albany's town beach, she was the only surf club member around.

Alan Playford, who has won more civilian bravery awards than any other Australian, inspects the aftermath of the Canberra bushfires at Mount Stromlo. 'He's fuckin' mad you know,' a colleague said of him. 'He won't stop till he's got everyone out.'

Alan meets the second last group of people he got out of the bushfires, the Naraines, at their Percy Street home. A huge fireball flew over them, hitting the house on the other side of the street, bursting the house's windows and exploding like it had been doused in petrol. That's when he decided he'd pushed his luck far enough.

Linton Jones took the lift down from his Gold Coast apartment when he heard screams on the street at 3 am.

Tim Britten ran towards the blazing Sari Club in Bali while others ran away. He was extremely frightened until, inside the flaming club, he resigned himself to death. After that, there was nothing more to be afraid of.

Coralee Lever thought Martin Bryant was doing some sort of re-enactment inside Port Arthur's Broad Arrow Café and told him she thought he was an idiot before her husband saved her life by sacrificing his own.

'Stay down. I love you,' Carolyn Loughton whispered as she lay on top of her daughter, Sarah, while Port Arthur gunman Martin Bryant walked by. She didn't know she'd been shot until she tried to raise her head and realised her shoulder was hanging off.

Rob Elliott had the opportunity to run at Martin Bryant. He paid the price.

I approach Pam Davidson's door with slight trepidation. I wonder what sort of heavy scarring she might have incurred. I have images in my head of those World War II pilots with their faces burnt off. But her law-student daughter Nicky opens the door instead and I'm ushered into a delightful timber house in the hills on the north side of inner Brisbane.

Pam comes out moments later and to my surprise there's no scarring at all. I presume her face must have been spared the burns. It's only later when she points them out that I see the marks. And, on closer inspection, the skin on her hands has an unusual texture. Her feet, showing through open shoes, also have barely noticeable wrinkles that are unusually small and close together.

We talk out on the jungly verandah while her daughter makes some flat whites in the coffee machine. It's clear Pam's life has arrived at a good place. Nicky brings us a plate of little cakes and pastries and joins us in our chat on the verandah. Pam is explaining that she probably had post-traumatic stress disorder for about a decade but that it had developed now into a 'generalised anxiety', the most obvious symptom of which is still hypervigilance. 'If a truck goes past and my car wobbles, I go, zing! And I can feel all my burns burning, just that shot of adrenaline. I'm tingling now where my burns were, just thinking about it. But the difference is that I'm not overwhelmed by it any more. I can function. I'm mindful that it's there, but I don't let it interfere.'

'But it does interfere,' Nicky chimes in. 'You just have to allude to danger and she cuts in, "I hope you were wearing your seatbelt." And I'm like that, too, now. And I know that I've got it from Mum. Like, growing up, I thought it was normal that when you get on a school bus you don't sit in certain seats.'

'She couldn't sit on the driver's side,' says Pam.

Nicky is laughing: 'And she would stand – this is bad – she would stand on the outside of the bus and before we got on for an excursion she'd be saying quietly, "You're going to sit in that seat, and I'll be standing here and you'll wave to me once you sit down and you get that seat." Cos if I didn't get that seat Mum would have caused a scene.'

'No I wouldn't,' says Pam, also laughing.

'Yes you would have. You would have done it quietly, but you would have done something. So we always sat in those seats.'

'Poor kids. They both had generalised anxiety disorders as a result of me.'

'When we fly now, Mum will ask, "What did you fly in?" And I'll tell her the materials of my clothes. "Oh yes, that would burn well," she says.'

Pam's version of how she regularly flew to Bathurst takes on a new dimension when Nicky adds her part. 'Up until probably two years ago, when we flew together, we'd get to the airport and Mum would just turn into a different person. She would become completely helpless. It's like her mind switches off.' Pam would get into the wrong queues as her subconscious battled for her to miss the flight. 'We're walking around the airport, looking for gate six, and the sign will clearly say "Gates 1–7" that way, and Mum will look at it and go the other way. And I'll say, "Mum, we're at gate six." She goes, "Yeah, that way. Let's go." And she'll walk away.'

'I'd sabotage it. Self-sabotage,' Pam explains. 'But I wasn't aware of it. I would literally think gate six was that way. I would misread the sign for my protection. I'm fine now. I've been going for the last eighteen months every fortnight on a small plane on my own. Not as small as a Piper Navajo. It's a sixteen-seater.'

'But it's only recent,' says Nicky, 'because I remember in

2004 I was speaking to Mum on the phone. She was in Sydney and she had a flight to connect to and she was talking to me and I said, "Mum, I think you're meant to have boarded by now." She said, "No, no, no, they haven't called it yet." I said, "Mum, where are you?" She said, "I'm sitting down, I'm at the coffee shop. I can see my gate." I said, "Can you please go and ask somebody while you're on the phone to me? Anybody in a uniform. Show them your ticket." So she did. And straight away she says, "I've got to go, I've got to go, the plane's about to leave." They'd been calling her name. They were about to take her bags off the plane.'

'Basically, I realise now, that's a panic attack,' Pam says.

Such behaviour does come with advantages. There was the time in 2005 when they were travelling to Beijing. The captain announced a delay because of some unspecified problem. Pam asked to be told exactly what the problem was. When the steward came back with some bland answer, Pam said, 'No, you have to go and find out from the captain exactly what is wrong. Don't lie to me. Tell me the truth or I'll get off the plane.' Nicky had to explain to the steward about the crash and the steward came back with the precise reason for the delay – and a bottle of champagne. Pam remembers none of this. It's been erased from her memory.

Pam's children have had to cope with other burdens beyond their anxiety.

When Jackie was doing her law degree, she went to the coroner's court as part of a project. The class was shown graphic images of a burns victim. Outside afterwards, Jackie was noticeably upset, as was an older woman sitting on the same bench. They each asked the other if they were okay. Jackie explained that her mum had been badly burnt and the woman explained that her husband had been burnt alive in a plane crash.

They exchanged stories and realised that it was the same crash. The woman's husband had been the pilot of Pam's plane. Pam had crawled out right next to him, unaware that his still-breathing body had been tucked down in the nose.

'The next time Jackie came home we talked about it,' says Pam. 'And I remember she was sitting on my knee. This twenty-four-year-old girl, sitting on my knee, crying for the first time. It took her that long to talk about how it was for her. And it was horrific. She'd seen me on TV the morning after it happened being wheeled out when the plane arrived in Sydney. No one had told her. Then she went to school and some kid said, "My mum told me your mum's dead."'

*

Pam practises a psychological model called mindfulness, based on Buddhist concepts. Unlike cognitive behavioural therapy, which would try to train her mind to get rid of the anxiety, mindfulness doesn't try to work it out of her brain, more to live with it. 'It's about accepting the anxiety but also being mindful that you can function and get on with things by keeping in mind what's important and keeping that as your focus. It absolutely felt right from my experience. I can get on an aeroplane even though I know I don't like it. She kept her practice in Coffs Harbour even after moving to Brisbane and opening a practice there, and for the eighteen months before we met, she had been flying to Coffs every week or fortnight.

'I can go into an airport and handle myself now. Just zip in and zip out. I love that.'

Even when her plane got diverted recently because of fog and three unsuccessful landing attempts, she remained cool. Her burns might have tingled but she held it together.

She has had one bravery award winner through her practice. 'It was difficult because he knew who I was.' She wouldn't normally tell a patient about her own experience. 'It becomes more about me and not about them. It's just not appropriate. When it's informal, sure, it might be okay. But it can make people feel, "Oh gosh, my stuff's so trivial compared to what you've been through." But they've lost something. It might be their dog, but some people experience that like others experience losing a family member. There's no hierarchy to the depth of feeling.'

Coincidentally she got to know the boy who Allan Sparkes rescued from the drain, Jai Galloway, during her time as a school counsellor in the district. 'He was one of the naughty lads around Coffs Harbour. We had programmes to help kids like that, but a lot of them fall through the net.' She is happy to hear the news that his life seems to have turned around. Perhaps a little surprised, too.

Here I am, talking to her twenty years after her incident, and her face might have mended itself with nothing more than oodles of antibiotic cream, but it feels like it's only now her mind has come close to recovery.

I mention a study that showed that while 46 per cent of heart attack survivors found that life got worse after their trauma, 43 per cent found it got better. The researchers called it post-traumatic growth.

'I can really understand that group where life gets worse,' Pam says. 'Life could have been really ordinary. I think where you are in your life when that event occurs is so important because you're going to have a huge struggle after that. If people can get help, if they can get a supportive network around them, it can make such a difference. There wasn't that understanding in 1988. The military get support, bills get paid, the police and ambos get support, but civilians don't. There's just nothing.'

She's proud of her medals now, but there was a time when they represented the ruination of her life. She threw the medal box into a brick wall at one point – 'when life was really shit, when it was really, really hard' – smashing it to pieces. 'I was probably being irritable,' she explains.

'We were being pains in the neck,' says Nicky. 'I remember it. It was awful.'

'It was a very symbolic thing to wreck the box. The medals were fine. It was like, "All of this has ruined my life." I remember feeling very different for a long time. Like people couldn't understand. It's a very isolating thing. That's where being in touch with something like the bravery association would have been very therapeutic for me and probably would have saved me five years of working through it. I would have met people who'd done something unique and had all this fallout, the repercussions, the healing. You just don't know anybody. Somebody pins a medal on you and that's great, but feeling understood is so important.'

We get talking about various other cases and Pam remembers another fellow who now lives in Coffs Harbour.

'Should I chase him up?' I ask.

'What are you looking for?'

'Interesting stories. Especially ones that have an interesting aftermath.'

'He got his medal two years ago. Star of Courage. Maybe I'll contact him and see if he'd like to speak to you. He probably would. I think it would do him good. His outcome hasn't been too good.'

And that's how I came into contact with Ron Wall. Up to then, the people I interviewed had a lot of time since their incidents to look back at their lives with a degree of perspective. Ron hadn't got that far yet.

FOURTEEN

Ron Wall

The willingness to die for another person is a form of love that even religions fail to inspire, and the experience of it changes a person profoundly.
Sebastian Junger, *War*

Talking to Ron Wall on the phone for the first time, I think that I probably won't get much out of him. He seems bright and friendly. Robust. A very Aussie kind of bloke and so I suspect he won't give much away on the emotions front.

We arrange to meet at his small business, a furniture warehouse on an industrial estate in Coffs Harbour.

Upon meeting, first impressions seem correct. He appears to be a straight-up-and-down businessman. Short-sleeved shirt and tie. We sit down at a table on the footpath outside his warehouse. I'm offered coffee as he starts telling his story. And I soon realise that appearances really do count for nothing.

'I always used to think things happened for a reason,' he begins, 'but, ahh, shit just happens. It was just coincidental that all these things happened at the same time. My mother and father had both just died. Mum lasted five days. I was there for the full five days. Dad had a fall and got golden staph about six days later. He lasted nine days. My wife left me not long after that, after twenty-one and a half years of marriage. I was in litigation over another matter. I had just stopped gambling, trying to get my life back on track. Here I was pottering along the highway. For once in my life I wasn't being a selfish gambling cunt. I was a normal person. Thinking clearly.'

And so begins Ron's extraordinary story.

*

In another universe that day, driving in the opposite direction on the Logan Motorway in Brisbane's south-west, is a young woman whose life by comparison seems perfect. She is happily married with two sons, aged seven and almost two. The oldest loves his soccer and cricket, the youngest with his blond curly hair is into The Wiggles and ice cream. She has taken seven weeks off her job as a police officer to move into a house that she and her policeman husband have just finished building. The day has been a typical Saturday in paradise. She read the papers while the kids watched cartoons before nagging her to take them for a swim at Grandma's. Why not? She packed them in the RAV4, told her husband she loved him, kissed him goodbye and drove off into the Brisbane summer heat.

*

Ron is going home to Toowoomba, heading west on the Logan Motorway, when he hears an explosion. Seconds later, the ordinariness of the motorway passes into chaos. Across the nature strip of broken shrubs and young trees he sees scattered cars, a truck, smoke.

He pulls over and runs down into the ditch dividing the motorway. There is a baby lying there on top of a bush. Two people arrive at the same time. They stand, looking at the child, dazed. Ron looks at them wondering if they'd been in the crash.

'You okay?'

'Yeah, we're all right.'

He looks at the infant – blond curly hair – lying there like he's asleep, wearing only a nappy. There isn't a mark on him. His colour is good. Everything looks good, but something inside Ron tells him, 'Don't touch this baby.' He races off to the shattered vehicles, through a litter of metal, plastic, glass and broken bushes. There is a truck and two other vehicles. One of the vehicles is lying on its side with flames coming out of the obliterated and flattened bonnet area. The back is all caved in, too – like it has been sandwiched.

Ron is the only person there. *Is anybody inside?*

Because the vehicle is on its side and the front and rear windscreens are shattered, he can't see in to look for survivors. But as he circles the flaming wreck, he sees that the sunroof has popped out a little. He gets down and peers inside. A woman is lying on the driver's side, hard against the road. Behind her is a boy. Looks about seven.

So he climbs up onto the passenger's side door, 1.7 metres off the ground. There is only one door up there. He thinks it is the front door of a van. The vehicle is so badly smashed up he can't tell that it is actually the rear door of a RAV4. He opens it and lowers his body into the vehicle. The door swings closed on top of him. Flames are just a metre away now, where the engine is pressed into the dash.

The little boy is unconscious. Ron talks to him anyway. 'You'll be okay, little fella. I'll get you out of here.'

Ron takes off the kid's seatbelt and with some difficulty lifts his body as gently as possible out of the compressed back-seat area. Another man has climbed up on the side of the vehicle and is holding the door open. Ron hands the boy's limp but breathing body up to him, before turning his attention to the unconscious woman in the driver's seat.

She is blonde, beautiful, helpless.

'I've got your boy out,' he tells her. 'Now I'm going to get you out.' He grapples with her seatbelt and gets it off, then starts pulling her body back through the gap between the front seats. But it won't come through. Her feet are wedged up under the dash.

He stands there on the broken glass of the rear passenger window in his bare feet – he'd lost his thongs racing across the nature strip – wondering what to do. The flames are getting larger. People outside the vehicle are screaming: 'Get out! Get out! It's going to blow.' He is more than aware of what might be about to happen. He managed a wrecking yard for ten years and had seen plenty of cars where the flames had devoured all the plastic interiors or gone down through the fuel lines to the tank and *kaboom*. *If I'm really quick I might just make it out.*

He grabs her under her arms and tries again. No good. She moans.

'You'll be right, baby,' he says. 'I'll get you out.'

He tries again, hard as he can pull, straining with all his strength. But she won't budge.

All the while, the flames are building in intensity. Plastic melting from the dashboard is dripping onto her legs. He brushes it off. Foul chemical smoke fills the cabin. The bloke holding the door is telling him to get out.

'Don't worry, baby. I'm not going to leave you.' He tries again, yanking on her armpits with all that he has. But he is feeling weaker as the smoke fills his lungs.

He puts her body back into the seat and tries to rip the seat out. He knows from the wrecking yard that seats are bolted down and he has no chance, but he has to try.

And as the voices outside continue urging him to get out, he gets a dreamlike feeling. Like this is meant to be. Almost like he's been here before.

'I won't leave ya, baby,' he says.

He has failed to keep his promise to get her out, but he feels bound by that promise, so he decides he will die with her. He starts readying for the explosion, figuring out where he can lie on top of her to protect her from it, reasoning that at least she might be able to survive. The clarity of his mind feels good.

*

'Crazy, I know,' he says, sitting out on the Coffs Harbour footpath with his mug of coffee. 'I was in there about five minutes at that stage. I wasn't going to leave her. I was just going to die with her. That's what's fucked me, see. We were both going to die. I couldn't leave her so I had to stay there and die with her.'

I ask him what was behind that reasoning? What had so instantly committed him to this stranger?

'I'd told her I was going to get her out, but I couldn't get her out. So I could not leave her to die on her own. I don't know. This woman I've never seen before in my whole life and I can't leave her. I was just going to die with her. I know it doesn't make sense . . .

'I had my young bloke in Toowoomba, my son. He was eighteen or nineteen at the time, with mental problems – depression – no one to look after him, but I didn't think of any of that. When you make that decision that you're going to die, it's like a moment of peace.'

He launches back into the story. 'I was exhausted. Buggered. I was having trouble breathing. But it was like I got this big shot of adrenaline. *Give it one last go. Just get HER out.* I tried her knees in a different position and I gave it a bit of extra tug, and with all the heat and the fire, the metal must have stretched a bit up under the dash and one foot came out, then the other one. [He delivers this line with excitement, wonder.] *How's that!* You know that was the happiest moment of my life. One moment I'm about to die, two moments later her feet come out and . . . Can you imagine the emotional ride of it all? I pulled her out and I screamed, "I got her." I got my hands under her real carefully and lifted her up to the top and they took her. I looked around and her handbag was down there, her mobile. I stuck them all under the door. "There's her handbag." I searched around in the back to make sure there was no one else in there and I opened up the console and saw all these CDs. I thought, I've got to get all this stuff out of the car before it catches on fire.' He's laughing now, just a little, but the muscles down the back of his shoulders are tingling.

'Then I remember saying to myself, "What the fuck are you doing? GET OUT OF HERE!" I was really going into shock. I couldn't quite climb out. I was half out and they dragged me out of the vehicle.'

*

Just as they hauled him out, somebody came over with a fire extinguisher and put the fire out, but seconds later, as he walked away, it burst back into flames. Ron went over to the baby. A woman was working on him. He went over to the woman he'd just saved who'd been laid out next to her older son. Her breast was partly exposed and Ron leant over and covered it.

There were cars parked all over the place now, but it seemed that most of the people were just looking. A bloke was dragging his guts along the ground, getting away from his car, on his own. It turned out that he was the driver who'd caused it all. He had been heading in the same direction as Ron. Witnesses saw his vehicle pull over to the left of the road and slow down, before suddenly and violently veering off to the right, accelerating through the bushes of the median strip full bore and colliding head-on with the RAV4, which was then rear-ended by a one-tonne truck and rolled. The guy had suffered an epileptic fit. Now here he was, dragging his innards along the ground with no one to help him. But eventually the guy who'd been on top of the car helping Ron went over to help him.

Police came a little later and took Ron's name and address. He got back in his car and it took him three hours to drive the hour's trip back to Toowoomba. He made it home and started ringing the hospital. They told him they don't normally give out details of people's condition, but they must have sensed something in the manic guy down the end of the line because they told him the baby had died. That really screwed with Ron's head. He'd done nothing to help the baby. *I should have saved the baby.* He threw it all back on himself. It was his fault.

Over the coming days, as he hobbled around on his cut-up feet, all bent over from the muscles he tore down his back pulling so hard at the woman and her seat – the muscles that would years later still tingle when memories fired up his brain's amygdala – he kept ringing the hospital to find out about the other two as their conditions remained in the balance. 'They've gotta live. They've gotta live.' The older boy hung between life and death for a couple of days. He had broken his arm, his leg and his back. He would never walk again. The mother had suffered massive internal injuries. She broke both legs, both knees, both ankles. She had bad burns to her left arm and cuts to her face. She woke up in hospital a week later.

*

Ron had to go to Beenleigh police station to make a statement but four times he found himself driving to the coast instead, getting pissed and maybe staying in a motel overnight before going home. He was afraid of being asked questions about the baby's seat. He presumed the thing had been put in wrong because he figured there was no other way that the baby could have come out. He didn't want to say anything that might cause any trouble for whoever had installed it. (The inquest found no problem with the seat but heard that the boy would often undo his own seatbelt.)

'The police rang me up. The coppers were good. They came out to my house. They patted me on the back. "Do you need any help?" I said, "I'm not going well." They offered me free counselling. I went to her once. I didn't like her. What has annoyed me, the reason I'm talking to you, was I was left out there on my own. If I'd been a policeman, ambulanceman, rescue worker or something, I would have been on workers comp. The system would have helped me. Although, those police I spoke to in Canberra [at a bravery association function] say they were treated like shit, too.'

He hit the booze hard. One night, he became so afraid of what he might do, he went to the police station and asked to be locked up. He cried to the cops about how much he loved the woman he had saved. 'How screwed up was that?' Ron says. 'Thinking that I loved this woman I never met.'

The police calmed him and took him home.

When he tells his family – or pretty much anybody – what he did in the rescue, they look at him funny and he can see them backing off like he's weird or scary.

*

Sixteen months after the incident Ron was awarded the Star of Courage, the country's second highest bravery medal. He joined the Australian Bravery Association, thinking that at least the people there would understand. And they did. They did. He went to Canberra for their annual meeting and heard snippets of other people's stories and he was going, 'Crikey! How'd you do that?' Then he'd tell a bit of his story which seemed pretty mundane to him by this stage but they'd all react the same.

'But it just goes from bad to worse,' he says. 'One of the blokes that got Sophie Delezio out of the Roundhouse was there and he was treating people like shit. I first saw him when there was an old bloke walking around, and this Roundhouse bloke said, "What are you doing here, you old fuck?" And all this sort of stuff. And he latched onto me, started following me around. I thought he may as well stay with me and leave all the other people alone. We went from the government reception to a big club around the corner for dinner. He walked along with me, driving me mad. We got there and they were all having dinner. I took my coat off and hung it on the chair with the big Star of Courage pinned to it. He was looking at it: "Geez that's good. You musta sucked a lot of cocks to get that."

'There were blokes there with medals all across their chests, dignitaries, and this bloke was talking like this. I said, "Mate, you're pushing the boundaries now. Be careful." This went on all night. I kept threatening. Never touched him. We walked out at the end of the night. I shook his hand after all these hours of crap. A couple of us were sharing a van back to the hotel. We were about to get in. "See ya later, mate, all the best," I said to him. He said, "You're a fuckin' wuss." I took my coat off, gave it to my girlfriend, and gave him two left crosses both in his mouth. "C'mon. C'mon." You know what he did? He ran. And I was after him, "Fuck, I'll kill him." I couldn't catch him. He ran around a little alcove and across the road. I tripped over and took all the skin off my hands and down my arms.'

Ron shows me the scars and if he had said he'd got them in the car fire, I'd have believed him. But no, he got them running across a Canberra street chasing a screwed-up hero. 'So next morning there was this other thing on at Government House and there I was with all this skin off my face. All up my arms. Word had spread around about what had happened. They all jumped to conclusions. They all understand now, but I don't go back to any bravery association things any more.'

That afternoon Ron got talking to Colin Brooks and he was blown away by his story of the plane crash off Cairns. He thought the guy was a legend and couldn't believe that Colin only got a Commendation for Brave Conduct.

Telling his story in this crowd was so different to telling it to his family and friends. They didn't look at him like a freak when he told them of his intention to die with a stranger. They understood.

He later mentioned his family's reaction to Pam Davidson. 'Do they look at me like that because they're wondering whether they would be able to do the same thing?'

'They know they wouldn't be able to do the same thing,' she said.

*

Gradually, Ron got himself together enough to go back to work. He put everything on the line to buy the little furniture warehouse in Coffs Harbour. The business is hanging in there. What, with the economy the way it is, people are hardly knocking down his door. He does a bit of security work at a local pub on the side. He might be past 50 now but he can still handle himself. He's also doing a private investigations course and has almost got his licence.

He's talking fast now. 'It cost five- or six-hundred bucks for a new suit to go to the investiture in Brisbane. I knew I'd probably be on TV. I wanted to look respectable. I wanted people to think I was a decent bloke rather than turn up like a feral. It cost a fortune to go to Canberra. It was like I got nothing except a box of medals . . . I go to psychiatrists and all that costs money. But the most hurtful thing was that I haven't got so much as a Christmas card from that woman. I haven't got a phone call. I don't expect 'em to clean my shoes, but they knew I wasn't well. Her mother and father knew from when I was at the hospital that I got hurt, physically and psychologically, but they never rang me to see how I was. Pam [Davidson] tells me that they think I'm a big tough fella who can do that job, that I'm okay.'

But he understands they've suffered worse than him. 'When I think of the losses they've had, maybe she hates me. Maybe she wishes she did die. I can imagine all those things.'

*

It is a short interview with Ron Wall. Less than 45 minutes. Ron needs to get back to work, but he has imparted his story with such speed and intensity that I can't think of any more questions.

Later that evening I receive a text message from Ron: 'Sorry about rave on so much 2day.i do really appreciate t medal, but meant to tel u I am only talking about it all in t hope that there may b more help in t future 4 others 2 recover fr t ordeal.im still suicidal as not save t baby.I will never forgive myself.'

I realise I can't just cruise into people's lives, delve into their inner turmoil and walk away. Here I am, I've got this bloke – a blokes' bloke – admitting that he's suicidal and I don't know what to say.

I reply: 'ron. every word was fascinating today. I am sure your story will help others. I'll be in touch in coming weeks. I'll just have a few questions about details. All the best and thanks again. Mark'

Half an hour after my limp response, my phone beeps again. 'i live on t edge all my life. Why was i there?fkd if i know.there was something, a higher power perhaps.i am so fn angry but I only want peace.'

I reply: 'gday mate. I do know that if you hadn't been there that woman would be dead. Everything has a purpose.'

The next day, he responds: 'Hey tiger. Sorry about silly msgs, had few ale last nite.get bit stressy wh I talk about it.'

Minutes later he texts again. 'Last msg. I SOLD MY MEDALS.i had 2.no money as couldn't work.it tore me apart.i hate myself 4 it.i loved those medals.But t baby die.i had 2 get rid of em anyway.'

After that, we speak on the phone and he's apologetic about the messages. Says he has a few beers and just gibbers away. He obviously feels bad for having crossed a line with me. I feel bad for the inadequacy of my responses.

He seems right as rain and I don't hear from him again for almost a month when he tells me via text that he's trying to buy his medal back. 'i need it.fkd without it.'

In later conversations with Ron, he is most concerned that I will portray him as a loony. I really hope I haven't. He has gone through what so many of the others in this book have experienced, but he was at an earlier stage of the progression. And he had a writer taking notes while he plumbed some of the depths. I'm sure he has come through the worst of it. He is a top bloke. One you'd want beside you in a foxhole . . . or a burning car.

FIFTEEN

Joanne Lucas

'It was a magnificent day,' Joanne Lucas begins, as so many of these stories seem to.

The 54-year-old mother of three arrives early at Albany's town beach, Middleton Beach, for a surfboat training row. Her mixed-sex crew usually trains on Sundays but they'd moved it forward to Saturday to avoid a clash with Mother's Day, the next day. The surf club season has finished, so nobody is on patrol, but her crew is training for a surfboat carnival next month.

The morning is still. The mighty Southern Ocean off the south coast of Western Australia is like a lake. The usuals are down there for their regular morning swims. The clubbies call them 'bobbers' because they tend to walk a few steps, swim a few strokes, have a bit of a chat.

Joanne opens up the surf club with her key, ready to start getting the boat out. An old bobber comes up for a shower. 'What a beautiful morning for a row,' he says. 'The dolphins have been out there all morning.'

'Yeah, it's a perfect day,' Joanne replies, as the sound of shouting drifts up from the beach. She doesn't pay much attention to the noise because people are always calling out and saying hello across the water in early morning bonhomie.

Then, a woman runs up. 'There's someone in the water and they need help. They're in trouble.' Joanne looks around. As far as the surf club goes, she is it, so she races down to the water's edge. A man is out there, waving his arms, with a dolphin nearby. 'Help! Can someone please help?' he calls.

'Can anyone help me?' Joanne asks, looking around.

'Sorry, I can't swim,' says the woman who had run to fetch her.

It looks like it's up to her. Joanne has only been in the surf club since she was 47 years old. She started out just taking her daughter down to Nippers before she and Rob steadily got more involved. She isn't a strong swimmer by surf club standards. She usually comes second last or third last in the club swims. Her forte is running – beach sprinting and flag races – but that isn't much good to her now as she strips off her tracksuit and thongs and steps into the shallows.

A woman in a wetsuit comes out of the water towards her. 'He's been attacked by a shark,' she says.

Joanne lets a little thought cross her mind: *Well why have you left him there?* But she stuffs that one back in. 'No. No, there are dolphins out there,' she answers.

'No, it's a shark,' the woman in the wetsuit insists.

Joanne hears the information but she doesn't allow it to register. She plunges into the water and swims a few strokes of freestyle before switching to breaststroke so she can see where the guy is.

She sees two people swimming further out who are clearly unaware of what is going on. And there is a fin – in between the two swimmers and the struggling man. She can see it in front of her the whole time as she breaststrokes towards it. Hardly takes her eyes off it. But there is something in her brain that refuses to recognise it as a shark fin. She just doesn't think about it. There is a guy in the water. She is going to get him out, just like her club training and the drills have taught her.

Joanne has only been involved in one rescue before, but she doesn't think it was much of a rescue. A guy was caught in a rip. She paddled out on a board and brought him back in. She has, however, done plenty of patrol hours and is always up with her training and retraining.

She glides up to the guy and says the lines as per the life-savers' manual, designed to keep the situation calm. 'Hi, my name's Joanne and I've come to get you.'

'Thank you so much for coming,' he says, or words to that effect, calm and cool-headed. 'A shark got my leg.'

Oh no, maybe I'm going to have to look for a leg floating about. But still she does not think about that fin. If there is any blood in the water, her brain does not allow her to see it. She grabs him tight from behind with both arms so that she is swimming backwards, looking over his shoulder. She is amazed at how he keeps his cool despite what he's been through.

*

Minutes earlier, the swimmer, Jason Cull, had seen a grey shape coming towards him. A dolphin, he'd presumed. But then it banged hard into him and he knew it was a shark. It dragged him backwards and down. His hands were free and he felt around for its gills but found its eye instead. He squelched his finger in hard and suddenly he was free. It had swum off towards other swimmers and he had begun to swim back to shore, calling out to others to warn them, feeling weaker with every stroke, doubting that he was going to make it until Joanne turned up.

She was sure that his coolness was going to make her job a lot easier. And he wasn't a big bloke either so that was going to help, too, since she was only five-feet-one (155 centimetres) and 54 kilograms. And as she started to scissor kick and frog kick her way back to shore, there was the fin again, not far away. She sees herself as hopeless at estimating distances. This fin was 'not very far, quite close'. But still her brain wasn't telling her to kick with all her might to get away from the beast.

'Can you get me back? Can you get me in?' Jason asked.

'Yeah. No worries. I'll get you in.'

Looking back out to sea, keeping an eye on the fin, Joanne saw the two other swimmers, maybe 30 or 40 metres away, heading straight for the fin. She saw the fin go right up to them and as it did, she saw the swimmers come together and splash like crazy – just as you'd do if a shark was attacking you. *A shark!*

Suddenly, the predator registered in her mind. It was real now – and it could turn around at any moment and charge her. She started kicking as hard as she could, finding every last ounce of oomph in her beach sprinter's legs, wondering what she'd do if it attacked the other two swimmers and she had to bring them in as well.

At that moment, way back on the boardwalk, a man raised his mobile phone and took a photo of the unfolding drama, unaware of what he was witnessing, thinking it to be some sort of drill. His picture shows the beautiful pastel light of the morning rising over Albany's rugged coastline and the still water, with two heads – Jason and Joanne – closest to the beach. Everything is calm. They could be two people having a chat while treading water. Further out, perhaps 30 metres, you can make out a very large vertical splash and three dark shapes – the nearest of which appears to be a shark fin.

'Can you get me back?' the injured man kept repeating.

'We're getting closer. We're getting back.'

As Joanne neared the shore, she did not try to put her feet down because she didn't want to go under if she couldn't touch bottom. He was getting heavy now, but she kept kicking until she was very close. When she eventually stood, the water was knee height.

She called out to a man standing on the beach and he rolled his trousers up and came in. She kept hold of the victim's armpits while the man lifted him by the legs, enabling Joanne to see the shark bites for the first time. His left leg was completely open, like blubber, from the ankle to above the knee. The jagged tear marks looked as if they had been torn by an old-fashioned tin opener. Curiously, there was no blood. Just white blubber. She grabbed a towel and threw it at the guy helping her. 'Put a pressure bandage on.' Her training was coming back to her. She made sure his airways were clear.

Her surfboat crew mates had arrived by now and one of them went and got the oxygen from the club, and all the while Joanne sat there talking to the victim. 'Don't close your eyes. Don't close your eyes.'

Just as the oxygen got there, the two swimmers who had been out with the shark reached the shore. They'd been followed all the way in, but were left unmolested. 'They'd swum in very quickly, I found out later,' Joanne would recall. 'The shark had nearly beached itself. They came straight away to my side.' One of them, Sally Malone, was a nurse. She pinched her fingers onto the man's femoral artery to stop the bleeding.

Joanne just kept talking to him and he talked back. 'Can we contact someone to let them know what's happened?' she asked him.

'My wife,' he said. Someone pulled out a phone and he called out the number, then spoke to her. The ambulance arrived and Joanne kept holding his hand until he was into the vehicle and away.

It was only then that somebody said, 'That was Jason. You know Jason, he goes in the swims.' It dawned on Joanne that she actually knew him. He was a club member and his wife was a patrol member. Someone else came up to her, 'You did a wonderful thing.'

'Oh shit,' she thought, 'what have I actually done?' She never usually swears. Not even in her thoughts, but that was the moment when her brain finally allowed her to process all the information about the shark and the fin and the danger that she'd swum into. It finally allowed her to contemplate what could have gone wrong.

One of her team mates, Tom Marron, the local head of emergency services, arrived and was told what had happened. He looked at Joanne. 'You?' he asked. Not in a nasty way. He was just shocked because she wasn't a great swimmer.

Tom organised a crew to go up the beach in the club ute to clear the water. Joanne went to get in.

'What the hell do you think you're doing?' Tom asked. 'You're not going anywhere.'

But she was so hyped, she was ready for anything. The police arrived and asked if she was all right. She sure was.

*

'I thought I was quite okay. Then after everybody had been cleared off the beach, Tom said we had to do an incident report. It was then that I started crying. I don't cry very often and that's when it sort of hit me. Everybody kept coming in the room. "What happened?" Within fifteen minutes of Jason being in the ambulance, the local media guy was there. Somebody had got me a cup of tea and every time somebody asked me something, I'd start blubbing, which was pathetic.

'I went to a friend's place, had a cup of tea. We talked about it and every time I'd cry she'd cry because she was so over-wrought by it. My son took me home and by that stage the [Perth] *Sunday Times* had got hold of the story. "Can we do an interview?" So they flew down by helicopter. They came more or less within an hour and a half. I was okay by then. It didn't take long to get myself under control.

'The next day, Sunday, I got a phone call at 5.30 am from an eastern-state lot saying they wanted an interview. The phone didn't stop ringing for twenty-four hours. That was the worst part. Having to recount it every time. We went and got the paper and the picture taken by the guy on the phone was on the front page. My son was playing football that day, so every-body there had seen the paper and wanted to talk about it. And I just kept getting phone calls – from people who had known me years ago to fairly close people. Just hundreds of phone calls. It was a lovely feeling. It was all positive, but also so exhausting, bringing it back each time.

'I went to see Jason that afternoon and had a chat. He said, "Thank you so much. Thank you so much." He told me there'd been so much blood he couldn't see what was under-neath him in the water, but I didn't see any of that. He said he was trying to warn people there was a shark in there and nobody would believe him. "No, no, it's a dolphin." He said he could still feel its eye from when he'd gouged it to make it let go. He was trying to get himself back to shore and shout out at the same time. I think he thought he did so much try-ing to get people out he should be getting the big hero thing, too. I've never considered myself a hero. When I look back I didn't have any thought processes. I honestly didn't. I just jumped in.'

*

That Sunday afternoon, Jason Cull gave a bedside interview to the massed media. He told of his escape from the four-metre white pointer's jaws and how it had circled him as he tried to backstroke the 80 metres to shore, before it turned its attention to the two other swimmers. 'I'm just grateful he didn't come back for seconds,' he said. And he heaped praise on Joanne for coming out to get him. 'I do not think I would have made it the rest of the way.'

The day that interview appeared in the press, Joanne decided she couldn't do any more interviews. She was fine when she was talking to people, but afterwards she'd get a huge surge of blood to the head. She went to Perth and turned the phone off, leaving Rob to fend off about 60 more callers.

'Even now, almost two years later,' she says, 'I don't mind talking about it. It's just that there's a bit of exhaustion – the blood pumping through your brain. Since then I have been great. I think about it quite often but I don't get flashbacks. The first night I didn't sleep. The good thing was, about a month after, the awards started coming. The first was from Surf Life Saving WA. After that, my husband and I had booked to go away to eastern Europe for three months. That was perfect. It took me a while to wind down.

'Jason was very heroic in what he did, but it's not my story to tell. Jason hasn't given any stories at all since that interview in hospital. He won't do any others and I won't give out his phone number either. I just don't want to burden him with that. Every time an award has come up there's always a big hoo-ha afterwards and I've felt . . . not guilty, but awful for the fact that he has to relive it every time it comes up. I've been really loathe to do anything that's specifically about me. I'm happy to talk but I really don't want to be the focus.

'Jason and I got reasonably close. I'd ring him quite often and, you know, send Christmas cards and how-you-going cards, but I've pulled right back now because I understand, really, I'm a bit of a nightmare on legs in a way.' She laughs. 'Every time he sees me or hears my voice, he must think, "God no". And it all comes back to him. I've cut right back. If I bump into him, we have a big hug and a chat, but I don't seek him out any more and he doesn't seek me out either and that's been fine.'

When I speak to Joanne, it's just a few weeks before her presentation with the Star of Courage. She hopes the ceremony will be the last of the hoo-ha. But, of course, people will ask her again about the nature of her bravery. So I get in first. 'If you'd stopped to think about it, do you think you would have done it?'

But she seems no more able to explain her heroics than the other brave people I have interviewed. Her answer is smattered with the same phrases: 'We'd all like to think we could . . . It was just an instant reaction . . . If I'd stopped and thought, maybe I wouldn't have done it . . . Maybe I'm just the sort of person who . . . I just felt I had to . . . If it happened again I'd probably do it again . . . I guess it's just the type of person you are.'

I have tended not to include a lot of those types of answers in previous chapters because I don't find them particularly illuminating. But I'm starting to realise they're the only answers I'm likely to get. There is one other response, of course, and that is, 'It's my job'.

SIXTEEN

Alan Playford

*Because we're in a uniform people think we're just doing a
job, but somewhere in there, the normal job ends and it's up
to you whether you can go a bit further.*
John Gleeson, ambulance officer

Alan Playford has seen more people die than anyone else
I'm likely to meet. Unknowable thousands of people.
He's smelt more death, too. It has seeped into his clothes and
his hair. He's watched mangy dogs devour corpses too numer-
ous to be cleared by human hands, and he's had death and
faeces fill his every waking moment till he knew he was in hell.

He's also helped saved unknowable thousands of people,
and he's got more civilian bravery medals than anyone else in
the country.

And Alan Playford is fine.

He'll be hitting retirement from the ambulance service
around the time of publication of this book in mid 2011. They
don't want 60-year-olds jumping out of helicopters.

*

I arrive at Alan's home in Newcastle, a few hours north of Sydney, not knowing much about him, other than the bit about him having three bravery awards. Jim Runham had thought he might be good to talk to. I walk out four hours later with a book's worth of stories.

Alan was a young ambo when the New South Wales Ambulance Service copied the American system of training their people up to paramedic level in the mid 1970s. Then those paramedics got put into helicopters in the late 70s. They were suddenly saving a lot of people who would previously have died in earth-bound ambulances or small country hospitals a long way from the major trauma hospitals.

Which brings us to a day in the late 1980s when Alan was on duty in one of those earth-bound ambulances, sent to a job in the Newcastle suburb of Mayfield.

He arrived to find an electricity linesman on fire, lying underneath a cherry picker. A neighbour was squirting a garden hose at him, which normally would have been good, but lying between the neighbour and the injured man were 11,000-volt powerlines on the ground. And the lines were moving; coiling up then straightening out with a whip crack. The current running through them was acting like water through a loose garden hose.

'Put it away, mate. You'll electrocute yourself,' Alan told the neighbour. 'The current'll backtrack along the water and kill you.'

'No, no. I'll keep it above the wire.'

Alan's ambulance partner chipped in – 'Put it away or I'll shove it up your arse' – before bending the hose and cutting off the stream. The linesman looked pretty much cooked. Alan thought he'd leave him where he was because it would be suicidal to attempt to jump the writhing powerlines to get to him. There was too much energy in there. Too much water lying about. And then he heard screaming. He stepped back a bit and saw a second man lying on the ground. Lumps of molten fibreglass were falling onto him from the cherry picker above. He was on fire, too. And he was obviously alive.

The ambos were later told that the linesmen had been up in the cherry picker working on the wires when current arced into the cherry picker and exploded a bottle of hydraulic oil they had in there. The first of them, Graeme Hards (Alan remembers the names off the top of his head more than twenty years later), was burnt 100 per cent from head to foot. It was unclear if he jumped or was blown out, but he had landed 25 metres below, on fire. The cherry picker was meant to be fireproof, but this one caught fire and the other linesman, Steven Truebody, had jumped over the side and clung to it until he could no longer hold on to the melting fibreglass.

The ambos had arrived soon after he fell. When Alan saw he was alive, he felt he had no choice. He had to get to him, live wires or not. He waited for the powerline to lengthen and flatten out. Then he sprinted and jumped before it recoiled back again.

He cleared the dancing wires and went straight to Steven's side, grabbing his arms, thinking that he'd drag him down the footpath away from the powerlines. But as Alan pulled, the linesman let out a scream that would have been heard in Sydney. He'd broken his arm in the fall, and now Alan had dislocated his shoulder as well. Steven was a big fellow and Alan wasn't – 174 centimetres tall and slim.

'I can't move him,' Alan called to his partner. 'You'll have to jump over.'

But his partner didn't move. He was rooted to the spot, facing the snaking wires. 'I can't do it,' he said. 'I can't.'

Another ambulance pulled up and one of the officers from

it, Dave Fitzclarence, ran and leapt. He cleared the wires and together they dragged the injured man by the belt down the footpath away from the power. Steven was still screaming in agony and all the while the ambos were yelling at the county council foreman to turn off the bloody juice.

When it was eventually switched off, they carried Steven over the wires and got the fireys to put a slow trickle of water on him. Alan got the intravenous line, the IV, into his foot and bowled him over with a big shot of morphine and at last his screams quietened. His right arm and leg were 100 per cent burnt.

It was the only time in his long career Alan ever got a police escort to hospital and they got him there quickly, but Steven Truebody died three weeks later from infection. 'My partner that day still feels bad about it to this day,' recalls Alan. 'He came off the road as a result of that job. He's in the control room now. I always questioned why Steven Truebody didn't live. And he should have. I consoled myself that we'd done absolutely as much as we could, considering the wires and everything. There wasn't physically another thing we could have done.'

*

Not long after, on 28 December 1989, Alan was off duty with the ambos when the Newcastle earthquake struck. He was called in to duty with the fire brigade – on top of being an ambo, he was an on-call fireman with the New Lambton fire station. Their truck was directed into the centre of Newcastle but there wasn't much fire action going on, so his fire captain told him he might be more useful as a paramedic than a fireman. The truck dropped him at ambulance headquarters and he got changed into his gear. He initially went to Beaumont Street where there were people trapped under rubble from a collapsed awning. Then a call came through that a paramedic was needed at the Newcastle Workers Club.

Alan arrived to see clouds of cement dust billowing out every aperture of the club, even though it was more than half an hour since the western wall had collapsed, leading to a cascading failure of the concrete slab floors. If anybody had survived in there, it seemed likely the dust would have suffocated them.

The way into the building was a driveway entrance where the slab had collapsed, creating a slippery dip at 45 degrees. The dust was billowing out at an improbable rate. *How can you go in there?* It didn't seem possible but he tied a rag around his mouth and in he went, sliding down the fallen slab on his backside, carrying Plano boxes of drugs and medical equipment in each hand, trying to use his feet for brakes as he accelerated down into the dusty pit. He hit bottom and walked out into some space where he could hear people screaming and calling out, but it was hard to tell where the voices were coming from.

Steel reinforcing had sprung out of the concrete, creating a labyrinth of metal spaghetti. Large pieces of concrete were attached to the dangling strands of reinforcing steel and they wobbled as the building continued to move. Alan thought it was aftershocks but it turned out to be the building still shifting. And every time it moved the reinforcing steel twanged a disconcerting twang. Just don't think about it, he told himself.

But the police *were* thinking about it and before he'd gone very far, they had ordered everyone out of the club, fearing an aftershock. Rescue workers gathered on the street where intense frustration festered. The voices still called for help, yet they could do nothing. Those voices, however, convinced the police to allow a limited force of police rescue and paramedics back in. (The fire brigade was ropeable that it was excluded.)

Alan descended the fallen slab again and found fellow

ambo Mal Martin with an IV bag in each hand, hooked up to an old bloke who was crushed below the waist by a large chunk of concrete floor, yet was still talking.

'Have a go at this, Scoop,' Mal said as he pumped away at the plasma extractor. 'You watch when I stop.'

Mal stopped pumping and the old bloke stopped talking and slumped back unconscious. Mal resumed pumping and, like a ventriloquist's doll, the old guy sat back up and resumed the conversation.

'I reckon I've got about fifteen minutes here with him,' Mal said.

'Where do you want us to go?' Alan asked.

'I can hear voices down there under this reo.'

Alan looked at the tangle of steel. 'The only way we'll get through there is with oxyacetylene torches.'

'The place is full of gas, Al. You'll blow us all up.'

'Of course. I didn't think. How we gunna get 'em out?'

Mal pointed to the slab above. It seemed that it had collapsed at an angle and all the poker machines and the people playing them had slid down into this hole and they were now below the level that Alan was on, stuck in some sort of cavern. Mal suggested that if they got up to the next level, maybe they could get back down the hole where the people had fallen in.

Alan cautiously climbed up. He found a man up there in State Emergency Service (SES) overalls, spread-eagled over the poker machines fallen across the hole.

'G'day, mate,' Alan said. 'What's going on?'

'I'm doing a good job. I'm talking to these people below and nothing you say is going to make me leave.'

'Mate, I don't want to make you leave. We've got to start burrowing our way through to them. You can help us move these pokies. Are you with the SES?'

'Yeah.'

'Come down and help.'

But the bloke point-blank refused. 'I'm doing a good job, you can fuck off and leave me alone. I'm here talking to them. They haven't got much longer to live and I'm going to stay with them.'

'Well, we'll make up our minds if they've got much longer to live, but we need you to get off.'

The bloke still refused. So Alan turned to a mate of his in police rescue, Meathead, and said, 'I've got a job for you.' Meathead grabbed the bloke, squealing and squirming, and frogmarched him out of the rubble. (Years later Alan learned he was put in a police car, driven out of town and dumped by the side of a road. It turned out he was a nutter who'd stolen the SES uniform.)

The small crew inside started pulling at the poker machines and dismantling them, standing in puddles of money, passing the bits and pieces along in a chain as coins continued to tinkle out. When the hole was cleared of pokies, a fire hose was wrapped around Alan (they didn't have any rope) and he was lowered into the cavern where the voices were. The cement dust rendered the torch useless, so he descended blind. The first indication that he'd hit bottom was a woman's scream. He'd trodden on her and she was clearly badly injured. He tried to reposition himself, but his stumbling efforts just seemed to make it worse. Her squeals echoed through the rubble as he tried to find a spot to ease himself down.

It took him a few minutes to feel around and orientate himself. He had come down about three metres into a V-shaped crevice filled with rubble and covered with a layer of cement dust about fifteen-centimetres thick. The screaming woman was buried among it almost as if she were part of it. And as Alan's hands pushed through the rubble, exploring the surrounds, he felt flesh – lifeless but not yet cold. He eased the dust and cement chunks away as gently as he could, trying to not stir it up any more. He got enough away to ascertain by feel that it was a woman and that a large chunk of concrete had smashed her head.

There were other voices around, a cheerful older man and another woman, but he didn't know if they were in the same cavity as him. He needed to get to work on the screaming woman, but first he had to pacify her. 'It's going to take some time to get you out,' he said. 'But we're here now. You're going to be okay. Who else is here?'

She was too wound up to answer, and just screamed and sobbed. And every time he moved, he stirred up more dust, taking visibility back to zero. He called to the rescuers above. 'I'm going to have a lot of trouble uncovering this patient, but it's too tight for anyone else to fit down here. I'll keep you appraised of how it's going.'

All the while, the older man's voice chipped in with words of encouragement. 'I can see the sun. We'll be out in the sunshine soon.'

Alan's plan was to first get an IV into the woman – get the fluids in to keep her going. His gear was lowered down and he tried to get to her skin, but the dust layer on it was about five centimetres thick and every time he wiped it away a cloud would go up blocking his view before settling back onto her skin. When he put an alcohol swab on her arm to try to sterilise it, he just created a concrete slurry. He thought of how much she looked like the Goroka mud men from New Guinea. And the old man's voice kept up the encouragement from his unknown cranny. 'We'll be out of here soon. I can see the sun. Did you hear that, Miriam? Won't be long now.'

Some towels were sent down and Alan eventually cleared a spot on the woman's arm, but then he had to find somewhere to balance the bag and tape the needle in. When it was all set up, he pumped the drip flat out to get it all into her so he could start clearing the rubble. She was under a lot of loose material and was partially covered by the dead woman whose body he had to move to the side. He passed the larger rocks up to a rescuer leaning in from above supported by a fire hose.

There was no way to fit any sort of stretcher down there so when the woman was clear of rubble, he got a fire hose under her armpits. 'I realise your pelvis is in a lot of trouble but there's nothing I can get down here to get you up,' he told her. But she was so busy expressing herself, so involved in her pain, that there wasn't any reasoning to be done. She was lifted out screaming as Alan held her arms down over the fire hose.

With her out of the way, he was able to see what else was down in the hole. He ran his hands through the rubble below where the woman had been and felt warm flesh.

'My name's Norm,' said the encouraging voice from under a thick layer of cement dust.

'Hello, Norm. My name's Alan.'

'G'day, Alan. How are you?'

'I'm good. What's your story, Norm?'

'I'm here with Miriam,' he said, forthright and matter of fact. 'We're playing the poker machines.'

Alan didn't mention the dead woman he'd already found, in case that was Miriam (it was). Now that there was more room and quiet in the hole, Alan realised there was another woman on the lower side of Norm as well – trapped and badly injured, but conscious and talking.

He thought he'd get Norm first, but Norm insisted, 'Make me last. Make me last.' He cleared the dust from Norm and got a drip into him, then set to work getting the woman out while Norm continued his casual, hopeful banter. Alan, however, could sense that Norm's spirit was getting lower and lower. By the time Alan got the second woman out and was able to turn his attention to Norm, it was well into the afternoon, after the quake had struck at 10.27 am.

Norm was a recently retired bus driver, council worker, you name it. He and Miriam had come in to pay their annual membership fees and put a few bob through the machines. When the quake had struck, they had gone from the flashing and spinning normality of the pokies on the second floor to this black, silent, suffocating hole in the basement.

Alan cleared the dust and stones away from Norm's torso, with more room to move now that the two women were gone. The dust was still a problem, kicking up every time he shifted anything as he worked his way down to a large slab of concrete and saw that it had crushed Norm's legs below the thighs. Alan had already been impressed by Norm's stoicism, but now he saw how badly hurt he was, the ambo was in awe.

Norm's blood pressure was falling. Alan put a second IV line in, and continued to work at the slab. A crowbar had been lowered down and he levered and hacked at the already cracked concrete. As he slowly manhandled the pieces off Norm, he noticed him suddenly go flat. His eyes had rolled back a little. *I'm going to lose this guy.* It was a sense you developed in the ambulance business. Norm was about to have a cardiac arrest.

Alan knew that when a body is crushed, acids unable to get back to the heart to be processed by the body build up behind the crush. When the crush is released, those acids flow en masse to the heart and stop it. It is called crush syndrome.

He quickly levered the last big piece away. Revealing legs like dishrags – flat, mottled and raggedy. The men above had lowered a Stokes litter (a basket-like stretcher) now that there was more room. Alan quickly strapped Norm in and called out to Mal Martin – 'I think he's going.' And as the men above raised the litter, Norm went into cardiac arrest.

He was gone. It hit Alan hard. To have spent so much time with such a strong, inspiring character, only to see him lose the battle was tough. He stayed in the hole to see if there was anything he could do for the other woman but he confirmed she was dead and it was too dangerous to hang around. The building was still shaking periodically, shimmering the steel reinforcing bars. So about half an hour after he got Norm out, he climbed up the hose and came out of the building. It was about 3 pm.

He was put straight into a cherry picker with colleague Terry McDermott to check the top floor. But before they went up, then prime minister Bob Hawke came along and shook their hands. Up on the top level, they squeezed in between the slabs and found the bodies of some roadies killed while setting up for that night's planned Battle of the Bands. They'd sought shelter under chairs which had been crushed like bottle tops. There would have been 2000 kids in the place later that night.

They descended in the cherry picker about 5 pm. Alan felt drained. Norm's performance had left a profound impression on him. Someone asked him how he was travelling. 'The one I feel worst about is a bloke called Norm. We got him out but lost him. He went into cardiac arrest.'

'We got him going again,' he was told.

'You've got to be kidding. Mate, that's the best Christmas present I ever received.'

The outside medical team had given Norm sodium bicarbonate, which neutralised the acids, and brought him back to life. Alan felt suddenly elated.

*

Early in Alan's career, he used to go to hospital to visit people he had brought in. When you're nursing someone on death's door on a long drive or helicopter flight, there is an openness of communication. You cut through all the stages of friendship and go straight to total intimacy. They tell you *everything*. You tell them a lot, too, and they cry with you and on you. But the hospital visits hurt too much. He realised he had to stay away to protect himself and he soon developed what he calls 'sympathetic detachment'.

'To talk to people over the years that have been crushed under trains, in mining accidents, in cave-ins, it's always been something that lingers because you've had that long conversation with them,' he says. 'We had a grain silo explosion in the Hunter Valley about twelve years ago. Three blokes were talking to us; they were 100 per cent burnt. You put them in the helicopter and they're talking about their last will and testament to you. You fly them home and you know they're all going to die because they've got not a shred of skin on them — and the conversations you had with them linger.

'It happens all the time. I had a woman down at Cams Wharf only six or eight weeks ago. She had a monumental blue with her husband and went out and poured mower fuel all over herself and set herself alight. She had almost no skin left. I got an IV into her foot because she'd had a sock and shoe on and that was the only place the fire hadn't destroyed the skin; the only spot I could give her pain relief. We were treating her in the driveway and the husband had locked himself in the bathroom. You could hear him screaming at the top of his voice while the police were trying to persuade him, reason with him, that he should come out. Finally, when we were just packaging her up to get her in the helicopter, they were wrestling with him on the front lawn. They had the handcuffs on him and she leant over and watched it all through her burntness. We talked to her all the way down to Royal North Shore. They tell you everything in the helicopter. She had combinations of remorse, anger, "What have I done?", "Am I going to live?". She died about four days later. It just remains with you.

But sympathetic detachment always works for me. I can reflect on it but I can let it go.'

That detachment went out the window with Norm, however. 'I had to meet this bloke. He was one of those remarkable people in life and you know you'll never meet anyone like him again. He turned out to be the most wonderful man – a Welshman who had the best attitude to life. We became life-long friends. We exchanged Christmas cards every year.'

The doctors saved Norm's legs but he was never able to walk properly again.

Far from feeling any psychological trauma from that day, Alan felt good, buoyed by Norm's survival and by what his colleagues had done to save many other people. 'I think the overwhelming feeling was one of success – that we'd saved lives. Your ego is stimulated. *If I can save lives in a situation like that, I can do anything. Nothing's going to faze me in pre-hospital world ever again*. But six ambos who were in the workers club left the service shortly after. They thought it was too much.'

Interestingly, one of the world's first studies of the efficacy of debriefing looked at emergency workers from the Newcastle earthquake and found that those who received debriefing had slightly worse outcomes than those like Alan who had none.

'Norm was probably the most satisfying save of my whole career. Then, bugger me down, two years ago he had a cardiac arrest and my boss, Nev, revived him and got him to John Hunter Hospital [in Newcastle]. They tried to helicopter him to Sydney for major cardiac work, but he died a day later. He was eighty-three.'

*

A little over four years after the earthquake, in April 1994, a long fomenting civil war in Rwanda turned into all-out genocide. The United Nations asked for Australian paramedics to help, and Alan Playford put up his hand. At the end of June, Alan touched down with sixteen Australians – paramedics, nurses and a few doctors – at the airport in the Rwandan capital, Kigali.

The airport terminal was like a standing sieve, blasted full of holes with AK47s. There were no officials to stamp passports. The Australian contingent walked through the building over broken glass and past a shattered display case in which a stuffed gorilla had been hacked to pieces with machetes. *What sort of madness had this place been through?*

As they drove through the capital on an Irish army truck, they saw and smelt the corpses of thousands of dead while the skinny dogs grew fat, their heads deep in the carcasses. The truck came under fire from one of the many hills and the truck driver put his foot down and got through it. There was nothing else for it. One of the doctors on board had already lost the plot. The day before, he'd tried to use an ice dispenser to send a fax to the authorities to tell them it was too dangerous and they had to be withdrawn. And that was before they'd even touched down in the country.

It was later estimated there were 55,000 dead in the capital, but the medical team had no one to treat. The wounded had either cleared out or were hiding.

It was decided to send the team to a refugee camp over the border in Zaire. The conflict was still well underway, but whereas the ruling Hutus had massacred the minority Tutsis in the first part of the genocide, now Tutsi rebels who had massed over the border in Uganda had re-entered the country and were pushing the Hutus back and taking revenge.

'The Hutus clogged all the roads, trying to get out,' recalls Alan. 'That's where our real work started – on the Ruhengeri road from Kigali out to the Zairean border and the town of

Goma. They estimated there were a hundred and thirty thousand dead on that road. They died in biblical proportions. They had no water. It was hot as Hades. They were digging at the side of the roads to get water. It rains a lot. There's a high water table. They dug through faeces and what have you. They were passing the border at ten thousand an hour. There was a slope from the road down to Lake Kivu right on the border. The lake was just awash with bodies. Thousands. All bloated and bobbing around and this biblical flow of people through the border. We were in vehicles trying to nose up the Ruhengeri road through them. We were under severe apprehension because we thought we were going to be taken at gunpoint – they were in such dire straits – but they were so weak and dishevelled they couldn't put up a fight.

'We were in Goma to start with because it was too dangerous to go any further on. Then Médecins Sans Frontières had a camp at a place called Rutshuru and they asked if we'd join them up there. So there were thirty-two Belgians and Frenchmen from the Médecins Sans Frontières and sixteen Australians, with one million people. We established this camp in the middle of them. It was just an extraordinary place. In our immediate vicinity we had something like seven thousand a day dying. The smell was . . . just . . . the smell of death was just everywhere. If ever in my life I wanted to get out of somewhere, it was there. For the first three weeks, I was like, "I've made the biggest blue of my life. I gotta go home."

'Cholera was killing them. It took five hours to die. If you've ever seen a baboon – that exposed skin on its backside – that's what someone dying of cholera looks like. They shit the lining of their bowel out through their bum. It's explosive diarrhoea. None survived. They were emaciated. There was nothing to drink.'

The United States had declined to put people on the ground after the heavy losses incurred in Somalia, but they agreed to parachute water into the camp. Clean water was crucial to saving lives. And Alan watched as the transport planes disgorged the cargo – giant water containers on pallets supported by three parachutes. They came down, great pendulums swinging earthward, with an ecstatic mob racing towards the salvation from the sky. And he saw the bodies being flung like skittles as the giant pendulums swung into the throng. Perhaps 200 died with each water container.

'There was a million people. They were charging over the remains of the dead to get to the water. We'd have been killed had we gone near it. They were a maddened mob. They were beyond reason. It was an extremely dangerous place. And the mountain behind us was a volcano exploding. It was presumed that it was going to erupt. Every night you'd see the red rim of the volcano. It was like hell.'

The enormous numbers meant there was no way to give the sick a drip to replace their fluids. The paramedics and nurses used a simple triage tool. The ones who were thought likely to live were put on one side of the road running through the camp, and those who looked like they would die were put on the other. And they weren't often wrong. Those on the bad side didn't complain. Most were incapable of speech, incapable of movement. All they could do was look, and they'd look with knowing eyes. That would be hard to forget. Especially the kids.

The Australians had been there for three weeks when the parachutes stopped and water began to arrive by truck from Uganda. The clean water had an instant effect. The 7000 deaths a day slowed to *only* about 500 a day over the following three weeks.

A camp orphanage was started. A PVC pipe was rigged up with holes drilled in it. Water was forced through it by a pump hooked up to a generator and they'd line up a dozen kids at a time to stand under it for a shower, ankle deep in diarrhoea.

Conditions improved and Alan was eventually moved back to Kigali and found himself treating trauma injuries as the fighting continued. One day he was trying to treat a line of patients, perhaps 200 metres long, while gunshots rang out in the distance followed by a much closer explosion. Soon after, he was asked to please come to the back of the queue where he found a twelve-year-old boy in the arms of a man. The boy's leg was missing and what was left was shredded bone and gristle, bleeding profusely.

'What's this from?' Alan asked.

An interpreter explained that it was the last explosion they had heard. A landmine.

'Come on, we'll pick you up and carry you down.'

But the adult protested. No, no, no. He didn't want to jump the queue.

Alan picked the boy up, got him into his ambulance and off to a hospital.

He tells the story shaking his head: *'Didn't want to jump the queue!'*

*

Alan was asked to extend his four-month tour by a month and so he did. But eventually came the time to go home. 'You just had a feeling of a fish plucked out of a pond – taken from a society out of control and placed back in normality where everyone's got three feeds a day and the biggest thing on a child's agenda is what he's getting for his birthday. But people still find trivial things to whinge about. It was very hard to assimilate back into. I needed a break but didn't get it. There was a lot of support services behind us. We were looked after, but we had a nasty superintendent here. Before we went, we'd been promised we'd be paid as volunteers to go. And when we came back that was withdrawn. I had to take it out of my own long-service leave. I've still not gotten over that.'

Alan says that those among his first group of paramedics were doing okay now, but a lot of the other Australians who came in later hadn't fared so well. 'Some have committed suicide, I believe. It's taken a toll. Particularly those who had an extended stay in Rutshuru with the cholera. Some of them have done really badly. The preparation that ambulance officers get from seeing death in the street had prepared us in some way for it. The nurses who went there straight from wards in Australia did very badly. You can't take people out of a staid life and subject them to a war zone. They're never going to do well. I think it's a lesson that we put to the authorities when we came back — if you're going to take people to these places, choose them well.

'Rwanda finished my marriage as well. It's remarkable what an effect those things have. My wife couldn't connect with me. She said that I wasn't myself. My kids concurred. I was very remote, not connecting. At work they tell me I was a different person. I wasn't the bubbly person I'd been before. I'd become withdrawn and "introverted". I've heard that term used. After Rwanda I was left wondering, "What if? If I'd done this, would more have survived? If I'd gone left, would more have survived?" It's all you're left with. "Could I have done more?" That has a lasting effect.

'It took a good two years till I started to feel myself again and that's when the next event occurred. I think I was probably in an unsettled state at that time. I'm pretty sure I wasn't thinking straight from Rwanda.'

*

Alan was attending a minor road accident in Newcastle's western suburbs when a call came through of a woman trapped in a house fire in the lakeside suburb of Eleebana. He looked up and saw the plume. They were close. He and his partner rushed to the scene, expecting to see fire engines as they turned into the nice new street, but all they saw was people tugging a side door to the flaming house.

'Mrs Marshall is trapped inside!' someone said to him.

Alan looked at the modern brick house. *God, it's well and truly on fire.* Not just one room alight, it was the whole building. He called on the radio for the fire brigade to expedite, then went back to the house.

'She'll be in the front bedroom,' a neighbour said. 'We know her well.'

The doorway and the hall were already burning. Flames licked through the roof. He reached in a front window where the glass had blown out and dragged out a curtain. Dousing it under the garden tap, he put it over his head and crawled in the front door on hands and knees. The smoke layer came down below knee height, allowing just enough air to see and breathe. To his right, the flames were intense, but the left seemed clearer. And that's where the woman's bedroom was. *If I stick left I should have a good chance of passing her out the front window.* He crawled down the hallway and turned left into the bedroom. He patted around searching the room, but there was no sign of her. The bathroom was next door. *A lot of people crawl into bathrooms, I'll search there.* No one there either. He came back into the hallway and looked to the right side of the house and there, sticking out of the kitchenette, he saw two legs, three to five metres away. There was a good chance she'd still be alive. People often collapse from smoke inhalation but then survive in the air pocket at their feet. *I'll do a quick snatch- and-grab and drag her out feet first.* He crawled in and just as he reached her, he heard a fearsome noise. The roof was falling in on the lounge room at the front of the house – tiles, beams, ceiling. And as it all came down, the rest of the roof followed in an horrendous boom.

He felt himself go unconscious. It felt pleasant.

Alan regained consciousness in an ambulance. The fire brigade had arrived and gone in with breathing apparatus and pulled him out. 'I had been knocked away by the blast. The roof fell on Mrs Marshall. The weight of everything hitting the ground had blown me back into a wall. They've picked me up and dragged me out onto the front lawn. I was unconscious and I wasn't breathing. My heart was still going ten to the dozen. Two of my mates resuscitated me there on the front lawn. Got me going and packaged me up and off to John Hunter Hospital.'

Afterwards, he beat himself up for not getting Mrs Marshall out. Another 30 seconds, another minute, and he would have had her. Had he looked right at the beginning he would have seen her. Had he not gone in the bedroom, the bathroom. Then again, what if he'd been in the hall when it collapsed? So many what-ifs. At least he could console himself with the pleasantness of going unconscious. He had been there when so many others were in that state, it was good to know how nice it felt.

Still single after the marriage break-up, he left hospital to go home to an empty house and a few weeks off work. His kids, now in their late teens, were good to him. Kept him going. And soon he was back on his feet.

*

In September 1999, Australian soldiers landed in East Timor to curb the violent anti-independence militias that were running amok on the poor little island which had the temerity to vote for independence from Indonesia. An estimated 1400 people were killed in the fighting and many more were injured.

Three months later, Alan was on a plane flying there. It was the horse he had to get back on after being bucked by Rwanda. 'It was a terrible place to begin with. It was genocide on our doorstep. The Indonesians had perpetrated some real crimes . . . I got involved in a lot of gunshot wounds. The Indonesians spread a lot of munitions when they left so the kids would pick them up. A very hateful people. In Dili hospital they smashed all the ECG [electrocardiogram] machines, cut all the leads on the premise that if we can't have them you can't have them either.'

He worked on a lot of children and some of the less well-trained soldiers blown up by mines. He went out to five Portuguese hit by a single mine, some with shrapnel in the brain. Bangladeshi sappers were sent in to clear the minefield and suddenly there was another huge explosion and six more men down, hit by an antipersonnel mine wrapped in sheets of metal. One was killed straight away and Alan worked on another till he died on the way to hospital.

He was there eight months. Unpaid again, but at least this time he knew he was doing it for free. And when he came home he felt remarkably better. He'd shaken Rwanda. He felt strong and immediately set in motion plans to go back again the next year.

After returning from the first deployment to East Timor in 2000 he met his new wife, Trisha. I ask Trisha how she feels about being married to someone who so routinely puts his life on the line. 'I could never change him,' she says. 'It would be like chopping off his arm.' I sense that they have a very good relationship.

*

We have been talking for some hours and I think we are just about done when I ask which medals he got for which acts.

There was an ambulance service Distinguished Conduct award plus a Royal Humane Society bravery award for the cherry picker incident; nothing for the Newcastle earthquake; a National Medal (for diligent service in hazardous circumstances) for Rwanda; a Star of Courage for the house fire; a Humanitarian Overseas Service Medal for East Timor; plus a Commendation for Brave Conduct and a Group Bravery Citation for the Canberra bushfires. The Canberra bushfires?

I realise there is a whole other story we haven't touched on yet. I can sense Alan is tired of talking but he kindly pushes on.

For the first time he mentions the Special Casualty Access Team (SCAT) that he belongs to. They are trained in mainly 'vertical rescue' – treating people down cliffs, down holes and out of helicopters. Their work is routinely dangerous but of course it rarely earns bravery honours because society expects a baseline of courage from such people. They need to go 'above and beyond' that level to gain recognition.

Anyway, such a need was the last thing Alan and his SCAT colleague, John Gleeson, expected when they were deployed to two small fires burning west of Canberra in January 2003. They were there to help any firefighter who might be hurt in the rugged hills. It looked like a cushy week camping at the Mount Stromlo observatory with paid overtime.

Alan and John were on the night shift so they'd leave the fire service camp at 5 pm to go out to the fire in the Brindabella ranges and come back in the morning to sleep through the day in the ambulance. On the first two nights, the fires ticked along, posing little threat. But on their third afternoon, Friday, the air was different. The hot wind picked up. The pall of smoke was darker. The firefighters had been ordered to get stuck in and do what they could. Nearby pine forests were at risk. Helicopters thundered above in waves, dumping their Bambi Buckets into the blaze. And that night, the wind and the fires got worse.

The two ambulance officers got back to Mount Stromlo on the Saturday morning after their night shift and looked back to the three-kilometre-high plume. They had breakfast but decided not to sleep, taking all their gear out of the big white wedding-reception marquee which served as fire headquarters and loading it all into their four-wheel-drive. They drove into Canberra to bring in another SCAT team from Newcastle. And long before they got back to the camp they could see the fire had grown nasty. The two fires had united, creating a 35-kilometre front. At noon it was still twenty kilometres from the suburbs of Canberra, but the wind picked up further and strange things started to happen inside the fire which scientists would remain unable to explain.

As the flames grew in intensity, the fire sucked in more air and generated its own weather. Intense firestorms have been known to generate tornadoes, but something else was at work here. A fifteen-kilometre-long line of pine trees a few hundred metres wide was snapped like matchsticks. They were found afterwards lying flat and smouldering in a straight line pointing towards Canberra. It was estimated that it would have taken winds up to 250 kilometres an hour to knock them over like that. And they were lying straight so this was no tornado, which would have scattered them in all directions. This was inexplicable – a whole new disaster bearing down on the city.

The ambulance officers got back to Stromlo just in time to see 180-metre-high flames burst out of the pine forest tops and rip through the camp, destroying tents and semitrailers, and all the gear to support 400 men in the field, as well as the little village of Stromlo – all gone in an instant in front of their eyes. Some volunteer bushfire fighters came out of the blaze and said seven blokes had just been killed in the overrun camp. (It turned out they were wrong, but the mood had been shifted.)

There were some old women running around screaming, 'My husband's in there!'

There was nothing that could be done for them they told the women. 'You've got to get out!'

John and Alan were the last out, with the fire chasing them down the road. It was only years later that the thought occurred to John that the road ran in the same direction as the wind. If they'd had to switch back or run across it, they'd have been dead.

They retreated back towards Canberra and came to a police bomb squad sergeant, Phil Spence, manning an intersection on Cotter Road. Phil, 44, had served with the federal police on peacekeeping missions in Cyprus, Mozambique and the Solomon Islands. He knew a thing or two about crises. He had been told the fire was eighteen kilometres away but that didn't make sense with all the embers flying in on the wind. Alan confirmed to him that the fire was here already – and it was huge. Alan pointed at a cluster of tiled roofs nearby and asked what it was.

'That's Duffy,' Phil said.

'It's a bloody good thing those people are out of there. This fire'll eat that place.'

'No one's out of there,' the copper replied.

'You can't be serious. Somebody better start getting them out.'

'Would you come with us?' Phil asked.

*

The ambulance four-wheel-drive fell in behind the bomb squad van and by the time they got to Duffy, the firestorm was just about on it, looming out of the pine forest, turning off the sun. 'We drove up this road called Hindmarsh Drive. I remember it like yesterday,' Alan recalls. 'It was like a World War II refugee film – all these people coming down Hindmarsh Drive, driving over peoples' gardens, over footpaths. Cars on both sides of the road that should have been going either way were all coming down towards us while we tried to thread our way to the fire, and when we got there it was just pandemonium.'

They went to the street on the leading edge of suburbia, Eucumbene Drive. The ambos changed into their fire-resistant helicopter suits and put on their helmets. They fumbled around for torches to see in the 2 pm darkness. Alan and Phil went door to door on foot, getting people out of their houses. People would say they wanted their cars, but the power was out so the garage doors wouldn't open. The cars were locked in.

'You can't take your car. Quick, get in ours.' John and Rod Carnall, Phil's bomb squad colleague, would drive them to Hindmarsh Avenue which, though still close to the fire, seemed to somehow have clearer air.

An old man came up to them. 'My wife is trapped in our house. Number eleven Darwinia Terrace.'

Alan looked in that direction. *No way.* The smoke appeared impenetrable, the fire too intense. It looked hopeless. A teenager about seventeen said to John, 'I know where number eleven is.'

'Will you show us?'

'Yeah.'

The ambos and police looked at each other. 'We'll give it a go.'

But as they approached the street, the smoke and flames grew more intense. Grass was on fire, cars were on fire, gas bottles exploded, and flames made curious shapes on walls, burning along the gas pipes. The teenager suddenly stopped. 'I'm not going in there.' They could hardly blame him.

Alan would recall that it was the policeman Phil Spence who said, 'Let's do it.'

Phil remembers it as Alan saying, 'Come with me.' ('And me stupidly agreeing.')

And John turned to Phil to explain what Alan was like: 'He's fuckin' mad you know. He won't stop till he's got everyone out.'

For his part, John would have loved to have run away, but two things kept him going: One, there were people trapped; and, two, he didn't know where he was in the tangle of Canberra streets.

And so they went in. The world turned burnt orange. Street lights added to the eerie glow. Sparks flew in a snowstorm of embers. Flames swept the scene in sheets, devouring garden mulches and trees alike. And all the while the world roared with wind and fire. They only had to go down a few doors to find number eleven well alight. They opened the door and there she was, a 75-year-old woman crouched in the hallway. 'Come on, darling.' She didn't need encouragement. She sprinted to the police van, arms pumping, knees high.

On the way to number eleven, they had seen people still on their front lawns in nearby houses with garden hoses, like King Canutes in shorts trying to hold back the tide of flames. They approached a man with a hose. 'Come on, get in.'

'I can't come. My family's inside.'

Alan found the whole family huddled in the hallway of the burning house.

'What about our car?'

'Forget about the car.' It was stuck in the garage. 'Why didn't you clear out?' Alan asked.

'We were waiting for the radio to tell us to leave.'

Alan and Phil continued on foot, bashing doors and windows to bring the people out, while John followed in the ambulance four-wheel-drive with Rod in the bomb squad van. They'd load up with people, take them back to Hindmarsh

Drive and drop them off. 'Which way do we go?' they'd want to know.

'Just go that way.' John would say, pointing downwind. He didn't know. 'Away from the fire.' And for every family he got out, there'd be another trying to get back in to save some relative. 'No, you can't go in. We're trying to evacuate. Here, take these people away.' And then he'd return when his every inclination was to get far away. He'd reverse into the blast furnace so he didn't have to do a U-turn, making sure he didn't park under powerlines which he could see were about to come down.

In the bomb squad van, Rod's passengers crowded in amongst bomb suits and on top of the bomb disposal robot, blissfully unaware that the van was full of explosives for blowing up suspicious objects.

The rescuers worked their way down Darwinia Terrace, dodging fallen powerlines and downed trees. To their right was open paddock, to the left, houses. They commandeered cars, ordering the drivers to take more passengers. The feeling of chaos was only added to by winds that would blow you off your feet one way then knock down a tree in the other direction. It was hard enough staying balanced on their feet, let alone their thoughts. Hard enough to stay alive, let alone figure out how to save others. Phil had been in a cyclone on Christmas Island, and this wind was stronger. His father-in-law, the federal police commissioner Colin Winchester, had been murdered as a result of his duties and now Phil had the thought that his wife – Winchester's daughter – might be about to lose another man to the service.

Phil would remember one old bloke with a dribbling hose. His house was on fire, the trees were on fire. Phil thinks he just imagined it, but he'd keep an image in his head of the bloke's hair on fire. He was just standing there with a trickle of water achieving nothing. A zombie. They virtually carried him to the van. Phil would later ask a psychologist about it and was told the shock just overwhelms people and they shut down.

They moved down Darwinia Terrace into an area where there were houses on both sides of the street. Phil did the west, Alan the east, meeting up again back at the cars. They'd got an estimated 70 people out in the two vehicles by the time a highway patrol sergeant, Ray Fitzpatrick, pulled up in his Commodore. 'I've got a report that people are trapped in Percy Crescent.'

Alan decided to go with him to have a look, and said good-bye to John, both thinking they may never see each other again.

Alan and Ray drove up Kathner Street which jutted out into the paddocks, with houses on one side and open ground on the other. Sheets of fire washed down across the fields from Stromlo. Horses in the paddock were standing stock still. As the blaze hit them, their tails and manes burst into flames. And still they didn't move; just stood there and burnt to death. Four-legged zombies. Nothing seemed real. The flames flowed above ground, perhaps two or three metres up, running fast like wild rivers. Alan could barely stand against the cyclonic wind, yet these horses just didn't move. Fire scientists would later look at the hard-grazed open fields and admit they would have thought the houses behind them to be quite safe because there wasn't enough fuel there. But the winds were so strong the inferno defied all previous understanding of firestorms. Tiles ripped from roofs. Chunks of terracotta and flaming lumps of wood flew through the air. And always there was the terrible roar. It was later estimated that the energy produced in the pine forest was equivalent to 50,000 bar heaters per square metre – enough to generate colossal winds.

Alan and Ray filled the police car with people and shot them back to Hindmarsh Drive, pausing for a quick breath of the cleaner air before returning to the furnace for another load. And another. They watched flame pour overhead, leaping houses and exploding like a bomb in a house behind. The wind got so strong at times, Alan had to lie down on the road to avoid being blasted off his feet. Sometimes even that wasn't enough and he would nestle into the gutter to avoid being rolled over by the hurricane. A telegraph pole exploded and snapped in half. The wind tossed it away like straw on a breeze.

They saw a car coming down the hill towards them. It stopped, and Alan saw a family get out and run into the gloom towards Hindmarsh Drive. The empty car rolled ever so slowly down the hill and into a power pole where it suddenly seemed to erupt in a spontaneous combustion.

Alan and Ray worked their way around the loop in the street into Percy Crescent and reached an Indian family, the Naraines, in the second row of houses away from the paddock. The houses facing the paddock were all on fire now. This family's house backed on to those. Their garage and back fence were on fire but their house was okay. The wife had buckets, the husband a hose, fighting the flames on the back fence.

A noise loomed up like a freight train. It was another river of fire. It hit the already flaming house in front of them and seemed to bounce clean over the top of them, roaring as it went. It flew over the street and crashed into the abandoned house on the other side, bursting all the windows and unleashing a house full of fresh oxygen. The place blew up like someone had doused it in petrol.

Alan began to think he'd pushed his luck too far. This was unimaginable. After they got the Naraine family out, they returned and found a father with his son in a wheelchair. 'We aren't leaving,' said the boy. He wouldn't budge without his dog.

'Guys, you've got to leave. Your neighbours' houses have been destroyed. Yours is on fire.' Alan lifted the boy into the car, leaving his wheelchair on the footpath, and went back for the dog which jumped in on top of the boy. As they drove off, they saw a man and a woman abandon their burning house and get into a car. The rear windscreen exploded as they drove away.

'Is there anyone in there?' Alan yelled to them, motioning to the burning house next door.

'We know the man is inside it. We tried to get him out and we can't.' The place was too far alight. He was probably dead already. And with that Alan and Ray drove out for the last time. There were no more people alive left to get and they were glad of it. They didn't want to have to go back again.

*

Alan had been in the inferno for three or four hours. The reflective markers had melted off his fire-resistant helicopter jumpsuit. His hands and face were burnt like he'd been trapped in a solarium. His hair was singed. His eyebrows curled into little coils of brittle fibre.

When he found John Gleeson hours later there were tears. They'd both thought the other might have been dead. They had also both been reported missing – their families informed – because they'd gone off the ambulance service radar when they went with the police into Duffy.

Their lungs were full of what the doctors said was a million cigarettes worth of smoke and they came down with adult respiratory distress syndrome and spent the next week in hospital. Alan had a chest infection for three weeks and he could hardly open his eyes for a fortnight, all gummed up with grit and goop. His skin peeled while John's blistered.

*

After Alan Playford had gone to Percy Crescent, Phil Spence had gone with another officer, Jane McKenzie, to Doyle

Crescent where there were reports of people trapped. Together they got a lot more people out and then there was a report that the bomb squad's headquarters at nearby Weston was on fire. Phil rushed back there. He found the shooting range next to the bomb squad was on fire with small-calibre bullets exploding. He knew they weren't too dangerous without the pressure of a barrel to force them along, but there was larger stuff there that he didn't want to be near if it exploded. And next door was the scientific unit where every piece of scientific evidence from the Bali bombings was being worked on. Phil knew it would be a national tragedy if that was destroyed, opening the possibility for the accused terrorists to walk.

Phil would be awarded a Bravery Medal for his efforts to secure the building, along with constables Allan Bell and Stephen Cross who received Commendations for Brave Conduct.

I ask Phil how he pulled up and he said he was fine. But when he got posted to Afghanistan in 2007–08, he had definitely become more aware of his own mortality. And whereas once he used to love driving hard through the back bush, he doesn't do that any more. He's a more cautious person.

He and Alan have become good friends. He says of Alan: 'He's fantastic on his feet. You've got to be in balance in those pressure situations. Your skills come to the fore. It's highly stimulating to be under that pressure and using your skills to their maximum ability. He's extremely efficient in emergencies. He gets on with it and gets it done.'

Of the more than 100 people who they got out of the fire, Phil has no idea how many of them they may have saved. 'Most would probably have got out, we just gave them a means to do it, but some of them would have died, like the old bloke with the hose. That's not grandiose pissing in the wind, it's just a simple statement of fact.'

*

'How'd you pull up?' I ask Alan.

'Not too bad. We had the satisfaction of getting a lot of people out,' he says before changing the subject.

I ask why he puts his life at risk.

'I think in my case it's expected of me. You just can't stand back if you're charged with looking after the public. How far do you go? When you can, you can.'

What makes you act though? Can you explain it?

'I can't. It's a cross between impulsiveness and a calculated immediate decision that you can get away with it – or you've got a reasonable chance of getting away with it – and not holding back. Doing it. We'll see what happens after that. If you're lucky enough you'll get away with it. There's a fine line between that and stupidity.'

When he retires, he plans to keep going back to East Timor with Aspen Medical, the company contracted to support Australian soldiers up there. He's gone back in his own time every year since 2000. And each time he has gone it has become easier as the country has slipped towards the normality of motorbike accidents and medical illnesses. Although there might still be the odd crossbow payback attack.

He'll also stick with his position as the retained fire captain at the New Lambton on-call fire station. 'I love the fireys. It keeps me young.'

And Rwanda? Will he return there?

'That's on the bucket list.'

SEVENTEEN

Linton Jones and the Bystander Effect

Talking to Sharon O'Leary about the upshot of her actions at the West Wynnum shooting, she said she'd do it all again, even though it had sent her life into such an anxious, insular shell. 'They've done tests where there are people dying and other people walk over and around them,' she said. 'How can you do that? Why wouldn't I help somebody again? I don't know what's wrong with the world when you see people walking around someone who's lying there dying.'

I presumed she was talking about a much-publicised incident the month before in New York, where a homeless man, Hugo Alfredo Tale-Yax, had gone to help a woman being confronted by an angry man. Tale-Yax had stumbled away from the confrontation and fallen to the footpath where he lay for an hour and a half. Security video showed pedestrians walking past, mostly ignoring him. One man stopped, shook the body, partially lifting it to reveal a pool of blood, before walking on.

Another man stopped and took a photo on his mobile phone. By the time paramedics arrived, the 31-year-old was dead from stab wounds.

Did this death reveal another callus on modern human nature? Did the passers-by in this poor Queens neighbourhood think he was drunk? Were they afraid of him? 'Or perhaps they had just learned a lesson that Mr Tale-Yax so clearly had not: better to keep to oneself than to risk the trouble that comes from extending a helping hand,' the *New York Times* commented.

In the psychological literature, New York City was the birthplace of the study of this unwillingness to help thy neighbour. It all began in 1964 with the murder of Kitty Genovese less than two kilometres from where Tale-Yax died.

It is doubtful the world would have heard of Tale-Yax if there had been no footage of him dying (you can watch it on YouTube). And it is doubtful anyone would have heard of Kitty Genovese back in 1964 if the *New York Times* had not run a story headed, 'Thirty-eight who saw murder didn't call the police'.

'For more than half an hour thirty-eight respectable, law-abiding citizens in Queens watched a killer stalk and stab a woman in three separate attacks,' the story began. The article included a quote from an unidentified neighbour who saw part of the attack: 'I didn't want to get involved.'

How could this be? The question prompted social psychologists John Darley and Bibb Latane to find out. In their first experiment, a group of volunteers were asked to fill in questionnaires. While they did so, the room began filling with smoke. The more people present each time they did this experiment, the more likely the volunteers were to ignore the smoke and keep on filling in the questionnaires. In the second experiment, the volunteers heard crashing noises in an adjoining room, then a woman screaming, 'Oh my God, my foot . . . I . . . I . . . can't move it. Oh my ankle. I . . . can't get this . . . thing off me.' In the third, the volunteers were having a discussion over an intercom with an actor pretending to be a volunteer when the actor suddenly gasped, made a choking noise and called for help.

Darley and Latane found that as the number of people present increased, the likelihood of an individual attempting to help the distressed person decreased. The lesson here is that if you're going to have a heart attack in the street, do it when one person is walking towards you, not twenty. Darley and Latane labelled the phenomenon 'the bystander effect', hypothesising that if there are a lot of people present we feel that somebody else will be better able to help than us. And we also know that responsibility is diluted. The lone bystander on a quiet street knows he or she is it.

Recall Scott Black when he saw the car go through the window of the Roundhouse Childcare Centre. After battling with the initial disbelief, he looked around and the normally busy road was empty of cars and pedestrians. 'Did somebody else see this? Am I the only one? Where is everybody? Shit! You are kidding me. Someone's gotta do something.'

In another variation of their experiments, Darley and Latane put stooges in the room filling with smoke. The stooges did not react, but just kept on filling in the questionnaires. This prompted the volunteer subjects to doubt their own perceptions and they also tended to continue filling in the questionnaires.

And so Kitty Genovese, a 28-year-old bar manager, was written into the psychology textbooks where she remains. The original story that prompted it all has been called into question. There were not 38 witnesses, perhaps as few as ten. Nobody saw the whole incident. Only two realised there was a knife involved. Some did call the police but they didn't realise the seriousness of the situation and were ignored. Only one woman, Greta Schwartz, ventured out into the night to investigate, discovering the dying Genovese, who had been stabbed and raped by a necrophilic man who had previously stabbed, raped and murdered two others.

Regardless, the story's importance as a parable for high-rise alienation and social decay defies the nitpicking. The fact remains that the bystanders did not do enough to save Kitty Genovese. But even when most people choose to stay out of harm's way, perhaps feeling they have done enough by calling the police, there will always remain those who are prepared to act decisively. One such individual is Linton Jones.

*

It was about 3 am on 23 April 2004. Linton Jones had been woken by the pain in his elbows. He'd been a plasterer for 30 years, but that had come to an end with a fall from a three-metre ladder. The surgery to fix his arms had not yet healed. He put the kettle on to make coffee to wash down the heavy-duty painkillers he was about to take. He planned to watch television while waiting for the drugs to kick in.

That's when he heard the scream. Not that there was anything so unusual about a scream in the night. He'd hear them all the time in his unit at the southern end of the Surfers Paradise strip where the massive high-rises start to give way to a few little old blocks of units holding out against progress. The detritus of any good night will tend to wail it up on the walk home.

But this scream was different. He hurried out to his sixth-floor balcony to have a look. Down on the street, he saw a man pushing a woman into the back seat of a car.

Shirtless, shoeless and wearing only trackie dacks, Linton bolted for the lifts and pushed the button. The elevator was quick to arrive, but it dropped slowly to the ground floor. He feared he wouldn't get to the street in time. The doors opened and he ran. It was 40 metres from the lobby, across Vista Street, to the corner of Garfield Terrace. There, he saw a big bald bloke pushing something under a blanket on the floor of a red Mazda.

'What's going on here, mate?' he asked.

'Nothing, mate,' said the bald guy, stooping in at the Mazda's back door.

Linton kept coming and reached over the guy's back, grabbing the blanket and pulling it up. And there she was. A girl. Her hands were bound. There was blood. A gag covered her mouth. But his view of her was fleeting, because the guy whose back he was leaning over rose with an uppercut. Linton, who has never seen himself as a fighter, threw one back without much effect. The big guy was standing up straight now, revealing himself as a 100-kilogram tank, dressed all in black like a bouncer. He landed a string of rights on Linton's left temple, pummelling him back across the footpath into a fence, until he suddenly broke off the attack.

The girl was running away across the street. When the bald guy saw her flee, he ran back to his car and tried to get away. Linton ran to the front of the vehicle to get the numberplate and car colour. The car revved hard as the bald guy tried to mount the kerb to hit Linton, but the tyres were too close to the gutter and couldn't get up. He drove off.

Linton saw now that neighbours had the girl safe and were bringing her back, dishevelled and bleeding. He'd later learn that her hands had been cut by the attacker's knife and he realised how lucky he was that the blade hadn't ended up in his own ribs.

He didn't talk to the girl. He was too busy pacing the street, repeating the numberplate and car colour to himself, searching his memory for other useful bits of description.

He went to the police station to make a statement and didn't get home until late morning. He learned that friends who were staying in the unit next door had barricaded themselves in their room, thinking some madman had been on the loose.

Linton suffered concussion and bruising and broken bones in the front of his foot where the perpetrator's boot stomped his unshod feet.

But there were some pay-offs. The licence number and description he gave police led to the arrest of Simon Anthony von Pearson. Police then linked von Pearson to an attack two months earlier when a 22-year-old woman had been abducted at Southport on the Gold Coast. Von Pearson, high on booze and speed, had grabbed her off the street at 3.30 am and bundled her into his boot, threatening to kill her if she didn't get in. She'd managed to unlock it from the inside and jump from the Mazda as they drove through Nerang, suffering severe gravel rash.

*

A letter arrived for Linton in the mail.

Dear Linton

I would like to start by introducing myself. My name is Natalie, the mother of Rebecca, the young lady you saved a few weeks ago in Surfers Paradise from abduction. Our heartfelt thanks go to you for saving Rebecca. After reading articles in Queensland papers and speaking with police, we at home in Sydney are eternally grateful for your heroic kindness. You saved our daughter's life.

Rebecca is back home with us, recovering both physically and mentally. The scars obviously will need quite a time to heal. She sustained cut tendons in her right hand

and at this time, even after surgery and many many hours
of therapy, has no use in her hand. She is right-handed
and we are very worried. She continues counselling as she
has very many bad days and nights. She hopes to return
to uni next September to resume her own nursing studies.
Rebecca is at a loss for words to you but I know her sincere
thanks and loving gratitude goes to you.

Again, many thanks, Natalie and Rebecca.

So there was a lot of satisfaction for Linton that he'd saved a
girl and stopped a very bad piece of work. He went to the court
and saw von Pearson plead guilty to the two attacks but wasn't
impressed by the eight-year sentence he was given.

*

Linton Jones has never heard of Kitty Genovese. What his act
demands, though, is not so much research on why people do
not react to help strangers, but rather research on those who
do step up. The research apparently doesn't exist for civilians, but what does exist is some astute observation by Major
Samuel 'Slam' Marshall, a World War I veteran and newspaper man who joined the US army's historical division in
World War II. He took part in beach landings in the Pacific
and interviewed soldiers straight after battle. He published
figures that only about fifteen per cent of ordinary infantry
soldiers fired their rifles in battle, perhaps a quarter in the better units. He recognised that only a few men in each platoon
did the fighting. When they came under heavy fire, all men
went to ground. They lost their group identity and so didn't
feel the need to stick their heads up again until roused, usually
45 minutes to an hour later, by a leader to go forwards again.
Marshall found:

> The majority are unwilling to take extraordinary risks and do
> not aspire to a hero's role, but they are equally unwilling
> that they should be considered the least worthy among
> those present . . . Personal honour is the one thing valued
> more than life itself by the majority of the men.

Like Marshall, Lieutenant-Colonel Lionel Wigram, a British School of Infantry tactician, observed in the Sicily campaign that every platoon of around 22 men had about 'six gutful men who will go anywhere and do anything, 12 "sheep", who will follow a short distance behind if they are well led, [and] four to six who will run away.'

He wanted tactics and training to be revised to recognise that modern battles were not won by generals pushing men around a chessboard, but by just a few courageous men thinking for themselves. Wigram's insights were taken as a personal insult by General Montgomery who demoted him to command of a field company. Wigram was killed soon after, leading a frontal assault against the Germans.

Linton Jones explains his actions like so many of the other people in this book: 'It's just the way I was brought up. You hear a scream, someone in trouble, you go to help. You do it by instinct. It's either in you or it's not. Other people heard it but didn't move.'

Ever since World War I, the military has tried to find ways of figuring out which men will perform when that moment comes and which men will crumble. They learned early on to weed out obvious mental defectives – those with a very low IQ or a pre-existing mental condition – but more concrete predictors proved difficult to pin down.

In 1973, the Israelis studied high-performing soldiers during the Yom Kippur War. They found them to be more intelligent, more masculine, more emotionally stable and more socially mature than the average soldier. But to find out who those 'gutful' individuals are going to be, we still have to wait till the bullets start flying – or there's a scream on a lonely street.

*

There's a video on YouTube called 'Battle at Kruger' which a lot of people obviously connect with – at the time of writing it had 57 million hits. It shows a pride of lions taking a young buffalo at the edge of a waterhole in South Africa's Kruger National Park. Eighty seconds after the initial attack, a crocodile starts wrestling with the lions for the calf in the shallows. The lions win that 40-second tug of war and it appears that we are about to watch a feeding frenzy, but then, as the tourist video camera pans back, we see the buffalo herd approaching, packed tight and tentative. They crowd around the lions until one 'gutful' buffalo comes forward and charges. It is clearly not one of the big bulls. Is it the calf's mother, or perhaps a young bull? The buffalo chases one lion away then returns to the pride which is still huddled around the calf, with the herd looking on just metres away. That same buffalo charges in and tosses a lion in the air, before other members of the herd chase the lion away. The buffaloes continue harassing and you see that some are braver than others, until, more than four minutes after the calf was taken, it gets to its feet and walks away, disappearing into the herd without even a limp. The lions break and run. Only then do the big bulls press home the attack, pursuing them off to the fringes.

In a buffalo herd, with its harem structures and each buffalo's high probability of being related to the animal next to it, you can easily understand the benefit of such behaviour.

So, too, it would have been for early man, evolving on the same African savanna. But humans developed the ability to talk about heroic feats. Whereas that brave buffalo's action would bring it no lasting benefits beyond saving some of its own genes, a brave human's status could be elevated for the rest of his or her life. Children would hear the stories and be inspired to act similarly.

That inspiration has survived into the high-rise alienation of the big city. It is worth remembering that we've only heard of Kitty Genovese because even despite the thickly calloused souls of New Yorkers, they were still outraged at the story that nobody had come to her aid as she was murdered and raped. That altruism and courage – and maybe the sense of justice, too – have persisted from the savanna when we were all related to each other. Perhaps cities could never have existed without those traits. They make us human.

EIGHTEEN

Rob Ryder

Rob Ryder came home on a drizzly Friday afternoon at the end of another day as a roof plumber, working at height on large commercial buildings. Inside his granny flat, he pulled the wallet and phone from his pockets and threw them on the fridge before grabbing a stubby of XXXX. Still standing at the fridge, he heard yelling, a dog barking, maybe a scream. He lived in a very quiet little street in the quiet Brisbane suburb of Bracken Ridge, so the noises were unusual, but he didn't do anything about them. He remembered he had his boss's extension ladder on his one-tonne ute parked out the front so he thought he'd better bring it in for the weekend. He went out the sliding glass doors and through a gate into the front yard. As he passed a broad-leafed tropical tree, the view to the street opened up and there, diagonally across the road, was a great big bastard in a sports coat hitting a kid in the head with a machete. *Nahhhhhhh.* He didn't believe it. *You've lost it.* But then he thought about it – he'd hardly had his first sip of beer. He looked and looked again. And here was this big bastard going at the kid, hitting him hard, like he was driving in a three-inch nail. *Fuck off! You are kidding.* His brain could no longer deny what his eyes saw.

He sprinted across the road, still spinning out at the absurdity of it all, running right up to this bloke so fast that when he tried to stop, his sandshoes slipped on the wet grass and he fell onto his arse, stopping just a metre or two short of the attacker who momentarily paused. The big guy turned and looked at Rob, raising the machete like he was about to start on him. But he didn't, and Rob wriggled his way backwards onto his feet while the big bloke resumed his attack on the kid who Rob now saw was a tall thin teenager, maybe older than he'd first thought. The kid was on his backside trying to crawl away on hands and feet. Closer now, Rob could also see that the kid wasn't getting the blows in the head but across the arms and legs. One blow was so hard it almost chopped his arm off. And now he could also see another person slumped against the brick pier of the garage door. There was blood all over the second guy's face and hair, blood pouring out of his limp limbs and pooling on the concrete. Despite the blood, Rob recognised him as the bloke who lived in the place, Dennis. They knew each other well enough to nod hello.

As Rob would later say, it was as if someone had plucked him out of the dead-still ordinariness of suburbia and dropped him into a battlefield. And his brain just couldn't cope with the change.

The kid was still sliding across the grass and Rob started screaming at the big dark-haired bloke. 'What the fucking hell? Come on, mate, stop.' He pleaded, begged, panicked full-on. 'Stop, mate, please.' But the bloke just kept going, kept laying into this kid, calm as could be. He was in control. Rob saw that aside from the nice sports coat and slacks, the bloke wore a thick gold necklace with links the size of Cheezels. The rings on his fingers were just as solid.

If Rob had owned a gun he would've shot him. He looked around to see what weapons he did have. The only thing that wasn't tied down was a wheelie bin, so he ran back to it, maybe ten or fifteen metres away, and got it. He pushed the bin towards the bloke then, when he was about four metres away, he leant around and picked up the front and charged at him like he was hitting a footy tackling bag.

The big bloke saw him coming and straightened just as the bin hit him on the left hip. Rob thought he was going to send the bloke arse over for sure, but he hardly even budged. *You are kidding.* The guy rocked back a little, regained his balance and resumed the attack on the kid who was still sliding on his backside across the grass.

Every second on that lawn felt like two hours. And the noises coming from the two victims — guttural animal sounds — made those two hours feel like two days.

'What are you doing this for, mate?' Rob pleaded.

'They stoled off me,' he said.

'What are you talking about?'

Dennis yelled out, 'I don't know what you're talking about.'

The wheelie-bin attack had jolted the big bloke's momentum. He straightened and looked around. Rob seized the opportunity and bolted back across the road. His neighbour, Ron, was a bit of a bushman and Rob thought he might have a gun so they could shoot this bastard. He knocked on the door so hard he was surprised the hinges didn't fall off. Nobody was home. So he ran next door to his own place, bolted inside, grabbed the mobile off the fridge and punched in triple-0 as he ran back across the road.

He expected the bloke to have taken the opportunity to slip away. But he was still there, standing over Dennis now, hacking at his head. Dennis, still slumped by the garage door, had his hands on his head trying to protect it and Rob watched as fingers were cleaved off – *'phit, phit'*.

Rob was talking to an emergency operator by this time, apologising to her for his swearing. 'I'm sorry, lady.' She asked him to please calm down, but he swears a lot at the best of times. He gave her his name and address. 'Please send an ambulance and the police. This is fucking fair dinkum.'

Maybe it was the phone, but something made the big bastard stop. He turned and walked over to the corner of the yard towards a black leather bag that Rob hadn't noticed until now. His movements were steady and deliberate, no hint of a rush. *The bastard's gunna pull a gun.* But he just put the machete inside the bag, zipped it up and, cool as you like, walked out onto the middle of the road. He strolled down the short street, around the corner, and was gone.

A garbage truck came swinging around the corner and the driver yelled out a licence plate number and Rob relayed it to the woman on the phone.

'He's just gone around the corner. Do you want me to follow him?' Rob asked her, thinking that there was nothing he could do to stop the bleeding of the victims. He would have needed 50 bandages.

'Yes, follow him,' she said.

So he jumped in his Holden ute and saw a little hatchback speed past the end of the street. He swung in behind it, but the Holden was no match for the sporty little car. 'I've lost him,' he told the woman still on the triple-0 line. 'I'm going home now.'

He pulled the ute back into the same spot, got out the driver's door, walked back behind the tray and saw two blokes in khaki with guns out in front, moving like he'd seen in the movies, with one going forwards while the other covered him.

One of them saw Rob and ran up to him sideways like a crab. He shoved the gun close up into Rob's face. 'Don't move!'

Rob could see his hand shaking. 'No, mate, not me. It's not me, mate.'

A marked police car came hurtling around the corner and pulled up next to them. A female constable got out and Rob explained to her who he was.

'Sorry we couldn't get here any quicker, Mr Ryder,' she said. 'We only got the call three and a half minutes ago.'

The two blokes in khaki disappeared and Rob never did find out who they were.

He was standing at the rear of the ute with the two officers when they looked across the street and saw Dennis staggering towards them like he'd just drunk 40,000 beers. Barely holding his feet, he made it to the bonnet of the ute and slid along it, smearing a red trail along the white paint with both hands as he made his way towards them . . . until his body hit the aluminium tray which almost knocked him over. He kept sliding along the tray, looking hard into Rob's eyes.

'Look! Look!' he said in a gasping, croaking voice. Dennis's head looked like it had been dipped in a tin of red paint – the eyes being the only part unpainted. Rob looked straight back into those eyes.

'Look! Look!' Dennis implored again.

'What do you mean?'

'Look. He's cut my fingers off.' Dennis lifted his hands. Blood squirted out the stumps onto Rob's clothes.

*

'That spun me out,' Rob says, fourteen years later as we talk in the dark on a balmy Darwin night. 'I don't know what post-traumatic disorders do to you, but that spun me out.'

He's never spoken publicly about it before and it took

months of toing and froing between us before he'd say yes to an interview. It had been Jim Runham's idea to talk to Rob. Jim had met him the day he was awarded his Star of Courage and knew he'd done it tough.

Rob lives with his son, Jess, in an old caravan under a tin roof on a block outside Darwin. There are five small quad bikes under the roof with us, plus a trike and a big black dune buggy with lots of headlights. As we talk, sirens and helicopters wail from Jess's Xbox as if we're talking on a New York sidewalk, only belied by the squeak of geckos and the occasional shriek of a bush stone-curlew out in the scrub.

'I was showing the detectives what happened, when the nine-year-old girl who lived in the house above my flat came home from school,' he says. 'She was walking up the street. I said to the coppers, "I gotta get her out of here." I grabbed her and took her inside. She didn't see anything.

'When I took the detectives over the road, Dennis and his son had moved a few doors down and got themselves in under this speccy house. There were two ambulances there. We stood a little bit off to the side, not getting in anyone's way, just look- ing to see how they were going. The ambos were working on them. They had both of them turned on their sides with their knees in their chest, covered by these small ambulance blan- kets. They had two drips in each of them. Just full-on blood. There was blood right around them, about a foot out from their bodies and at least a centimetre deep. If the ambos hadn't got there so quickly, they would have bled to death.

'Then the detectives said they had to take me to the police station. They were standing there quivering. So was I. Nerves got the better of everyone. They took me back over the road and said, "You'd better have a shower."

'When I was at the police station, I had a nervous break- down. I couldn't help it.'

'What happened?' I ask.

'I'm nearly having one now. Things build up on you. Nothing goes right. I tried to ask that bastard to stop chopping people up in front of me, if you can understand what I'm saying.

'Later that night, the woman who lived upstairs came down to see me. "Are you right, mate?" And then I just sorta . . . It's easier to cry in front of blokes than it is in front of sheilas. And I got real upset from that. She said, "Are you right?"

'"Yeah, no worries." She went and I just started getting muddled up a bit, if you know what I mean. I rang a few of my work mates up and told 'em what happened. Back then I was earning a thousand dollars a week. Not doing well, but cruising. They thought I was bullshitting.

'A bloke called John King from the Victims of Crime Association came over – a Vietnam vet who'd been round the track. He was good to talk to. He made a lot of sense to me. I went to a few counselling things they'd line up for me, but it doesn't fix you up, mate. You might think it does, but it doesn't. I went and saw a psychiatrist. He put me down as having "very severe" post-traumatic stress disorder. I got a debilitating condition. The older I get the worse it gets. You see post office workers get three hundred thousand for stress. I can't justify that. It's shit. You ever tried to eat a medal? It's pretty bloody hard . . . You want another beer, mate?'

Jess comes in and Rob stops talking because he doesn't want the kid hearing this stuff. Jess wants some dinner.

'He wants to drive this down the road,' says Rob, pointing at the gnarly black dune buggy. 'You wanna come for a drive?'

'Yep.'

'You do? He's driving,' says Rob, pointing at Jess, giving me a chance to back out.

'Is it safe?'

'Too right it is.'

Jess gets behind the wheel and Rob and I squeeze into the single passenger seat. Rob talks him through the switches and the gears, shouting over the engine noise. 'He drives the thing better than I do,' he yells to me.

We bush-bash our way to the pub and arrive too late for dinner. Rob's not hungry. Jess doesn't seem to mind. We sit while the bingo is called and Jess sips on a pink lemonade.

'What class are you in at school?' I ask him.

'Five–six,' he says.

'Do you like it?'

'Yep,' he nods vigorously.

'All his mates are there,' says Rob, sensing that such an unlikely answer requires explanation.

Rob, who has been careful not to discuss his story while Jess has been in earshot, tells me that he used to find it easier talking to older blokes about it. A Changi survivor lived around the corner. He understood. He told Rob he'd seen a man's head cleaved in two by a Jap guard. The machete had split the skull down to the shoulders.

The detective in Rob's case had said the machete was very sharp so Rob couldn't understand why it hadn't gone deeper. The copper said the skull bone slowed it down.

Jess drives us home. Rob and I crack another longneck each and resume the conversation. I ask when did he start to realise the post-traumatic stresses were going to hang around.

'I'd never heard of post-traumatic stress disorder. But I just wasn't thinking normal, something doesn't click. Basically what happened to me is like getting plucked out of suburbia, getting dropped in Iraq or some war zone. It's not normal to see what I saw. I'm not Rambo or nothing . . . Even him [pointing towards Jess], he's always going, "How come you never go out anywhere, Dad?", "How come we can't go there?", "You're a caveman, Dad." It's very hard to explain to him that if we go out I might see something and have to go in and help again. "How come you got that medal, Dad? Can you tell me what happened?" How can I tell him what I'm telling you? And it's very hard to lie to him.

'If I won Lotto tomorrow night, I'd buy a block of land out in the middle of nowhere, the furthest away I could get that still had water and electricity, and I'd go there and keep right away from every bastard. The way I've worked it out, people cause you trouble in life. People. Other people.'

'What happened at the court case?' I ask.

'A couple of weeks afterwards, the detective came and took me down to Sandgate police station to identify this bloke. "What's going to happen to him?" I asked. The detective said he had given himself up a couple of hours after it happened. He said he'd been charged on three attempted murders – one on me – plus five or six grievous bodily harm charges. "Don't worry, he won't see daylight." The bloke was looking at fifty-odd years in jail.'

The big bloke, however, was found to be of unsound mind and didn't face trial. He was locked up in an institution, but twelve months later he was being allowed out on leave, much to the dismay of Dennis and his son.

I ask if Rob saw the victims when they came out of hospital. How did they look?

'Bandaged. It was about three or four months afterwards. The old bloke, Dennis, came over and talked to me. He wasn't too bad. He thanked me. His son came over about a month later. His arm had been sewn back on. I was sitting on the fence where I usually sat and he came over and thanked me for saving him and I said to him, "Why did this bloke do this to you?" He said, "I don't know." "The police won't believe that, mate." Then I just looked at him like, "Get away from me." It just didn't add up.'

*

A copy of this story was shown to Dennis. He corrected a few minor details and gave me a copy of his police statement. He came across as a perfectly decent fellow – a draughtsman who heads a local writers' group and who builds miniature trains. He'd been studying for an engineering diploma exam when he heard his son's screams from below. His eighteen-year-old son – just back from six months with the army reserve – was doing up an old car in the garage when the perpetrator had lifted the tilt door.

'Can I help you?' Peter had asked.

'You rob me,' the dark-haired middle-aged man in black had said, holding a black bag and something wrapped in newspaper.

'What?'

'You robbed me. You stole my VCR.'

'I haven't done anything.'

'You robbed me,' he said, the agitation rising.

'I don't know what you are talking about, I haven't robbed you at all.'

'Well, I'll have to kill you anyway.' The newspaper fell to the floor, revealing a 60-centimetre machete blade.

Soon after I speak with Dennis, an email arrives.

Hi Mark,

My name is Peter . . . I was the teenage kid whose life was saved by Robert.

I've read your story on Rob's experience and would like to commend and thank you for going to the effort to publish the ordeals that ordinary blokes like Rob endured and hope that it gives some recognition and hopefully some kind of release from the hell he had thrust upon him.

I only spoke to Robert once in my life . . . The day I tried to thank him for saving my life and coming to my aid . . . I could tell from Rob's reaction towards me that he did indeed blame me for what happened that day regardless of the truth . . .

I just wanted Robert to know I am grateful for him stepping up and helping me that day. I, too, have been diagnosed with post-traumatic stress disorder and under-stand how debilitating an illness it is even when you think you've got it under control. Hopefully he can get some peace in this world soon, I really wish him all the best.

Robert's reaction towards me is something I've encoun-tered from others any time I've ever relayed my story, in that 'I must have done something' to have made this bloke target me . . . My only crime was living 6 or 7 houses away from the offender as a kid. In fact the perpetrator's chil-dren used to come and play with us other kids down the road. So I find it easier to not tell anyone what happened and if anyone asks about my scars I say I was in a car acci-dent . . . If you could let Robert know I did appreciate his courage and there's a very good chance I wouldn't be typing this email to you today if it wasn't for his efforts, that would be great. A Star of Courage medal is well deserved.

*

When Rob Ryder received his Star of Courage in February 1998, the Governor, Major General Peter Arnison, said to him, 'You shouldn't have seen what you saw.'

Rob didn't understand what he meant at the time. 'Now I know,' he says.

Rob stayed in the granny flat in Bracken Ridge for a few

years. 'But I had to get out. I had to move. I don't think the people upstairs wanted me to move, but I was just in their way. Nobody understood what happened there. I wouldn't say the people felt uncomfortable around me. I'm not blaming them. Maybe I lost it a bit. Things happen and they build up inside you. It's very hard to admit you've got something wrong with you. You get your anxieties. You get very emotional around things. I do . . . You just don't trust no cunt. Whether it's your bank manager or your missus or your cat. Actually cats and dogs are pretty good because they can't talk. That's how it gets you. It pretty well fucked me. I don't sleep very much at all. The only time I sleep is when I'm pissed as.'

I say that he must be tired most of the time.

'I work eight- to ten-hour days. I sleep then. But I don't relax. I haven't relaxed in years. As far as seeing social workers or psychologists, I might as well talk to that post because they don't make sense to me. Won't fix me up. I'm just wasting your money. Plus I can't earn a living if I take the medication. It's a very hard road.'

'Is your main symptom that you can't relax?' I ask.

'Nah. I get sick of having hallucinations. Flashbacks, whatever you want to call them. When you shut the eyes you see, like, bubbles. It's blood, I think. It used to happen at night when I was sleeping but the last couple of years it sometimes happens in the daytime. It's like you're on drugs. I don't know what you call it. I constantly think about what happened that day. I mean constantly. When I shut my eyes I'm thinking it.'

'Are you right back there in the moment?'

'Oh yeah. I lie in bed, comfortable as, then I just wake up and – whoa. You can't fix it. Like the governor told me, "You shouldn't have seen that."'

I tell him that some of the people I've interviewed had got their post-traumatic stress disorder under control.

'Fucked if I know how,' he says. 'It's a bit like rolling in blood, you just can't get rid of it. You can roll around in the dirt. You can go swimming. You can go and get pissed. You can go and get stoned. You can do whatever you want, but you won't get rid of the stink, if that makes any sense to you. You can't get rid of it . . . A lot of people have told me I should forgive him and I'll feel better. But I can't. How can I?'

Jess had come in and interrupted a few times to get the torch to go out to the loo. There is always the chance of stepping on a snake out there.

'I'm trying as hard as I can with Jess. Don't think he's easy to get along with. He's worse than me. I'll never ever give up on him. No way. I'll be there until I die. I didn't even know he was my son until about five years ago. Him and me, we've got a pretty good thing going. But he thinks you shove your card in the wall and it just gives you money. He had a fair bit of trouble with his mum. I haven't got guardianship of him. The department's got guardianship. I relinquished guardianship when I first found out he was my son, but I've been told they'll give it back. He's a good little dude. Or he can be. When he plays up, you wanna look out.'

It's 10.30 pm and Rob puts out a mattress for me under the tin roof. Jess is still spinning wheels, running from the cops. But Rob has let him play the game so he wouldn't be listening to our conversation through the thin caravan walls. 'Bed. Now!' he orders. Jess is slow to react. 'Nooooow!'

I tell Rob I won't see him again because I have to leave for the airport at 4.30 am.

'Nah, I'll be awake,' he says. 'How do you like your coffee?'

NINETEEN

Bill Lowther

On the impossibly lush lawns of Government House at Yarralumla, Royce Thompson, wearing a formal naval uniform and a distinguished, clipped-moustache bearing, is saying how odd it seems to have, say, a police inspector who might have won a Bravery Medal 30 years earlier, sitting next to some long-hair covered in tattoos, who, in another place, might be regarded as a 'person of interest'. But the bravery association brings them together like that.

We are heading in to the service of remembrance for bravery award recipients hosted by the Governor-General, Quentin Bryce. Held annually since the association was formed in 2000, it is the bravery medallist's Anzac Day. A chance to get kitted up, to remember the fallen and to be honoured themselves in turn. Royce, a naval chaplain who is also honorary chaplain to the Australian Bravery Association, warns me to be delicate with the people I interview.

'You can't imagine the grief of somebody who dives into a river to save three drowning kids. He drags two out, but can't get the other. And he remembers the look on that kid's face when he had to leave him. Then he gets home to a wife, "How dare you risk your life when you've got me and the kids here at home." His marriage breaks up over it. So he's lost his family and home and he's still beating himself up over not saving the child.'

We file in and all the medals are on display. Sally Gregory stumbles on her heels in the soft lawn and makes a big gregarious joke of it. She is with Alicia Sorohan, the 60-something grandmother from Brisbane who wrestled a crocodile that was pulling a fellow camper out of the tent next to hers on the Cape York Peninsula. The deep scars on her arm where the crocodile clamped down on her are clearly visible with her short-sleeved frock.

The formalities over, we make our way to a marquee where I am introduced to Vic Boreham. Vic was on a bus in Perth in 1994 when a gang of hooligans set fire to something next to the bus. And as the driver was trying to collect some unpaid fares, they yelled out to 'Get him! Get him!' The thugs piled onto the driver and Vic, a Vietnam veteran, got up to help him. Nobody else on the bus moved. 'I put three of them in hospital, but then I was on the ground copping blows to my head and everything went white. I was still conscious, I could hear them saying, "Kill him! Kill him!" I just couldn't do anything about it.'

Alan and Brenda Cochrane wander into the conversation and the two of them recite some of their adventures for me as the little sweets and savouries float around on silver trays. There was the knife incident in the caravan park where Alan intervened, the shotgun incident, those people being attacked in the street when he went to help and that time Alan jumped in to save a couple of kids trapped in an enclosed stormwater drain. When he took them home their parents just shrugged over their beers, 'They would have got themselves out.'

Alan, silver-haired and full of Aussie wit, tells me how his favourite cousin got up him recently, 'Of course, you get yourself into these situations if you're always trying to be the hero.' That really annoyed him. He was suffering depression, but he really found a home in the bravery association, he says, even though he's never actually been awarded any formal bravery honours. 'When Jim Runham came up and gave me a big hug, I knew that I was home among like-minded people who do act when it's required.' Interestingly, though, he's found his nightmares have *increased* since joining the association as an associate member.

After the function, the day moves on to a barbecue by the side of Lake Burley Griffin. Jim Runham introduces me to Suzanne Leone from Melbourne. She was at work one day in a dress shop when her colleague's ex stormed in. He was just out of jail and mad as hell and he started stabbing her colleague. Suzanne grabbed the knife off him but then he just pulled out another and continued stabbing the poor girl to death. Suzanne tells me she herself wasn't wounded, 'not physically anyway'.

She doesn't like talking much about the incident, but she likes this crowd – even though to the outside observer you might think they are all defined by their 'incidents'.

'You don't have to say anything to anybody about it,' Suzanne says. 'Everybody just respects each other's space and you just have a good time. If somebody wants to say something, then you listen and try to help out. Otherwise you just have a good time.'

Port Arthur massacre survivor Coralee Lever is there, too. At the RSL club the previous night, she had manned the gift shop selling all manner of bravery association goods like T-shirts and ties. I ask her if she'd be up for a chat later on and she says she'd be happy to talk.

Every direction you turn there's a new story waiting to be told. But casting my eye around now that everybody has dropped the suits and the medals, there's a great dissonance between the ordinariness of their appearance and the extraordinary tales they have to tell. I secretly long for a catastrophe so I can watch them spring into action. Even a flat tyre would be fun to watch. I imagine they'd be pushing each other out of the way trying to get at the jack. For while every one of them has been labelled a hero, it seems to me that their essential nature is not heroic. They are, in essence, people who like to help.

Proceedings are stopped briefly while John Thurgar asks about a new line of merchandise. 'Who'd be interested in a bravery association stubby holder?' 'What's a stubby holder?' asks one wag, but half a dozen hands shoot up. They'll be into that.

*

Jim Runham steers me over to someone he says I should meet. He introduces me to Bill Lowther, a redhead from Adelaide who commences talking at me with energetic, wide eyes. Bill's in his early 70s but looks 60. He tells me how he works in outback Aboriginal communities in South Australia. When he goes to a new town and he's manning the bowser, a group of local toughs will invariably come in all sullen and surly. 'They'd hold a twenty-dollar note between two fingers and say, "Fuel." "Hi, my name's Bill, what's yours?" "*Fuel!*" "Excuse me, my name is Bill, what's your name?" "Fuel you f'en b' white fella." "Listen, fella, I'm in charge of the fuel. You're not getting it till you and I have had a talk. So get out of the car and have a talk." I pick out the loudest and challenge him to an arm wrestle. I've only ever lost once, but there was a story behind that.' He feels the muscle in his right bicep. ' "You want to tell people a *gilpy* beat you in an arm wrestle? Mr Bill, seventy years old." They have a lot of respect for elders. When they realise how

270

old I am, it's, "Sorry, Mr Bill." "How much fuel do you want?" "Twenty dollars, Mr Bill." '

He tells me something of the day in August 1987 that led to his Star of Courage. And I conclude that, yep, he's crazy enough to be in my book.

*

Bill Lowther had put his little boat in at the mouth of the Murray River at 4 pm to test a new waterski. His nineteen-year-old daughter Sharon was there with her friend Julie Patterson, along with his son Christopher and son-in-law Russell. They were all going to have a quick go on the ski – smallest first, through to largest – have some fun before the winter night swallowed them up.

Russell had also brought out his tinny with a fifteen-horsepower on the back. They put the boats in and motored across the Murray mouth where Australia's greatest river system drains into the ocean. Bill didn't know it at the time, but the authorities had opened the barrages to flush Lake Alexandrina so there was a lot of water flowing out. He saw three men fishing from a boat anchored near the mouth where the water was running hard. He pulled alongside. 'Listen, guys, you're in a very dangerous spot here. I don't know if you know, but three people lost their lives here in calm water a few months ago. Their engine failed and they were washed out to sea.'

'Thanks for that, mate. She's right.'

Bill continued on eastward across the mouth to a spot called the Mad Mile. They had some fun with the new ski, then headed back on dusk. The three men were still fishing about 500 metres from where the river crashed into a line of breakers.

Bill motored back to Sugars Beach on Hindmarsh Island to put the boats back on the cars. When they pulled in, Russell asked Bill to take his tinny out for a spin to see what he thought of it. So Bill got in and took it for a few circuits around the beach, leaning forwards to keep the nose in and the propellers from touching bottom in the barely 45 centimetres of water.

He came back in and saw the others on the beach signalling frantically. 'What's the matter?'

'The men in that boat are screaming.'

Bill spun the tinny around but couldn't see anybody in the fading light. He turned his wrist hard onto full throttle, leant forwards and bounced his way back to the mouth. The men's boat came into view, drifting towards the line of breakers. He thought that if he could reach them before they hit the waves he'd be able to nudge them into the eastern shore where the swirling current was collapsing the sandbank into the river. By the time he got there, they were in a stretch of whitewater in front of the breakers. Their outboard was missing. And so was one of the men. There were only two in the boat.

Bill saw a head rushing towards the surf and raced towards it at full speed, desperate to reach the man before the waves.

'Grab the bow! Not the side!' he shouted as he cut the throttle and the bow dug in.

But the floundering guy missed the pointy end and grabbed the gunwale on the side. Water gushed in as the 50 centimetres of freeboard disappeared under his weight and Bill thought the tinny was about to capsize. He struggled to get the guy's mid-section over the side as water poured in, while the rip pulled them further into the danger zone. A large wave was approaching and the guy still had his backside hanging over the gunwale, 'like a bumper on a tug'. There was no way over or around the wave. So Bill turned the boat and gave a burst of throttle. The wave lifted them and they rode the thing back in. Bill ran the boat up onto the eastern bank. The guy jumped out and shouted, 'Save my mates!'

Looking back out to sea at that moment, Bill saw the two blokes in the boat hit a wave and go up. Their little aluminium vessel seemed suddenly light as it caught the wind off the crest and fluttered away.

'Did you see what happened to that boat?' Bill said. 'The same thing'll happen to this one. I'll go back and see if I can get my other boat back in the water.'

He started the engine but the tinny didn't move. *Cor, thank goodness*. For that glorious second he thought he wasn't going to be able to do anything more. He had an excuse to not go out there. But then he realised he'd knocked the outboard out of gear. He put it into forward and went back out into the current, hugging the shore through the mouth, hardly moving against the flow. He'd later learn the propeller was bent and the transom – where the engine was mounted on the stern – had been cracked in his wave riding. But he got back to Sugars Beach where the others had put his boat back into the water. He jumped in and Sharon and Julie hopped in with him, while Russell and Christopher followed in the broken tinny.

Bill called Sea Rescue on the radio under the bow. 'Mayday! Mayday!' Something he'd always wanted to say, but now that he was actually saying it, it had lost its appeal. 'Two men have been washed out of the Murray mouth,' he told the operator. 'They're not in a boat and they don't have life jackets on.' The operator notified police and ambulance.

'What's the procedure for navigating through the mouth?' Bill asked.

'There is no procedure for going through the mouth at any time.'

A fisheries boat had motored up and the men on board were talking to the man who Bill had just rescued. He'd run across the dunes from the ocean side to the landward side. Bill sped towards the big new boat – probably 25 feet, covered with aerials, two engines on the back, pedestal seats – in his fourteen-and-a-half-foot tinny glorified with a windscreen and a canvas awning.

He pulled over and saw the men had put on two emergency yellow jackets. *Thank God. They're going to do it.*

'Hi, guys. Are you going out to rescue them?'

'No, mate. Not on your life. It's too dangerous out there.'

'Somebody's got to try.'

'Not us.'

There was no point wasting time with these blokes. Bill and the two girls put on their life jackets. 'I'm going to go and see if I can find a sea pattern,' he said. He was hoping that he might be able to zigzag through the breakers. But when they motored up close to the waves, perhaps 40 metres away, it was clear that the only pattern was a long straight line of continuous breakers.

A big wave came curling in and a line from a Patience Strong poem came to him: 'A mountain stood before me. There was no way to pass.' But then an idea struck him.

He turned around and headed back to the beach. 'Listen, girls, what I'm going to do is too dangerous to take you with me. I'm going to crash underneath those waves.'

*

Bill remembers it: 'My daughter took me by the hand. "Dad, we're family." ' He pauses, sucking in a breath. ' "And if you think I'm going to leave you now, you've got another think coming." And Julie her friend said, "Look, Mr Bill, you might need us out there. We're sticking together, mate." It was the first time my daughter had ever defied me. But it was beautiful. It's one of those things I can't talk too much about. It makes me upset. It takes me right to that point.'

Julie had been amazed that the fisheries blokes wouldn't

go. Their boat was so big. But she totally trusted 'Mr Bill' and knew he would have made them get off if he thought he was going to kill them.

Bill turned the boat around again and stood off the breakers, perhaps 20 metres back, watching, waiting for a big wave on which to execute his plan. He saw one loom up, maybe three or four metres high down the face. He pushed the throttle full forward and gunned it straight for the wave. The girls held on tight as the bow burrowed into the wave and for a brief moment they were underwater, submarining. Julie was thinking about the movie *Blue Fin* in which a South Australian trawler is wrecked in a storm. *We're swamped. We're dead.*

Then they burst out the other side.

Bill's son Christopher, watching in the tinny, not far back, later told him they came out of the wave vertical, with about a metre and a half clearance between the engine and the top of the wave. They landed vertically on the stern, too.

But the boat stayed afloat. Bill rammed it forwards into the next wave. Same thing. Straight through and out, the little bow creating enough vortex to pull the windscreen and the canvas awning through the wall of water.

Then the next one. Same thing . . . and suddenly they were clear. Swells were still rolling towards them, breaking white on top, but there was room now to dodge them. It was time to start looking for the two men. The sun was long gone. There was just a strip of red on the horizon. Bill headed south-east along the coast, following what he thought might be the path of the current. They scanned the horizon as they rolled across the cold southern swells for about a kilometre.

Suddenly, there was an irregular shape silhouetted on the red horizon line. *Flotsam?* He steered towards it and two heads came into view. One was cuddling the bow of the boat, kept afloat by a little pocket of air in the point. He had his feet on a submerged seat. The other was alongside, wrapped around the petrol tank.

Bill steered to the far side of them. They looked nearly finished.

'Don't let go, boys. You wait till you drift into us. Don't you dare let go.'

They drifted in. The girls pulled one man over the front and the other over the stern. Julie remembers one missing a lot of clothing. Their whole bodies shook hard, vibrating through an arc of about three centimetres, as a towel was draped around them. They'd been in the frigid water for more than half an hour.

'The boat!' one of them said. 'We can't leave the boat. It's not ours.'

'Stuff the boat.'

The men kept saying, 'Thank you, thank you.' They said something about having seen fins out there. Julie wished she had some warm gear to throw on their shaking bodies.

Bill got back on the radio. 'Mayday. Mayday.'

'Go ahead, mayday.'

'I've got the men in my boat.'

'We thought you said they were in the sea.'

'They were.'

'*You're* out at sea?' the operator asked with disbelief.

'Affirmative. The only thing we've got wrong now, I'm looking back to shore and I can't see the mouth. There's no light anywhere. I can't see where to bring this back.' He knew that if it got desperate he could just drive the boat up onto the beach but he didn't want to lose his boat.

'Sea Rescue Four has just arrived at the Murray mouth. It's a four-wheel-drive. We'll ask him to put his lights on and shine them out to sea.'

Soon, the tiny lights came on in the distance. 'The Murray mouth is fifty metres to the starboard of those lights,' the operator said.

As they steered in, guided by the fluorescence on the back of the swells, Julie dreaded the thought of facing the huge waves at the mouth again. She periodically wiped the spray off Bill's spectacles so he could see as they approached the thunderous waves again. *We're going to die. We're going to die.* It suddenly seemed much scarier to her now she had time to think about it. But much to her surprise they surfed on through the mouth with ease and were soon dropping the men off at the four-wheel-drive.

Afterwards, Julie just remembers the buzz of being interviewed and of having done something important. Having a Bravery Medal seemed totally normal. There was no comedown. 'We made it back so there was no need to look on the sad side. And I never look on the sad side.'

Sharon had a few weeks where she'd lie in bed and be just drifting off to sleep when she'd be airborne again, going through the back of those waves, then feel the thud as the boat crashed down. It wasn't a good feeling. She dwelt on what might have been, but that passed. She thought it seemed a bit odd that she got a Bravery Medal. She didn't want to be in the limelight but she knew she was entitled to it. She can look back at it now and know that it is special.

And what was it like growing up with your dad, I can't help but ask.

'Dad's good. He's got a good heart and he's always trying to do his best for everybody.'

*

As for Bill, he remembers that after the rescue they went and got the biggest pizza he'd ever bought. Two of the blokes phoned him later and thanked him, but neither apologised for not listening to his advice earlier in the afternoon. The third bloke never called. Bill received the Star of Courage for his actions and it rankles him that the citation says the girls begged him to rescue the men as though he'd been reluctant to do it, rather than them begging him to let them go with him on the rescue.

I ask what made him act when he had every right to do nothing. Bill launches into one of his stories. 'My mother was a midwife in Portsmouth during the war. Three hundred and thirty-five thousand soldiers came home from Dunkirk. The injured went to hospital but all the others went home and saw their girlfriends and their wives and whoever. So you can imagine what their situation was like. From conception to birth is two hundred and eighty days. So nine months later she had a list of all these impending births. There were no telephones, all the husbands were off in North Africa by this time. So she came to me and said, "Billy, you're going to stay with Susan tonight and you'll stay with her for two days, and if she cries twice, you're to come and get me." I became a telephone for ladies having babies during the Blitz. Irrespective of whether there was an air raid on, I had to run and get my mother. It just gave me a feeling for adventure. I felt I was doing something worthwhile.'

He says he didn't speak about the Murray mouth incident for years. That's what he was taught during the war. But the incident kept coming back into his head. 'People don't understand what it's like to see that wave night in and night out, night in, night out. It was a pain in the neck.'

He eventually did start talking about it and now he's a public speaker telling the story of the incident and other experiences. He still sees the wave, though. 'It's amazing how it impresses on your mind. I might go to bed tonight and see it so vividly.' But it's not a problem any more.

Like about half the people featured in this book, he tells me he had wanted to write an autobiography. He thought he didn't have the time or the literary skills. 'The Germans bombed Portsmouth sixty-seven times during the war and I wagged school for a year.' Spelling and grammar aren't his strong points. He didn't know about Microsoft Word or spell checks. 'And I didn't have time in the day to write a book. So I decided whatever time I woke up in the night I'd sit down and write for an hour.' The next night Bill woke up at 3.38 am and wrote for an hour. The night after he woke at 3.38 again, and wrote. For the next year he continued to wake up at 3.38 am exactly. 'I can't explain it but that's what happened.'

He wanted to call the book *Believe You Can and You Will*, but the publisher at first insisted on calling it *Courage*, then, after reading a few more chapters, *Step Beyond Courage* (available at stepbeyondcourage.com). Bill is keen to emphasise that this title was not his idea. The publisher also excised a lot of the religious stuff and put that into a second volume, to be called *Planned by God*. He doesn't have a problem with that title.

TWENTY

Graeme Samuels

Graeme Samuels was a security officer at Sydney airport in early 1991. It was the time of the first Gulf War. Fears were heightened.

The way the job worked, he might do two hours in a car patrolling the perimeter, two hours watching a building and two hours doing traffic control. This day, the 33-year-old was posted on the gate of the Australian Airlines cargo area and was due to change over into a car. But he was also the union rep and had to go to a meeting at the end of his stint in the car. If he did the car, he wasn't going to get a chance to have a break before the meeting, so he tried to convince a colleague to let him stay on the gate, but the colleague wouldn't be in it.

He'd just lost the debate when the walkie-talkie on his hip crackled to life. There was a disturbance at the Australian Airlines taxi rank. The message didn't say much. They never did, because you didn't know who was eavesdropping on scanners. So he jumped in the car, turned on the flashing light, and drove the 100 metres or so from the cargo gate to the terminal. He got out and saw a man – six feet, lean, about 45 years old, clean clothes – talking to himself, talking to everybody about the Gulf War and God, and Lord knows what else.

'What's going on?' Graeme asked a colleague already there.

'He's a crazy. He's trying to get himself shot. He's after someone with a gun.'

'Just let him get away from the terminal,' Graeme said. 'Let's get him down the street.'

They'd had crazies there before. The police would take them away but couldn't hold them so they'd be back in a few hours. The best you could do was herd them away.

The guy came towards the security car: 'Have you got a gun?'

'No. No. It's okay,' Graeme answered. 'No one here has any guns. Down the street they have.'

The guy was all worked up like he was high on drugs. Only later would Graeme learn that he was a long-term schizophrenic who was a member of a hard-core religious sect that believed in reincarnation. Death was going to be a way out of whatever nightmare he was living.

Graeme would also learn later that sometime before this incident the guy had attacked a city shop window with a pair of garden shears, then he'd turned on a parked car before going for the police who came to take him away. 'His brother was a high school principal. He said to the judge, "Don't release him because he refuses to take his medication and he's not responsible for himself." But a member of his religious group was a solicitor and got him released to his 86-year-old blind mother who had to make sure he took his medication and behaved himself.'

For Graeme, life was good at this time. He was happily married with a ten-year-old son. He'd always played a lot of sport and had also been an abseiling instructor with the Scouts and Adventurers. But he'd cut back on a lot of that to devote himself to taking his son to sport and to working more hours. He could double his wage on overtime.

The crazy's protest this day had started at the Ansett terminal, but it was a quiet time of day so he'd moved around to the Australian Airlines terminal and started lunging at people with a knife, and then on to the taxi rank where he poured the contents of a bottle over a taxi and tried to set it alight. That's when Graeme had arrived. Now, as they were getting him moving in the direction they wanted, the driver of the taxi was suddenly running towards them with a wheelchair ramp, trying to lumber the guy. A couple of the security guards stood between the two men and continued moving the guy away.

Graeme got on the radio and asked for police help, trying to play it down on the radio. The radio operator said he should handle it himself, but Graeme told him, 'No, I really think the police should be here.'

By the time he got off the radio, the guy was a block away, but he'd stopped. As Graeme drove up, the crowd around him was getting bigger. He was lunging out at people again with a Wiltshire StaySharp. The airport police office was only one more block away.

'Just keep the crowd back,' Graeme said. 'Let's keep him moving.'

Graeme expected the police to show at any moment, but after a few minutes, he jumped back in the car and drove to their office to give them a hurry-up. By the time he arrived back at the scene, the crowd had grown. People had come out of a nearby bank and the rental car wash. Others were stopping in the street. Still no sign of the police. So Graeme grabbed the heavy security torch and walked back into the drama.

The nutter drew the knife back over his shoulder and threw it into the crowd. As it landed harmlessly, he reached into his backpack and pulled out another.

'Keep the crowd back,' Graeme told the security guards. 'Get them moving. Get them out of here.' At last the police showed up. And when they did, the man reached into his backpack and pulled out a bottle filled with liquid. He lit a wick and threw the bottle at the police. The Molotov cocktail smashed on the ground but didn't explode.

'Stay away, stay away,' the guy said. 'Keep away from me.'

A female security officer looked at Graeme. 'Oh good, you've got a torch. We'll get around behind him.'

'Nah, just get the crowd back.'

The guy was backing in towards a garden bed. He was half in, half out and a police officer called to him to be careful he didn't trip. He looked around and saw the female security guard close behind him. He lunged at her with the knife.

Graeme had no time to think. He was perhaps two metres from his colleague and the guy. He put his shoulder down and charged, pushing her away as he drove into the guy's torso. At 98 kilograms, six feet tall and athletic, Graeme thought he hit him pretty hard, but it was like running into a brick wall. The guy's adrenaline and all the lunatic energy pumping through his sinewy frame seemed to give him a super strength. Graeme drove harder into the guy's middle and managed to topple him, but as they fell, witnesses would later tell Graeme, the guy switched the blade from the front of his left hand to the bottom of both hands and plunged with all his strength.

Graeme felt a thud in his lower back. He landed on top of the guy but suddenly couldn't move. Couldn't stand. Couldn't roll away.

'I told you to keep away from me,' the guy said, from underneath Graeme. 'I told you I'd get you . . .' and off he went rambling about God and the Gulf War again, a half sentence about something then another half sentence about something else.

The police moved in.

'Can you get him out from under me?'

The police handcuffed his attacker but didn't move them. Graeme looked down at his legs to try and see what the problem was. But his legs weren't there. Not where his brain was telling him they should be. They were actually heading off in a different direction and he knew then that he would never walk again. *It's a knife. It's obviously chopped my spinal cord.* But all his focus was on the guy still stuck beneath him. He wanted to get him out without doing any more damage. And he wanted to stay calm. He knew that the worse he appeared, the worse the people around him would be.

He heard someone say, 'The knife's still in his back. Should we take it out?'

'Noooo. Just leave it. Get an ambulance,' Graeme said.

The police got the guy out and the ambulance came.

'I think I had a bigger motorcade than the Queen. Just about every police motorbike was out in front of me,' Graeme recalls. 'The doctor came out to my wife and said I had a knife in my back and it'd severed the spinal cord and I'd never walk again. He was right up front about it. He said he was going to take the knife out, and see you later. The diplomacy wasn't the greatest. He'd told me the same thing when they tried to X-ray me. I couldn't fit through the scanner because of this knife sticking out of my back. They were trying to turn me round a bit. I was worried the slightest movement was going to do more damage.'

It was one spontaneous moment of courage that would in a matter of seconds change everything for Graeme Samuels, yet his greater acts of heroism lay ahead.

*

The police started taking statements straight away. 'My story to the police was a little different to what happened because this woman I pushed out of the way, I knew she was in tears and blaming herself and I didn't want her to share any of that blame. And I don't blame her. I knew what had happened to me was irreparable. Why affect other people with it? She was badly distressed. She had a lot of counselling and that sort of thing. So I always played that side down. I said to the police, "I heard someone call out, 'Get him now!' I pushed past one of my security officers and tackled the guy."

'The police weren't going to lay criminal charges against him because if they had, the guy would have gone for diminished responsibility and been back out on the street. So we had to just prove he was a danger to himself and the public and get him institutionalised. That's where he is to this day.'

In the hospital spinal unit, the counsellors brought the patients together to talk about their new predicaments and they told them it was all right to feel whatever they were feeling, but Graeme didn't agree with that. It gave people too much scope to dwell and wallow.

He was out of bed in five days. A week or so later he went over to the basketball court to watch a wheelchair game and soon he was doing wheelstands and rowing in the gym. He thought he was on the way back.

'I accepted what happened to me. Other people in the spinal ward were trying to blame someone or something for what happened to them. "Hey, you know, wake up. It's not going to change anything. The sooner you accept it and get on with your life the better you handle it." I can't say there was never a moment when I was upset. I did have a couple, but they were pretty quiet, I kept them to myself. I just went over to the park near the hospital heliport and sat there and thought all about it and had a whinge about it. We weren't meant to go too far from the ward but we'd go there and escape. One time, everyone was looking for me. They thought I'd gone off the deep end. I just needed time to myself.

'I did later give in and go to a psychiatrist that the airport wanted me to see. He said to me, "Graeme, if all my patients were like you I'd be out of a job."'

The mothers of some of the young guys in there used to ask him to have a word to their boys. Pep them up. He'd have competitions with them to see who could get up a little ramp in there. They called it Mount Everest. Some guys just needed waking up to what they could do. They ended up walking out of the place. But as these people were improving and leaving, Graeme started to go downhill. The 'spinal shock' wore off, and his body started going into spasms, and the spasticity just seemed to get worse, to the point where he couldn't sit in his chair any more. He'd move a few centimetres and all the muscles — including the paralysed leg muscles — would fire at once and hurl him onto the floor. He couldn't see himself living like that for the rest of his life. No way.

*

'While we speak here,' he says to me, 'the amount of pain that's going through me at the moment, you would be running to the doctor. You wouldn't be able to understand how you could live with it. That's from the rib cage. A constant state of pain. It races through you all the time. Your toes feel like someone dropped a brick on them. They throb. Spasticities will jump out all over the place. They lock out with that much vigour, it's like getting a cramp. It goes too far and your body releases and then it snaps back into that again. So it's a constant bang, bang, bang. My legs will fly up and nearly hit me in the face. I've got to be careful when I turn over in bed that I don't knee myself. There's no warning. Any sort of vibration sets it off, so I've got pump-up tyres on my wheelchair. If I sit absolutely still, it can drop off around the buttocks and legs but a small adjustment will set it off. Your messages from the brain to the body are getting screwed up. There are all these phantom messages going backwards and forwards.'

*

Even as Graeme's condition deteriorated, nurses still got him to talk to new arrivals in the spinal unit. He'd give them the positive talk, omitting the spasms and the agony. While still in hospital, he received a letter saying he'd been put in for a bravery award. It didn't change anything, but it at least made him feel there was a reason for him being there.

After seven months in hospital, he was sent home. He was running out of weeks on workers comp and needed to go back to work, but the spasticity made that impossible. The doctors suggested a pump implanted in his belly that could inject muscle relaxant up a tube directly into his spine at the back of his neck.

'No way!' was his initial reaction, but his body was out of control. He couldn't move fifteen centimetres without being thrown out of the chair. And he needed to work. He had a mortgage. So he went in for a trial of the pump and it made a difference.

When he was released from hospital his doctor wrote on a certificate that he was okay to return to full-time employment. Graeme queried him. He couldn't work five days a week. 'It's so they can't discriminate against you,' the doctor said.

He returned to work at the airport where he had a job waiting – in lost property. But the thought of spending the rest of his days in some poky office was not at all appealing. He could only work eight hours a week so he decided to enrol in a TAFE computer course. His taxi driver would wheel him into the classroom, right up to the desk – then come and wheel him out again at the end. The course was the most basic one possible. 'This is a computer. This is a mouse.' After that, he did another course in microcomputers. That qualification got him into the property management area of the airport. He was shunted into an office on the far side of the runways, where some days he was the only person in the building. He didn't even have a computer.

Eventually he carved out a niche working on the computer side of the business, making himself indispensable, getting all the different computers from the different departments linked up. Only then did he get a transfer to the information technology side of the company. The toilet was nine storeys down in the basement, he couldn't get in the kitchen because there was a bubbler in the way, but he put up with it all because he wanted to further himself. He never wanted to appear down. And that's been a problem because if he always looks happy, when he asks for help, people don't understand that he has problems. But that is better than the alternative. 'If you start telling people what you can't do, you'll stop being invited to things. Sometimes you'll turn up somewhere and here's twenty stairs. And they say, "But we saw you at so-and-so's." "Yeah, that's because I went next door and up their goods lift and in the back."'

In a company intent on cost cutting, he found himself controlling more computer systems – the ones no one else wanted. He had eleven or twelve of them and was only working 30 hours a week. Every day was a struggle. But there was no way he was going to tell his bosses that. They might cut back his hours. He'd become dispensable.

And he figured out how to get himself back into his chair after he'd been flung out by a spasm. He'd put his legs in first, then when he started lifting himself, his legs would go into spasm, pushing him up and into the chair. Unlike most people bound to a wheelchair, his legs never withered because they got constant exercise from the spasms.

'The garden needed doing so I got to know every blade of grass around this place. I used to cut it with a pair of scissors. I laid on my knees and just bent over in the garden. I had extension arms and just used to pull things from the garden. I spent hours and hours. It was just something to do. It kept me going. And then I saw a garden bed full of massive rocks and I ripped them all out by hand. Now I think, "How did I do that?" Your will and desire to not let this beat you is the whole thing. I can show you fences I put up, garden beds. I did them all while debilitated with the spasticity.'

He fought the pain with self-hypnosis, managing to tell himself not to associate the spasticity with the pain. The pain is still there, but the spasticity doesn't make it worse unless his legs hit something and cause worse spasms.

It took him five years to realise that he'd just have to live with the pain. Before then he couldn't have believed it possible. But his body has adjusted. Now he can graze his knuckles on a brick wall and not even notice. Someone will say, 'What have you done to your hand?' He'll look at it and see blood everywhere but the pain from it just hadn't been enough to register compared to the pain he lives and sleeps with every day.

He still sits on foam rather than the new-fangled cushions. He doesn't want to make life too easy. The foam wobbles around, making it hard to balance, but that works his muscles. His wheelchair is an old sports model that forces his body to work harder. He doesn't want to relax in it. He's never had a pressure sore.

If he doesn't do the stretches his spasms are worse. But how can he fit them all in daily? 'You either try and keep a mainstream job or you be a disabled person and do all your stretches and stay at home. I try to be mainstream.' By going to work he has to transfer himself in and out of his car, go downstairs to bathrooms in the basement, downstairs to have lunch or a cigarette. (He hangs on to the smokes. It's an excuse to go out and get some exercise.) The movement and interactions are his physiotherapy.

*

In the early days of World War I, when shell shock was emerging as a huge problem, it was hypothesised that the physical concussion of the explosion of shells caused the catatonic states, the 'hysterical dumbness', the amnesia, and the strange gaits that doctors were observing on a mass scale. But then, as the huge battles of 1916 produced ever more cases, it was realised that injured men rarely suffered the problem, including those who'd been blown up by shells. They had clearly been more exposed to the explosions than those uninjured men with shell shock, yet remained psychologically strong. Likewise, I was struck by how psychologically unaffected Graeme was despite his huge physical injuries. That's not to say he hasn't had other pressures to deal with.

'Over the years after the incident, my wife and I became just friends. She ended up going off with some guy. I was left to myself with two kids. It was getting to a time when they weren't paying too much attention to their mother and she had better places to go.'

His son, Ben, was then nineteen, and his stepson, Damien, was 27. Graeme cooked for them and tended to clean up for the boys. They'd say, 'It's not my turn to mow the lawn,' and there wasn't much he could do about it.

He doesn't blame his wife for leaving. 'It's hard to say if I was in that situation whether I'd do the same, because you've got no idea what it's like to live with a person with a disability.

290

I wasn't the person she married. That's why this current relationship is so good because Ramona has only known me in a chair.' He met Ramona, 'a part-Cherokee, part-Italian Yank from Rhode Island', on the internet. He told her of his predicament but she didn't care. There was just something about him which drew her to him, she says. She came to Australia for a trial run . . . and it clicked.

*

The evening I visit them in 2008, Graeme has just worked eleven hours straight on the computer at home, linked to the office. He'll be stuffed tonight, he says. He won't be able to sleep, his legs will kick out and fly up at his face. The computers take his mind off the pain but his body suffers for it. After a meal and a long chat, he drives me to the station in his modified Commodore.

When we speak again in 2010, he's feeling a lot better. It turns out the second pump inserted in his stomach in 1996 was faulty and had been leaking the muscle relaxant straight into his gut rather than into his spinal cord. So his dosage has been cut to one-seventh of his previous level and he's feeling good.

He's bought himself a four-wheel-drive wheelchair because he wants to show Ramona the country, and the new chair will make it easier to get from the car to the lookouts. 'I want to be able to do it properly. I don't want to leave it till it's too late. We'll do the harder places first, the outback and the bush, and go to the easy spots later.'

TWENTY-ONE

Tim Britten and Richard Joyes

Richard Joyes was on a mission with his mates to get some groceries and stock up on beer for their hotel room in the heart of Bali's Kuta district. They were just walking past the Sari Club when it hit him – nausea, light-headedness. 'Guys, I'm feeling crook. I'm going back to the hotel to get some sleep.'

By the time the others got back with the supplies, he was feeling worse and wanted to go to hospital. One of his mates, Tim Hawkins, volunteered to take him in a cab. He checked in and they put him under observation for an hour and a half before he was diagnosed with mild food poisoning and discharged.

He managed a bite to eat that night, then crashed while the boys downed a few more on the balcony. A bit after nine, one of them came in: 'Come on, Rich, we're going down the Sari Club. Do you want to come and have a drink?' He would have loved to have joined them but they'd been on it for three nights already.

'I'm going to give it a miss.'

His mates, being mates and with no respect for Bali belly, felt obliged to jump on the patient and fire him up for a big one, but he held out. They left, and he nodded off again, thinking that maybe he would pop down later and surprise them.

He woke to a noise. *What was that?* He wasn't sure. Seconds later, there came the loudest most powerful thing he'd ever heard – and being a mining geologist he'd heard a few blasts. The bed shook, the hotel shook, the big window over his bed burst in on him, showering him with glass. Whatever it was, it felt like it was right outside. Everything was in darkness and as his pulse thumped through his veins an awful feeling descended on him – something very bad had just happened. He walked around the hotel and saw a huge mushroom cloud blooming, roughly in the direction of the Sari Club. He could hear screaming, and people started coming back to the hotel in the eerie darkness. There was crying. It occurred to him that it could have been a bomb and, if so, the Sari Club would be a good place to target. He thought he'd better go find the boys.

*

Tim Britten only heard one explosion. He knows there were meant to have been two, about twenty seconds apart, but that's not what he heard. First, the lights had momentarily gone out as he walked back to his hotel, then followed the almighty boom. As glass came crashing and tinkling down, his first thought was that crooks had blown a safe in one of the many jewellery stores in the tourist strip. He melted into the shadows, ever the policeman, thinking he'd be able to nab the offenders as they decamped. *I'll get a free trip back to Bali for the court case.* That's how coppers think.

The 33-year-old West Australian was in Bali on leave from East Timor where he'd been serving in the United Nations peacekeeping force for the past four months. Some mates who'd been meant to join him hadn't arrived yet. And another was shacked up in a flash hotel with his girlfriend, having decided not to go out this first night on the island. So Tim was alone and hadn't quite shifted his head from the tensions and difficulties of life in East Timor to the freewheeling holiday spirit of Bali. He'd probably only had two beers at the Hard Rock Café, watching a local covers band, before giving up on the night about 11.30 pm.

Now, as he waited for the bandits, everything didn't quite gel. People pointed over the roofs at a mushroom cloud. The realisation dawned that it was a bomb – probably terrorists.

In East Timor, he'd been briefed on the terror threat in Indonesia. A large amount of ammonium nitrate fertiliser had been stolen. It looked like the stuff had turned up.

A wave of people appeared, running towards him, and he moved in the opposite direction. In the narrow crowded alleys it was impossible to tell exactly where he was heading. He took his bearings from the crowd, heading towards whatever it was that they were running from. And the closer he got, the thicker the crowd seemed to be. It was like trying to get into Subiaco Oval at the end of a big game when everybody else was leaving. 'Don't go down there,' someone said. 'There's another bomb going to go off.'

But he pushed on. He got a bit impatient with the oncoming tide, shoving them out of the way as he barged through. He came around a bend and suddenly flames towered above. He saw a man on the ground with his guts hanging out. It was slaughter. Hundreds dead or injured, all confined to a narrow street.

The smell of cordite – modern gunpowder – and burning meat hit his nostrils. And the sound was of a million car alarms wailing. They'd all been rocked by the percussion. And the motorbikes parked nearby seemed to have had their horns activated by the shock. People wandered, dazed and aimless.

It was a total assault on the senses.

He knew terrorists often exploded more bombs to clean up those who rushed in to help and he fully expected they'd do the same here. (He was unaware they had, in fact, already done just that – the first backpack bomb exploded in Paddy's Bar followed by a much larger one-tonne bomb detonated in a mini-van across the street, outside the Sari Club.)

'I'm an Australian police officer,' he said to the people standing around. 'Is everyone out of the building?'

A group of women off to the side were frantic. 'No, there's a woman in there burning. People have tried to get her and no one can.'

They begged him to go in and get her, and so he thought he'd give it a crack. He was a copper. This is what they did. He'd try to get as many people out as he could before any more bombs went off.

He waded into the inferno – his thongs, shorts and singlet offering no protection from the broiling heat. He stepped over burning debris and maybe 25 metres from the door he found a woman pinned by a piece of metal. She reached her arm out to him, imploring with her eyes. It was no longer a matter of 'Should I?' or 'Can I?' It was now a matter of 'I've got to'. He pulled at her, tried to move the metal, but she was stuck fast. The heat was getting to him now and he retreated to the street.

He saw a young bloke standing out there who looked like a copper. 'Mate, can you give us a hand to help this woman? She's going to die.'

*

Richard Joyes had pushed through the same sort of crowd as Tim Britten, looking for his mates. People in the blackness screamed at him: 'Don't go down there.' He was terrified. He had no idea what it was that he was heading towards but he had to find the boys. As he approached Jalan Legian – the main road the Sari Club was on – from Poppies Lane, he started to see the destruction. Aside from the shattered buildings, scaffolding laying around, broken glass and tiles, he noticed how the palm trees were all laid over in the same direction. He saw bike helmets strewn around. And heard the sound of a bike horn blasting.

A Balinese man lying on the footpath looked up at him. Richard could see from his stomach wound that he was going to die. But he didn't know what to think. It didn't feel real. He kept on walking – around a corner and into the full grotesque horror of it all – lots of people stumbling about, some carrying horrid wounds, all disorientated. Dead bodies, body parts.

He noticed some guys with big boxes full of water bottles handing them out to whomever, to drink or to splash on their burns. They asked him to help. 'Sure,' he said. He ran into the surf shop two doors up and grabbed some T-shirts through the broken window and started ripping them up to hand out for bandages, just trying to do what he could. He didn't know what he was doing but he had to do something. There were people dying. All those he was trying to help knew they were dying, but he kept telling them they were going to be okay.

And that's when the tall, lean short-haired guy came up and asked for a hand to save a woman trapped inside.

'Okay,' Richard said.

So, wearing T-shirt, shorts and sandals, he ran into the Sari Club with the stranger, Tim Britten.

*

Gas bottles exploded. Burning debris fell. The flames seemed to swirl around in inexplicable gales. They went in towards the woman on a clear path, but then looked back at the way

296

they'd just come and it was blocked by a wall of flame. It was hard to breathe, hard to see. The cop resigned himself to it. *Yep, this is where Tim Britten dies.* Then, suddenly, it went clear again. They tried to get to the woman but the heat was too intense. Their skin burnt, their hair frizzed. They retreated and got the guys with the water bottles to douse them. It felt wonderful and cool, washing over their skin, almost like it was going to protect them. And there was something about that near-death experience that changed Tim. Before it, he'd been shitting himself. Now that he was resigned to death, there was nothing to be afraid of. He got on with the task at hand. He would get as many out as he could before that next one went off. And in he went again with Richard Joyes.

They made their way the 25 metres or so from the door to the girl. They had another go at freeing her, but she was still pinned fast and her limbs were slippery with burns. The heat, overwhelming, searing into their lungs, was just about to beat them off again, when they had one last go and something gave. She came free. But she was a big girl and they probably would have struggled to lift her under normal circumstances. They grabbed her blistered arms and carried her out of the most intense heat. Then, as they struggled with the weight and the slipperiness, two other guys came in to help. Each grabbed a limb and they lifted. They got her to the street and someone suggested putting her in a puddle to cool the wounds but someone else pointed out the risk of infection would be too great. They took her over to where some other people were being cared for and put her down.

Both men were now cut and burnt themselves, but with people still inside, they turned and went back in. They clambered over rubble and cinders, the fire still raging, growing hotter all the time.

*

Ben Tullipan was in Bali on business. He and his fiancée were going to be joining her family's business, importing homewares, so he was learning how the stuff was made, buying product, seeing what was out there. He'd been touring the markets and was at the taxi rank to head home when he thought he'd grab a bottle of water in the Sari Club. He knew Bali well but he'd only ever been to the club once. Drinking and partying weren't his scene.

The front bar was way too crowded so he went to the side bar and got his water and was on the way out when he heard the bomb go off across the road in Paddy's Bar. Everyone looked around: 'What was that?' People started moving towards the front door, and he went with them in a big crowd. As he was coming down the front step, he looked out over the top of the fleeing heads and he'd remember seeing a van parked outside the metal gates. His eyes registered the word 'Mitsubishi' written on it.

At that point, his world went into slow motion.

Ben saw the van windows shatter and a hole appear in the van's side behind the driver's seat. A great fireball burst out of the hole and came at the crowd. He'd remember saying, 'You're fucking kidding!' as he covered his face and hoped. His body convulsed uncontrollably like he was being electrocuted for a long time, until he found himself on the ground with a log over his legs. He seemed to have been blown sideways, near the front bar. There were small fires burning around him. He heard explosions. *Machine guns?* He looked across and saw that it was a crate of bottles exploding in the flames. The hut area was on fire. He was aware of screaming but couldn't hear it properly because his eardrums had burst. There was nobody else alive around him. He craned his neck, but saw only flesh and body parts, bricks, tables and corrugated iron. He tried to get away but couldn't move. *This is it. It's over.* He lay on his back for a while. *Nah, stuff this. They're not getting me. I'm getting out.* He tried moving but burnt his hands on the iron.

His hands looked like sausages left way too long on the barbecue. He had no energy. He just couldn't shift this log on his legs and his legs didn't feel like they were working.

'Get me out!' he screamed. 'Get me fucking out of here!'

Two blokes ran in through where the front wall had been but which wasn't there any more. 'Are you an Aussie?' one of them asked.

'Yeah, yeah. Just get me out.'

They got the log off his legs. 'Can you walk?' one of them asked.

'No, look at his legs. They're smashed,' the other said.

It was probably Tim Britten and Richard Joyes. They found a man near the pillar just inside the front door.

'This is going to hurt,' they told Ben, 'but we'll get you the hell out of here.'

'Good idea,' Ben said. They picked him up under the armpits and carried him out, his legs dangling behind.

When Ben was laid down behind a car, he got his mobile phone out to call his fiancée, Kristin, but the little rubber buttons had all melted. (Ben later had both legs amputated.)

*

Tim and Richard went back in looking for more survivors, but all they could see inside now were bodies. The ever-growing heat pushed them out for the last time. No point risking their lives for the dead.

They stayed at the scene helping others, lifting and carrying wounded souls the 150 metres or so to where vehicles were waiting to ferry victims to the clinic. Tim would lift them in a fireman's carry while Richard supported their heads and spoke comforting words.

They found a woman on the footpath with some other injured people. She seemed in a bad way, a lot of burns and wounds. Tim lifted and Richard went behind, supporting as best he could because, again, she was a big woman. 'Everything's going to be okay. We're going to get you to hospital. You're going to be fine.' They got her onto a truck and just seconds later she died. It was deflating. But there was no time for conscious decisions on what to do with her. They took her off and laid her down on the footpath to make way for other injured people who needed to get on.

Richard hadn't had a chance to think about his three mates. It wasn't until about half an hour after it all began when they stopped to have a bit of a rest outside the metal gates in front of the inferno that he wondered where they might be. 'I've got to go back in,' he said to Tim. 'I've got three mates in there.'

'Look, mate,' said Tim, 'if there's anyone else in there, they're probably not going to make it. There's probably nothing more you can do.'

Wounded people were sprawled about. Others wandered in groups like zombies, lit by the bright yellow tower of flame. Tim tried to move people along to safety, but it was 'like mustering kittens'. They kept wandering back, looking for friends, getting themselves in harm's way. The Bali police had arrived. They were scared and on edge like everyone. Some had machine guns.

Tim and Richard continued carrying the wounded. They found a door and started using that as a stretcher. They did what they could for perhaps an hour until the street was cleared.

Richard was keen to go. 'Mate, I might shoot through and try to find my mates.'

'No worries, I'll catch you later.'

They swapped numbers but Tim had it in his head that

Richard was a copper and thought he was giving him his regimental number.

Tim helped the local police until there was nothing left to do then he headed back to his friend Troy's hotel. He sat in the bath for a long time. Troy and his girlfriend helped pull glass out of his feet and a hotel doctor later dressed his burns.

*

Richard made his way down the street just as a wave of mob hysteria hit. People yelled that another bomb was about to go off. People ran. Richard, terrified, ran with them. By the time the panic subsided, he was disorientated, a long way from his hotel in some back alley. He tried to find his way in the blackness. There was still screaming and panic in the air. The blinding lights of scooters came towards him as people hid in the shadows. It occurred to him that they could be the very same people who'd caused this. It was perhaps as terrifying as being inside the flaming club. But he found his way back to the hotel where the wounded were being helped in the foyer. He sat himself down by the side of the pool and didn't know what to do or think. *What have I just been through?*

Somebody said that everyone from the hotel was accounted for. That annoyed him because he knew the boys weren't back. He sat there for a long time. Someone offered him a cigarette. 'Sorry, mate, I don't smoke.'

'Do you want to start?'

'Now's as good a time as any.' He lit one up. It didn't make him feel any better but it took his mind off things. He borrowed a mobile phone off someone who seemed to be lending it out to just about everyone. It must have cost the guy a fortune on global roaming. Richard rang his father back in Tasmania and woke him. 'Dad, something really bad has happened but I want you to know that I'm okay. I can't find the boys but if

301

you turn the TV on tomorrow or if you hear of something happening over here, some sort of explosion, you know I'm okay and I'm going to try and find the boys . . . I'll give you a call as soon as I know anything, okay?'

The longer it went without any of the group showing up, the more he started to think he might be going home alone.

It was about half an hour after the phone call, about 3 am, that an Indonesian policeman came into the hotel, yelling, 'Richard Joyes. Richard Joyes.'

'Yeah, that's me.'

'Do you know a mister Ben Davis?'

'Yeah, I do, absolutely. You know where he is?'

'He's at Sanglah Hospital in Denpasar.'

Richard felt a surge of relief. He and Ben were very close. He grabbed all his cash and rushed into the street, found a taxi and went straight there in a crazy three-minute hell ride that should have taken about ten minutes.

He was greeted with mayhem and horror. Injured people, some with almost no skin left, filled the beds and corridors. In the twenty minutes he wandered around he had plenty of opportunity to observe the carnage and he dreaded what Ben might look like. But then there he was, lying in a bed, with a lot of shrapnel wounds, small burns and perforated eardrums. He was in a bad way, but good compared to what others were enduring. It felt great.

Richard rang Ben's dad back in Tasmania and got him out of bed to break the news. It was hard telling him what happened when he didn't really know himself, and how do you describe such injuries? On a normal scale, Ben was severely injured but compared to what Richard had seen he was so lucky.

He stayed with him for a few hours to do what he could, but about 7.30 am he told Ben, 'Look, I'm going to have to leave you and go and find the others.'

Richard walked out and grabbed the nearest taxi: 'Take me to all the hospitals.'

The driver took him to about six hospitals over the next three hours with no luck. There was only one hospital left to check – the military hospital. It had a list of names on a board out front and at number 22 was the name of his friend Stuart Anstee.

Richard felt overwhelmed with relief and joy. If he'd found Ben and Stuart, there was a good chance Tim Hawkins was going to be alive, too. He went in and saw that Stu was in a bad way, propped up in bed wearing only boxer shorts and with a lot of serious burns and shrapnel wounds. Two cotton pads covered his eyes. But while a lot of those around him were screaming out their pain and calling for help, Stu was sitting there, strong and quiet.

He stayed with Stu for a while before going back to the hotel and gathering up everyone's valuables. He spent the rest of Sunday on the back of a scooter, going back to all the hospitals looking for Tim Hawkins. The heat was extreme, probably 40 degrees, and the day-pack holding everyone's belongings soaked onto his back in the dripping humidity. More than once, battling the unusually heavy traffic, he experienced moments where he felt the full disconnect from his new reality. *Where am I? What am I doing here? Why have I been put in this situation?* But he tried to get his mind onto the business at hand – finding Tim Hawkins. He knew there'd be time down the track to think about the bigger picture.

But, unsuccessful again, he went back to the two hospitals to visit Ben and Stu. At Ben's hospital an Aussie came up and asked him for help: 'I'm here on my own. No one knows I've been injured. Can you try and get through to my mother in Melbourne?'

'I'll try and do what I can, mate,' Richard said, but he was struggling just getting information back to Ben and Stu's parents as it was.

And the bloke in the bed next to Ben was burnt all over. Richard felt so bad for him, knowing there was nothing he could do. (He later learned he died.)

They got Ben out on one of the first RAAF Hercules that night and then later got Stu out. With his two mates gone, Richard ended up falling asleep in the hospital foyer. A doctor came out and offered him a coffee and a couple of biscuits. Richard thought it was probably the nicest thing anyone had ever done for him because he was more than aware of what a hard time the doctor must have been going through as well.

He got back to his hotel sometime in the pre-dawn of Monday morning. He borrowed some candles because the electricity was still off and he got back to the room to find shattered glass still over the bed and belongings. The food they'd bought on Saturday had gone off in the warm fridge. He didn't want to shut his eyes because he knew it would all come pouring back into his head. The two candles flickered away, a symbol of light against the darkness. He knew it wasn't over yet. Not by a long shot. He had to find Tim Hawkins. But the candles eventually snuffed it and he nodded off – the memories flooding in like he knew they would. Sleep proved difficult and fleeting.

He woke early and did the round of hospitals once more, looking closely at every single patient, feeling very alone now. Again with no luck. So, the next day, Tuesday, he knew he had to go to the morgue. Tim Hawkins's family was coming over to search for him, too, but he didn't think they should have to do it. He didn't want to do it either. It terrified him. He was exhausted and hungry, still crook from the food poisoning, but it was another step that had to be taken if he was going to do everything possible to find his mate.

He went with some people he'd met but they'd only been inside looking at the bodies for five or ten minutes before someone from the Australian government came in and announced they were taking control of the morgue and they all had to get out. He hadn't found Tim Hawkins.

The next few days just got harder as the adrenaline subsided and the relatives arrived full of their own fresh pain. He sat through information sessions where angry relatives expressed their displeasure at what they were or were not being told. He'd look up at the aeroplanes flying overhead and he so wanted to get on one, but knew he couldn't because he had to see it out to help Tim Hawkins's family in whatever way he could. Tim Hawkins's body, however, was never found.

When Richard eventually came home, a week after the bombing, he felt crap. He had all the tests and was diagnosed with depression as a manifestation of post-traumatic stress disorder and all its associated anxieties and vigilance. He described it, too, as a broken heart, so sad for everybody.

And just when he thought he was coming good, about six months after, the coverage of the Iraq War shook him up. All that death served up in his face evoked a lot of odd thoughts and memories.

*

Tim Britten was sent home to Perth. The burns on his left arm got infected and that knocked him around for a few weeks but they came good and he went back to East Timor to finish his tour in November.

He doesn't know if the girl in the Sari Club survived. He got an email from someone with the picture of a corpse, thinking it might be her. He studied the dark hair but there wasn't a lot to go on. The burns on the hands and feet looked right, but there really was no way of identifying her.

He tried to find Richard Joyes but had no luck, until one of Richard's brothers saw him on the telly and realised his story was the same as his brother's and that's how they came to reconnect.

They both lived in Western Australia and started hooking up to surf, play golf and watch footy together. 'We have become very close mates since, and feel as though we can both talk freely and bounce any feelings, thoughts, memories off each other,' Richard said as the first anniversary of the bombings approached in 2003. 'I feel guilty that I have found such a close friend as a result of losing someone very dear to me,' he said.

*

I was nearing completion of the book and it was time to try to contact Tim Britten. I'd spoken to him back in early 2007 when I first sought out the five recipients of the Cross of Valour. He had been friendly and forthright, but he asked if I could tell his story from previously published interviews.

As I muddled my way through a yes-and-no type answer, Tim interrupted. 'What do you want to know, mate? You know, things don't go very well and I'm now divorced and my ex-wife thinks it's all to do with this and all the rest of the crap. How many pounds of flesh do people want from me now? The story of the day hasn't changed, but parts of my life have. It hasn't done me any favours mate, you know . . . They [the survivors] put up with having nightmares every October, all that sort of crap. I personally don't see there's anything differ-ent to talk about now. I still work. I'm going well, yeah. The people who are dead are still dead. The people who are alive are still alive and dealing with their scars, I suppose.'

I asked if he'd like to talk about the time since the bombings.

He paused a long time. 'I don't know, mate. I'm still a serving police officer. People don't understand unless they've been there.' He was happy for me to quote what he had said so far but felt awkward going further. 'It's a source of a bit of personal torment and I've got my own demons to deal with without having the whole of Australia know what they are.'

'Do you have regrets?' I asked.

'There's no regret that I did what I did, Mark. There's regret that it's had longer-term effects on me. I'd like to say I'd be able to do it again, but I don't know if I would.'

He said I had Buckley's of speaking to Richard Joyes. 'I know where he is and I can't even contact him half the time.'

I left it at that, until 2010 when I sent Tim an email in the hope I might get him on one of those good days. In the end, he did agree to talk.

*

Tim Britten seems in a better place now than when I spoke to him two and half years earlier. He's remarried with a child due to be born within days. 'There are certain things you do to get through it,' he says. 'I believe it's by addressing things as they come up and then washing your hands of it because there's nothing you can do. Let it go. If it gets stuck in your head it'll ruin your life. I've got a good mate who is ex-SAS from Vietnam. He's like my father. I say to him, "You've got to let it go or it'll ruin you," and he says to me, "It's already ruined me."'

Tim has been helped a lot by the police psychiatrist. 'But there's also my own personal beliefs on how to go about handling it – not getting caught up in the whole post-traumatic stress disorder thing. I desperately don't want a bar of that. Just get on with it. There's nothing you can do about it. Bad things happen. I was one of the blokes who was there. People live and people die. You don't choose the time or place, but when that time comes there's nothing you can do about it. It sounds callous. I'm trying not to sound that way, but it's the only way you can do it. I could wallow and cry for the kids. I allow that to happen for one week every year. I probably drink too much and get a bit down during that week coming up to the anniversary. But for me, that's the way to do it.'

His day job has plenty of scope for trauma but it also requires razor sharp performance. He is a sniper in the West Australian police Tactical Response Group. It's a good job, he says, although his head's a bit jangled today. He spent it on the range, assessing four new blokes who want to get into the 'cell'.

He sold his medal set. 'Just got rid of 'em. It felt like a bit of a cleansing thing. Part of the thing that kicked it off was that I kept them at work in my locker and the leather box got a bit of mould on it. I couldn't keep something worth a bit of money in my house. I thought I might as well get rid of them. I was recently divorced. If they can earn money now, what's the point of having the kids fight over them when I'm gone? They've gone to a private museum in Maryborough, Queensland [Maryborough Military & Colonial Museum]. Anyone can go and have a look at them. The bloke who runs it is a top bloke.'

*

Richard Joyes again declined to talk to me but what happened to him after Bali was covered by a Canadian magazine, *Real Weddings*. It reported that, 'spiralling downhill from post-traumatic stress', Richard left Australia in 2004. He'd booked a round-the-world ticket. First stop was Vancouver and on his second night there he walked into the Granville Room for a drink with his travelling companion. So did a local girl by the name of Heike Tiemann. Romance blossomed and a month later when it came time to get on the plane for rest of the trip to Montreal, London, Rome, Vienna and Bangkok, the plane left without him. He got work in Canada as a geologist. The magazine said:

> Heike knew he was 'the kindest and most romantic soul' she had ever met. He would surprise her with 'secret weekends' to BC (British Columbia) destinations such as Whistler or Salt Spring. When he took her to the airport one August weekend in 2007, she was intrigued to find they were en route to San Francisco. In a tiny park near Pier 39, Rich told Heike the story of how the garden they were admiring was constructed 'bucket by bucket'. 'This guy spent 25 years building something that meant the world to him,' he continued, 'and I'm ready to spend even more than that.' Down on the obligatory knee, he presented Heike with an enormous diamond ring he had designed himself. He laughs: 'It was corny and cheesy, but it worked.'

*

Acts of bravery abounded on that night in October 2002. Aside from Tim Britten and Richard Joyes's Crosses of Valour, three Stars of Courage were earned, plus twelve Bravery Medals and sixteen Commendations for Brave Conduct.

TWENTY-TWO

Carolyn Loughton, Rob Elliott and Dennis Lever

Some bloomin' great lump of a thing kept bumping into the back of Rob Elliott's knees as he stood in the queue at the Broad Arrow Café in Port Arthur. The distinguished-looking Melbourne property developer turned to see that it was a large blue sports bag carried by a young bloke with long blond hair. Must have had camera equipment in there, he thought. Tripods perhaps.

'Would you like to get in front of me?' Rob offered. 'I'm waiting for my friends. I don't know what they're doing.'

Rob's wife Aly was looking for a table in the Sunday-lunch crowd while the eight other people they were travelling with wandered in from the car park. The group of old friends had just arrived at the famous convict settlement as the last stop on their Anzac Day long-weekend trip to Tasmania from Melbourne. They planned to grab a quick bite and a coffee, see the sights, then head back to the airport and home.

310

The long-haired bloke took up Rob's offer to go in front in the servery queue. Rob watched him buy two plates of food and head to the tables outside. Two of the women from Rob's group, Carol Pearce and Carmel Edwards, opened the door for him and looked at his two plates. 'Gee, you must be hungry,' one of them said.

'Yeah, I've been surfing.'

The 28-year-old looked like a surfer. He even had a board on the roof racks of the unregistered yellow Volvo he'd parked illegally down by the water. But the surf was Nullarbor flat that day. The young man had, in fact, just come from murdering two people about an hour earlier at the Seascape guesthouse.

Other diners at the café noted how he gulped down the meal.

Aly had, meanwhile, secured a table – number thirteen. The Elliotts got their sandwiches and coffee and sat with most of their group who squeezed into the limited space. Rob's mate Ron Edwards, sitting next to the aisle, saw the young bloke walk back in with the two plates empty except for a big pile of carrots on each.

'You don't like carrots,' Ron quipped, but the surfie didn't answer, walking on into the servery, still carrying that ridiculously large bag.

*

Seated at the next table, number fourteen, Carolyn Loughton noticed the long, blond hair and the bag. *Why would you bring a bag like that in here? Surely you'd leave it on the bus or in the car.*

The 40-year-old knew that the blond man hadn't stayed on site at the youth hostel last night because that's where she'd been with her teenage daughter, Sarah, and her friend Graham Colyer. So why would he need that bag here?

Carolyn was in Tasmania as a fifteenth birthday present for Sarah. Like the Elliotts' group, they were taking advantage of the four-day long-weekend courtesy of Anzac Day having fallen on the Thursday. Carolyn was just about to leave for the airport to head back to Melbourne. They'd only stopped at the café at the urging of Sarah and it proved to be one of those pivots in life that would leave Carolyn pondering the what-ifs, blaming herself when there was no blame to apportion – *Why did I agree?* And it would leave her angry in future when people said to her they were just in the wrong place at the wrong time. She knows what they mean, but what was wrong with what she was doing and where she was doing it? *This is what you do on a Sunday. Or at least it's what you did.* Nothing would seem so ordinary, so normal, again.

*

Coralee Lever, 52, was in the gift shop adjoining the café with her husband, Dennis, and their friends Vera and Ron Jary. On the last day of a six-day driving holiday, they'd popped into the café because Dennis was a diabetic and needed to keep his energy up. They'd finished lunch and were browsing the souvenirs – the books about the convict days, the T-shirts and mugs with logos like 'I escaped Port Arthur' – when they heard explosions. They hit the floor, thinking that something had blown up in the kitchen.

*

Inside the café, Rob Elliott thought the same thing. But as he looked across the room, he saw people slumping over tables, crockery flying everywhere. One of their group, Ron, said, 'Quick, under the table.' And they all got under except Rob, who was too slow. There was no room for him, so he stood, frozen solid, his eyes fixed on the blond guy now shooting with a large rifle. People fell in quick succession. Nobody screamed. All was quiet but for those enormous explosions.

'The big thing that saved us was the fact he was left-handed so he shot to the right,' Rob recalled. 'Had he been right-handed he would have knocked us over first off.' He came out of the servery towards Rob, still firing, only about three metres away now.

Sixteen people had already been wounded, eleven of them fatally. It would later be estimated that this had all occurred in less than fifteen seconds.

'People just stood there and copped it. They were trans-fixed. Most of what he did was head shots. It took a bit of time for me to react, but then I did react and tried to get to him because he had his back to me as he walked through. I had a chance to get to him. I tried to get there, but I hesitated a little.'

Rob didn't know what he was going to do if he got to him. Maybe distract him, maybe grab him if he could. There wasn't time to think. He lunged towards the gunman. 'And he obviously sensed me and spun around and I was four feet away from him . . . five feet away, maybe. And he was so quick on his feet.' The gunman aimed, Rob threw up his left arm. The bullet struck it through the back inside part of the upper arm, took out ten centimetres of bone and the radial nerve before blasting a hole out the front. As Rob fell, a sec-ond bullet hit him in the head, carving a groove down the back of his skull.

*

At the next table, Carolyn Loughton's group had finished their meals and stood to put their coats on when the shooting began. She experienced the same disconnect. The noise was just so loud in such a confined space, it could only be a car backfiring.

But what car? No sooner had she had that thought than she saw plaster flying. She saw . . . It is the sort of thing she will shy away from describing in future.

Then she saw the blond guy. He had the gun and was doing what he was doing in that small café. She was facing him, but her daughter, Sarah, was on the other side of the table facing away. Carolyn would only be able to imagine what Sarah saw, but her daughter's expression turned to total terror and dread. And now Carolyn could see the gunman coming towards them behind her daughter, so she grabbed Sarah by the shoulders, spun her around and flattened her to the floor, face first, then threw her own body on top. They lay out in the aisle, completely exposed to fate as the blasts continued so loud it hurt. It might have been at this point that Rob Elliott had lunged, perhaps buying them an extra moment. Carolyn felt fluid running from her ears. It felt like her eardrums had been blown out. (And they had.) But the gunman's footsteps carried him past her as he headed towards the souvenir shop.

*

Coralee Lever and her husband got up off the souvenir shop floor. 'It's only a re-enactment,' Dennis said. The multiple explosions seemed to confirm that it wasn't the kitchen blowing up. By the time they'd stood, the blond man was at the souvenir shop door with the gun across his body. Coralee wasn't impressed. She let fly at the idiot doing the re-enactment. She told him he was a stupid . . . (She won't actually repeat the words to me at first. 'I wasn't a lady anyway,' she'd say.) 'What about the people with heart conditions?' she asked. Both Ron and Dennis had had operations. Coralee didn't look at the gunman's face so she didn't see how he reacted to her comments. She looked at the gun as her nostrils filled with the familiar smell of gunpowder. She'd done a bit of small-bore target shooting so she was no stranger to weapons. She turned in disgust to walk away when she felt Dennis's hand in the middle of her back, pushing her to the floor. As soon as she hit the ground, more shots boomed out and she realised the deadly reality of the situation.

Coralee crawled along the floor. A tall woman she didn't know – Jenny Moor – reached out and grabbed her hand. Coralee reached for Vera's hand, too. Vera had also been pushed to the ground by her husband, Ron. In seconds, the tall woman dragged the two older women behind a screen displaying jumpers and pulled it closed behind them. Coralee had already looked back, expecting to see Dennis right behind her, but he wasn't there.

*

Still lying in the aisle across her daughter, Carolyn Loughton thought of her family. *Everyone knows we're on holiday, but nobody knows this is happening now in such an isolated spot. My God, this is just like Dunblane. We're going to die here. This is it. This is it.* She could hear the gunman returning. The incredible noise. The footsteps. And he walked past her again, standing near her to shoot at Peter Crosswell who was lying across two female companions to protect them. Peter, who received a Bravery Medal, later spoke of his bitter resentment at people who weren't there, asking why nobody cracked a chair over his head.

'It happened so quickly. It was so far from what we'd consider reality.'

Winemaker Jason Winter had stood up, thinking the killer was gone. 'No, no,' Jason was heard to say when he saw him return. The gunman fired two fatal shots, then moved back to the souvenir shop.

A group of four people huddled against the locked exit in the souvenir shop were believed to have been shot at this point. An Asian man huddled there with them was about to be next. The gunman aimed, but the gun didn't fire. It was empty. All 29 shots in his magazine had been fired, so he returned to the big blue bag in the servery area to reload.

Coralee saw Vera's husband Ron lying shot on the floor, along with a woman lying on her back, obviously dead.

Vera struggled to get up. 'Let me out. Let me out. Ron's dying.' But Coralee and Jenny Moor wouldn't let her. They had to stay hidden. Coralee put her hand over Vera's mouth to quieten her screams and she held her tight to stop her moving. She could see there was nothing to be done for Ron. He'd taken on a strange wax-like quality – like a Tussauds dummy with a bloody wound on its neck.

And then the gunman was gone. He'd been firing for between 90 seconds and two minutes. Twenty people were dead or dying and another six wounded.

The killing was far from over, however. There was more firing outside and Carolyn whispered in her daughter's ear. 'Stay down, stay down. I love you I love you I love you. Just stay down.' Still feeling a terror so great she can't understand how the body survives it, she thought he might come back at any moment. The windows were low. He might fire at them from outside.

*

'Basically I'm going into shock,' Carolyn tells me as we sit at a conference table in a church building near her home. 'Look at me here!'

I don't need to look. When she had repeated the words she said to her daughter – 'Stay down. I love you' – the conference table had started shaking hard and would continue shaking for much of the rest of the interview, a constant reminder of the physical force of memory and grief.

*

Behind the screen, Coralee saw the Asian man, dressed all in cream and white, who had been saved by the empty magazine. She saw the fear on his face as he ran to the door then back again. (He later left the scene quickly and it was months before authorities tracked him down.) They could still hear shooting outside. Vera's bad knee was hurting as they crouched behind the carpeted partition. Coralee had to try to lift her to straighten it out and ease the pain, still with her hand over Vera's mouth so she wouldn't scream. *We'll all be gone if he hears us back here.*

*

Rob Elliott lay unconscious in a blood puddle. The nine other people in his group had all got out unscathed, all with their own tales of good fortune. Now they had the misfortune to be standing amid the carnage in the silence. They went amongst the dead and dying, doing what they could, trying to find towels, staying with people till life flickered away. Aly did what she could to stem the flow of her husband's blood, while trying to ignore the body next to him with its head blown out.

*

Carolyn Loughton tried to raise her head but realised her shoulder was hanging off. Still lying across her daughter, she hadn't even known she'd been shot until that moment. She dragged herself across the floor, thinking she might find help. Find somebody. People were coming in now. She slumped herself against a wall and noticed there was a woman there trying to hide behind a closed umbrella, like trying to hide behind a stick. Even then the absurdity struck her. Carolyn looked up and saw a green exit sign. *My God, if he comes back in this door he's going to see me and her sitting here, and I can't move.*

A woman grabbed a man and asked if he was all right. 'My wife's been shot, but I'm okay,' he answered.

'Go to the kitchen,' the woman told him, 'and grab some towels and put the towels down this lady's back,' she said, pointing at Carolyn. 'And keep talking to her. Keep her eyes open.'

They could still hear shooting and Carolyn still felt absolute terror. She didn't know how Sarah was. She couldn't get back to her across the room.

*

Coralee Lever, Vera Jary and Jenny Moor stayed behind the screen for perhaps fifteen minutes before people came in the room looking for survivors. One of them, Sue Burgess, found her own daughter, Nicole, dead behind the souvenir shop counter.

Coralee maintains that the bodies that were widely reported to have been piled up against the locked souvenir shop door were in fact piled up against the screen that the three women were hiding behind – next to the door. The three women struggled to get out from behind the partition because the bodies had them jammed in. 'I believe there was one young lass still alive under the pile, but she couldn't move.'

Coralee found her husband, Dennis, dead. He hadn't got far from the spot where he'd pushed her to the floor. It looked like he'd gone towards the shelter of a pillar but had been shot in the cheek.

'We all sat on the hat box with hats and scarves on it. You looked down into that café with all the bodies and the . . . . It was just horrid. People wounded and some were dead. You just didn't know which way to go. You couldn't believe it. I felt so useless. I was so numb, I couldn't help anybody else. I wasn't allowed to go over to Dennis. I had to step over him to get out.'

The overpowering smell of gunpowder and the deafness of her ears all added to the sense of unreality as they were led from the building, stepping over more bodies, to an outside balcony. 'All I wanted to do was go back in to Dennis but they wouldn't allow me to. We sat out there for an hour or two. They brought us cups of tea and said, "That'll make you feel better" – but how can it?'

She sat there thinking she was to blame. If only she hadn't sworn at the gunman he might not have started shooting again.

*

Leaning against the café wall, Carolyn Loughton said, 'See that little girl over there with the blonde hair? That's my daughter. That's my daughter.' But the people did not respond. They did not rush to the girl's body on the floor like she thought they would have. At the time it didn't make sense. And, hours later, as Carolyn was taken out to the first helicopter, she told them, 'You have to get *her* out.' But they left the girl on the floor and continued on to the waiting aircraft.

Earphones were put on her but they slipped off and the noise in her burst eardrum was unbearable. She was looking at the cuff of the copilot's trousers in front of her and she wanted to reached out and tug it to get his attention but couldn't. She'd remember the lights coming on in Hobart as they came in to land at dusk.

She was run into the hospital – lots of masked faces looking down at her, trying to find a vein and failing. 'How many dead?' they asked. But she didn't have words to convey the enormity of it.

'Everyone's dead,' she told them. 'Everyone's dead.'

*

319

Coralee Lever can still hear her daughter's scream when she rang that evening to tell her the terrible news. 'Not my dad. Not my dad.' Then Coralee had to call her two sons.

She and Vera huddled in a cottage on site, with the lights out and the crackling of the open fire sounding like gunshots. The killer's whereabouts were still unknown and it was a dark, unsettling time. She and Vera were moved to the police academy to stay the night.

A counsellor from Hobart, Claudette Wells, came and stayed with them. The counsellor didn't say much. Nobody seemed to know what to say. How could they? She just listened and comforted them through the night.

When Coralee's children arrived at the airport the next day, the police picked them up. Coralee had been too numb to cry but now the kids were there it became real.

Coralee had to identify Dennis. The adult children could have done it, but she figured that she'd already seen him, and there was no need to put them through that. Looking at him again in the morgue, with a small black bullet hole in the cheek and the back of his head exploded out, was perhaps the hardest part of the whole catastrophe.

*

Sarah Loughton had been shot dead on the floor of the café while lying underneath her mother but no one had told Carolyn. A day or so after the massacre, people came to Carolyn's hospital bed to inform her: 'Mrs Loughton, we must tell you . . .'

'And I just screamed,' Carolyn recalled. ' "Where is he [the killer]?" "He's down the corridor." And I just screamed. They shouldn't have told me. They should have lied. And then they got death threats. The hospital was evacuated because of bomb threats made because he was in there.'

*

Rob Elliott remembers becoming vaguely conscious in the hospital and hearing voices talking about amputating his arm. He couldn't open his eyes or talk, just listen as they discussed it. A woman said, 'No, I can save the arm.' He went into surgery and woke up with titanium rods holding the bottom part of his arm to the top, where bone had once been. But he was blind. His eyes didn't work. The bullet that fractured his skull had not entered the brain, but the part of the brain which controls vision had been damaged by the concussion so he couldn't see a thing.

His wife Aly slept in his room each night in the hospital. As the days went by, he slowly became aware of a shape on the wall, and after a few more days he realised it was a clock, and after a couple of weeks he was able to discern the numbers.

The police were keen to interview him because his eyes had prevented him seeing any media so he couldn't be accused of being influenced by pictures when he identified the suspect. And he'd had a very good look at the blond man. When he was later shown a collection of photos, he picked out Martin Bryant, the man arrested at the Seascape guesthouse and who now stood accused of 35 murders.

Rob was airlifted to the Monash hospital in Melbourne where he stayed for another three weeks. 'I wasn't strong enough to go home but I wanted to go home so badly. It was a bit of a shock to the system when I did get home. I couldn't get comfortable. Restless nights propped up in bed. I had to get the arm dressed for weeks because of the possible infections that could go into the bone with all the shrapnel and glass in there. Then I had to have a series of bone grafts from the hips to the arm. I eventually got my arm strong enough to have the tendons transferred from the wrist to the fingers. I'd had no radial nerve so my wrist had just been flopped loose and all the tendons had withered from lack of use. When the tendons went in, I got the use of my hand back. It's quite strong now. The recovery took eighteen months. I had thirteen operations. I got my eyesight back, but I lost my peripheral vision. I bump into things and trip over things. If I'm walking over broken ground, I usually have to hold Aly's arm. She's my seeing-eye dog.'

Rob is sitting out on his very wide green lawn, looking distinguished with silver hair and a generous silver moustache. He's approaching 70 when we speak, more than fourteen years after the incident, the first time he's granted an interview except for a brief one on the day he received his Star of Courage – the highest bravery award of all 28 arising out of Port Arthur. He agreed only because it is for a book and not the daily media.

He has come out of it remarkably well. And aside from the hard work of his wife, Aly, to nurse him back to health, he had the double good fortune that, firstly, his property development partner kept the business ticking over so he didn't have to worry financially and, secondly, he and Aly were part of a solid group of friends who'd all been through the same trauma. 'We stuck together and if anyone had a bit of a downer, we'd go to the group and do our own session, just gently talking things through. We didn't want external people. The girls were better at it than the boys, obviously. External counsellors say, "I know what you're going through," but they don't know at all.'

I ask if he's had nightmares or flashbacks but he says he's been fine. 'We decided as a group that we'd try to get this out of our minds as quickly as we can. That's why I don't want to regurgitate things. We try not to talk about it terribly much. We just want to get on with our lives. We don't want him to spoil our lives. I know some of the people – years and years have gone by and they still want to talk about it. Within eighteen months I was completely out of thinking about Port Arthur. We just put it down to an accident and left it at that. Having said that, I'm still very wary about anybody that looks suspicious. You become very aware of anything unusual around you. Initially I wouldn't sit with my back to a door . . . It was a rotten day but it's done and dusted now.'

*

Coralee Lever gave a number of statements to police and would continue to do so over the coming months as they went back over every detail, every moment, again and again, putting the brief of evidence together. 'It wasn't very nice giving the horrid details. I'll talk around it now to you, but I won't go too deep. It still hurts too much. I don't have to close my eyes to see the horror. I don't have to pass that on to people. They can just imagine what that's like.'

She came back to Red Cliffs, a town of about 4000 near Mildura in north-west Victoria, where she and Dennis had lived all their lives and where they owned a gift shop. She arrived home and found she didn't want to go inside. She couldn't. But the grandchildren came running out. 'Nana!' So she had to go in. She kept clearing the hurdles.

Dennis had also worked at the school and had been the president of the bowling club so everyone knew him. The first weeks back were hard. 'I found I was the one comforting other people. I had to have strength to pass it on to other people. It was very difficult . . . but I had a lot of wonderful people who came in and helped me run the shop for eighteen months. Just serving. They didn't want to take wages or anything. But I found I was counselling people all the time. It took me the whole weekend to get over it, then I had to start again. But I knew I was going to run that shop. I wasn't going to hide. He wasn't going to destroy my life.'

Dennis Lever and Ron Jary were awarded posthumous Bravery Medals for their actions of pushing their wives out of the way of the gunman. Coralee and Vera were bound closer together. Both women went to the inaugural meeting that formed the Australian Bravery Association. There were a few Port Arthur people there, but only Coralee has continued to be associated with it and it's become an important backstop in her life. She has become the Victorian president and one of her duties is to greet new bravery award recipients at their ceremonies. She invites me to join her.

TWENTY-THREE

Simon Tanti and the Aftermath
of Bravery

*I saved a fellow from drowning years ago. It's just me. I don't
know if it's built in you or not. Do you turn or do you try and
help? Then you do help and it's so horrific it destroys your life.
You get these medals from the Queen, then you're on your own.
We are the forgotten ones. What do we want? I don't know.
Do we need a march to be recognised like the Vietnam war
people? Are we worth that?*
Sharon O'Leary

Fifty award recipients file into the impossibly ornate ballroom of the Victorian Governor's residence, ushered into
their preordained seats by a man in full military dress uniform. They wear a mix of good and bad suits, good and bad
hair. One man – who later tells me he lives in his car – wears
a black T-shirt, jeans and runners. Only three of the 50 are
women. A group of teenagers involved in a surf rescue walk in

awkwardly, like they don't know what to do with their arms.

Port Arthur survivor Coralee Lever watches them file in and scans the little booklet with the names of the 50 recipients and the official stories – the citations – for each of them.

'I'm surprised how many there are,' I say to Coralee.

'Just shows you how many people put their lives on the line to save lives, doesn't it?' she says.

To see the 50 people really does bring it home and I wonder what hidden traumas lie behind these ordinary faces. Skimming the booklet, I am struck by how many have come from house fires (sixteen) and car fires (five), but there's four who thwarted suicides and four from cars in rivers. Ten of the awards come from three surf rescues.

The Governor, Professor David de Kretser, stands there, slim and gently smiling, shaking the hand of each recipient after their citation has been read, guiding their faces around to the in-house photographer.

*

Number eight in line is boatbuilder Mr Simon Victor Tanti – good suit, fresh-clipped hair, shiny shoes. He's standing at attention next to the military officer while his citation is read out.

> On the morning of 22 December 2007 . . . Mr Tanti was awoken by his neighbours' screams . . .

Standing there listening to the citation brings that horrible week back to Simon Tanti, that beautiful morning, 6.15 am, when the yelling and screaming comes through his bedroom window. Next door is housing commission crisis accommodation so the noises aren't unusual. 'Why don't you go and have a look?' says his wife, Joanne.

Simon gets out of bed, puts on his shorts and looks at his feet. He sees his toenails have been painted hot pink. He realises his daughter must have done it for a joke while he was asleep in front of the telly after he'd come home from his work's Christmas party the previous night. *Better put my runners on.* He looks over the back fence and three adult neighbours and two children are there – stunned mullets, doing nothing. 'What's going on?' he asks.

> . . . as windows exploded and their house became engulfed in fire. Mr Tanti learned that three children were trapped inside.

He feels instantly sober and alert. The hangover is gone. His training from his former career as a prison guard kicks in. 'Have you called the fire brigade yet?'

'Not yet.'

'How many are in there? Where are they?'

'There's three at the back of the house.'

He sees the fire is much worse at the back. *If they're in there, there's no way they're coming out.* The three neighbours are doing nothing. They seem helpless. It's up to him.

'Get the kids around the corner,' he barks to his wife, knowing it might be grisly. He doesn't want his children to see anything. He runs to the front and tries to smash a window with a rock but it doesn't work.

> He quickly grabbed a garden rake and used it to smash in a front bedroom window which immediately produced a fireball that roared through the opening.

He smells the thick black smoke come out. He's scared. He's got five kids of his own. But he looks around. *No one else is going to do it. Looks like it's me.* He sees his wife out of the corner of his eye as he goes in. She is thinking it will be the last time she sees him alive.

> As the flare subsided Mr Tanti climbed halfway into the house. Thick smoke created zero visibility, and such was the intensity of the flames and heat, that Mr Tanti was restricted in his movements. Without any protection and using the rake as a probe, Mr Tanti scoured the area as best he could . . .

He can't see any flame but people outside see it all around him – in the ceiling, licking walls. Maybe it's tunnel vision. He sees what he wants to see. The prison guards' fire training had them prodding around in darkness searching for people in the cell blocks. It all comes back – keep low, use the back of your hand to touch, and prod, prod, prod. He climbs over mattresses, crap all over the floor, until the rake hits something that feels different, softer.

> . . . and by touch was able to find a three-year-old girl.

It's pure arse. She feels dead. Keeping low, he holds her close and scrambles back over the mattresses and out of the house. It turns out she is alive but her nappy is on fire. 'Douse her in water and take her nappy off,' he orders the mother.

The whole house has gone up now, there's no way he can go back in. He sees two cars out the front. He smashes the window of one, puts it in neutral and pulls it by the bullbar out of the driveway and across the road so the fire truck can get in close when it arrives. It is a lonely feeling. Such a beautiful morning. Everyone else is in bed. He throws up.

The fire brigade go in with their masks and oxygen and find the boys just a metre or two from where Simon had found the girl. *If only I'd hung around and searched a bit more.* He beats himself up over that one.

It was so very bad and yet it's led to this – he's standing here about to shake the Governor's hand in this giant gilded ballroom. It's good. The emotion is flooding through him. He wants to cry but he stuffs it back in and manages half a smile, a big brave face.

He receives his Bravery Medal, poses for a photograph with the Governor, and walks smiling back to his seat.

*

Jim Runham, who used to come along to these sorts of functions for the bravery association in Queensland, had given me two warnings about such occasions. First: 'If the award recipient has tried to save the life of somebody who died, be aware that they'll be blaming themselves and feeling full of guilt. "Why are you giving me this when the person died?" It usually hits them at the investiture and they'll often go off into the gardens and have a cry. You've got to be sensitive about that but I'm sure you will be.' Second: 'Watch out for the drinks tray. The beer and wine flows freely and if you're not careful you can easily get a bit light-headed.'

I find Simon Tanti standing by the huge white fountain out on the lush lawn, and approach him tentatively – orange juice in hand – heeding Jim's warnings. But he seems cheerful enough. Bright and smiling. He agrees to have a chat and

I mention that there always seems to be more to these stories than the citation can convey. 'You can say that again,' he says, and his wife Joanne nods in agreement.

But Simon got out of it all right. The little girl, Phoebe, was in the burns unit for a long time. She had a hair transplant and will have breathing difficulties for the rest of her life but he'd saved her. He worried for a while that he should have gone deeper into the fire to look for the two boys. But he knew he had to save himself for his own five kids. 'There was nothing I could have done. I didn't know where they were. I couldn't see. I do believe I did my bit and I'm grateful I got Phoebe out. It's just a tragic event. You can't let it get to you.'

*

I talk to a couple more people who were awarded that day and then find Coralee who has been mingling with some old acquaintances and new recipients. We walk back towards the city along St Kilda Road and Coralee talks about her darker days.

Two things stayed with her after Port Arthur. One, that she'd called Bryant a stupid bastard. (She lets slip what she actually said.) She fretted that she had prompted him to resume shooting. And, two, holding her hand over Vera's mouth and not letting her go to Ron. That got to her. Even though Vera told her, 'You probably saved my life by not letting me out,' it took her a long time to get that perspective.

She's had other Port Arthur survivors come and visit her. 'I had a couple call into my shop and had a talk to me and no way could he ever work again. They didn't lose anyone. They were just there. I said, "Why can't you work? I'm here running a business. You can't live on sympathy." And you can't. It's up to you how you want to be. What would I do if I didn't work? I'd have nothing to do but dwell on it.

'I still have my days. I call them my dustbin days. I go round kicking plastic dustbins. I used to go up to the shop and throw boxes around and clean up around the back. I've become a workaholic. I do sporting trophies and do a lot of the engraving at night. I bolt myself in and work to about eleven o'clock. Dennis and I used to do it but now it's just me.'

When Dennis was first buried, Coralee would go to the gravesite to talk to him and she left a handprint in the bare earth, where his hand would be. So when the grave was done they did an outline of her hand and sandblasted the handprint in the concrete and now she can hold his hand all the time and feel close to him while she talks.

*

In Melbourne, I arrange to meet Coralee's fellow survivor, Carolyn Loughton. She is standing outside her local church hall waiting for me. She has not found solace in religion, she explains, but the people at the church have been good to her. Her figure and clothes – a luscious green velvet jacket, blue scarf, new jeans – are young. Yet her hair is snow white. Small talk over, she begins proceedings: 'I'm agreeing to be interviewed on the condition that I get to read what is going to be published and I get the opportunity to vet it before it is printed. Do you agree with that?'

I normally wouldn't consent to such terms. 'Yep,' I say.

'Okay. Would you like me to start?'

'Yeah. I'd like you to start at the very beginning,' I say. 'Can you talk about life before Port Arthur?'

'No. That's too personal, but, of everything I'm going to say, *that* is the most important.' She passes over a folded sheet. It is the funeral order of service for her daughter Sarah, a pretty, healthy teen.

331

'That is the greatest loss and that's what it's all about for me . . . This is going to be all fragmented. You've just got to bear with me.'

And so she begins a long account of her injuries. It is long because her medical troubles have been many and ongoing. She had operations every second day for the first few weeks after the massacre. And the wound was left open so they could clean it. Nurses picked out glass and shrapnel twice a day without anaesthetic while she screamed the place down, so they eventually gave her the horse tranquilliser ketamine and she'd be hallucinating before the needle had left the vein. Her shoulder got pinned together, and that should have been the start of the road to recovery.

Months after the incident, she returned to her empty home for the first time and – as if her faith in human nature hadn't been sufficiently shaken – the place had been robbed. Society wasn't holding, and neither was her shoulder. The bones were turning to jelly from a condition called osteomyelitis – 'gangrene of the bones' is her layman's explanation. Back in hospital, the doctors took out a large chunk of her hip bone and mashed it up to try to rebuild the shoulder with it. That put her in a wheelchair, and she had to cope with learning to walk again on top of the shoulder problems. They said to her that if the osteomyelitis returned, she'd know because of the pain. But she woke one morning at home to find her flannelette pyjama top stuck to her back. The wound had opened and gunk was oozing out. But there was no pain. It turned out the nerves were too damaged to feel anything.

She didn't have any hip bone to spare to rebuild the shoulder again, so this time they took out a fibula – one of the two leg bones below the knee. She tosses over some X-rays: 'A picture tells a thousand words.' Indeed it does. You can clearly see the two knobs of bone at the knee and ankle, but the rest of the bone is missing, cut clean off at either end. It is strangely stomach-turning to look at.

'Once again I was back in a wheelchair and learning to walk, and I couldn't even lift my arm to put a flannel under my armpit to wash. That particular surgery was done many years after the event. Can you bear with me while we go through this?' She takes me through a series of X-rays with scatterings of staples and various mechanisms that hold her shoulder together, something like a chain. 'I've also had skin grafts to replace the skin on my back and had major veins taken out of my neck to vascularise my back because there weren't enough blood vessels there. So my body has been farmed to fix the shoulder. And as a result of taking the fibula out of my leg, the tendons all pulled in and that pulled all my toes under. I had to have a screw put in my big toe.'

She pulls out a foot X-ray showing a large screw in there that looks very much like one from a hardware store.

'For six months I had Meals on Wheels. I would crawl from the bed to sit in the shower. I would then crawl to the couch and that was my life for six months. This was four years after Port Arthur.'

She pulls out more X-rays. 'The flecking there is shrapnel they can't get out of my back. The glass doesn't show on the X-rays, but it bubbles up every so often and I might be able to get a friend to pick it out with tweezers. It snags on my clothes. As I say, all of this fades into insignificance when compared to that.' She points again at the funeral order of service.

'I just wanted you to see all this because to look at me from the outside is different to that,' she points at the X-rays. 'And I think the public's perception of being shot is that if you're not killed, the bullet is removed and you recover.'

Carolyn has endured 30 operations in thirteen hospitals. She still suffers dizziness from her eardrum being blown out. She's been told you're never cured from osteomyelitis. It can lay dormant in your system. She lives in absolute dread of its return.

'My life is still dominated by medical practitioners, fourteen and a half years after the event. I had treatment on my back yesterday. I do physio and Pilates once a week to maintain my balance and strength.' Throw in X-rays and doctors appointments and there's not a lot of time left because if she visits a practitioner one day, she'll need to rest the next. 'I just go round and round. So I'm a bag of nerves. I can't handle loud noises – kids parties with balloons.'

When she's asleep she can see Sarah and smell and feel her, and it is real and wonderful. And then she'll wake to the reality of her pain and loneliness. Two years ago she woke from the magnificent dream and couldn't move. The pain was worse than being shot. She couldn't do a thing to help herself and had to stay at a friend's place for a week, her neck in a brace. One time in bed she was sure she heard gunshots. She was too scared to even sit up. So she just rolled onto the floor and sobbed. That's when she ended up in Heidelberg Repatriation Hospital being treated by the doctors who treat Vietnam vets with post-traumatic stress disorder.

After one of her long stays in hospital, she visited a friend's house and couldn't get over how there was no receptionist at the front counter. Hey, there wasn't even a front counter. Kids were allowed to play on the floor. She realised she was becoming institutionalised.

'Life used to be good. I'd get up, go to work, be happy. All of a sudden I'm in the world of scapulas and fibulas and ballistics.'

Had Carolyn been working on the day of the massacre, she'd be covered by workers compensation. There was money early on thanks to public donations, but that has long since been exhausted and most of her problems have arisen since. She's had to manage her own case so she's refused the painkillers the doctors want to give her. She needs to be alert. She needs to pay bills. 'The people who hold the purse strings do not know and do not seem to want to know what I've been through. And they don't seem to understand that people need to be looked after for life as recommended in [Special Commissioner] Max Doyle's report. But the report has been ignored. There is no one for me to send my medical receipts to. It should just be a straightforward process, but I can't even find out who owns Port Arthur or who the third party insurer was. In my case, it's not going to go away. I'm minus bones now, and as one gets older, problems might get worse. What happens if I end up in a wheelchair?'

The physical pain keeps pulling her back from psychological recovery. She adjusts to life without a daughter: what do you do with yourself when you're used to being a parent?

'At forty, you think you've got life pretty much sorted out, then something like this happens and you have to pretty much reconstruct your life. Everything you think you know is not true. I can remember thinking the only sure thing I know is that the sun will come up tomorrow. Everything else – the structure of the world as I've known it – I do not understand any more. And I remember it was like I was hanging on to life not with my fingertips but my fingernails. Sliding. Thinking, I've just got to hang on. I remember waving my arms around and saying to a clinical psychiatrist, "I can't get back."'

There are no Port Arthur support groups, so Carolyn has no way of gauging how well she is because she can't see what the others have been through. 'I would find it beneficial or even heartening to hear people have moved on. That people are coping. That would be nice.' By the time she was well enough to receive her Bravery Medal, it was years after the others. 'I was flipping out about it. *How can they give me a bravery award when I didn't save my daughter?* I felt like a failure. I said to them, "Can't you post it to me?" But protocol demands that you be there. At last I decided to accept it. It's part of my family history to pass on, so I went down and received the award. But then what do you do with it? It's not like an Anzac medal. There's no march.'

That's one of the reasons they formed the bravery association, I say, to give people an occasion to wear the medals.

'I've heard nothing from them since the meeting in Canberra in 2000. Then again I've moved and haven't even thought of them.'

I tell her I'll get Coralee to give her a call. 'Yes, please do.'

I ask if she can remember the conversation she had with Jim Runham which left such a lasting impression on him at the founding of the bravery association. She doesn't. But she does recall hearing a lot of stories that she already knew from the newspapers. 'So much of it was so incredibly remarkable. I sat there with the man with the electricity and the pole and the crane [Cross of Valour recipient Darrell Tree, Chapter Two]. I remember meeting him and hearing the story and thinking it was truly remarkable. I suppose it put it into perspective that maybe that's what people see when they see me. I've got so used to living with my story, it doesn't seem remarkable. The whole thing is so very, very humbling. I've seen the worst – the absolute worst – of what someone could do. And to hear the remarkable stories of bravery, survival and service, I understood what makes us human.'

Epilogue

Floods smash into Toowoomba, the Lockyer Valley and Brisbane in January 2011 just days before the completion of this book. The necessarily brief news stories contain glimpses of so much pain I am almost glad to be shielded from the full details – rescuers struggling to save families, succeeding with some and failing with others; a child wrenched from her mother's arms. There is so much grief still to be felt. And yet, amongst the worst traumas anyone could be expected to endure, emerge stories of extraordinary bravery, survival and community service. And this, as Carolyn Loughton understands it, is what make us human.

I ring Jim Runham in flood-hit Ipswich to see how he has fared. I know that in recent months post-traumatic stress disorder has returned to dog his life. When I phone he is in a debrief. He's spent the day manning a flood boat in his capacity as the commanding officer of the local Navy Cadets. They've rescued 56 people and assisted in four births. While taking an Indian-born family to safety, the father turned to Jim and told him, 'Australia is the best country in the world. In my country, a flood like this would kill a million people and nobody would care.' The Indian family had in fact helped save a woman suffering an angina attack while others had left her. She has nominated Jim's crew for bravery awards. It all helps reinforce my view that the people featured in this book don't have heroism at their core. What they have is a strong moral spine and a commitment to helping others. And when asked the question, how far would you go to save a life, or to right a wrong, these are the people who are prepared to go that one very large step further.

Acknowledgements

My sincerest thanks go to all those brave people whose stories appear in these pages and who gave their time and emotions so generously. My thanks and apologies too, to those who told me their stories, but who, owing to limited space, do not appear in the final book. You are all remarkable.

Special mention should go to Jim Runham whose assistance went way beyond the call of duty, but also to Sally Gregory and Coralee Lever who are wonderful examples of the fine people found at the Australian Bravery Association.

Also, Associate Professor Mal Hopwood at Austin Health helped me understand something of the workings of the mind under stress. Stephen White assisted on matters aviation. Adele Astley, Leanne Field, Sharron Arnold, Anne Marshall and Pete Doherty all went out of their way on my behalf.

My former bosses and colleagues at *The Weekend Australian Magazine*, Bruce Guthrie, Graham Erbacher, Petra Rees, Greg Callaghan, Christine Westwood and Kerry Taylor, all played a part in making this book happen though they may not be aware of it.

Special mention must go to Tom Gilliatt at Pan Macmillan for his always sound judgement and to Emma Rafferty and Susin Chow for their silky-smooth edit – like a good visit to the dentist.

Thanks to Lucy Willesee and Row Golledge, and to Maree Whittaker and James Chatfield, for the accommodation and to James for his manuscript advice.

My greatest thanks, though, are reserved for Amy Willesee, my editor-in-life, my inspiration and my wife. She had more than a passing contribution to the words that appear throughout, particularly the beginning and end. But most importantly she provided the impetus – the 'if that's what you want to do, do it'. A man could not ask for more.

Endnotes

Chapter Six

Page

76 'his postwar career was punctuated by long intervals of nervous collapse': Shephard B, *A War of Nerves: Soldiers and Psychiatrists 1914–1994*, Pimlico Books, London, 2002, p 294.

78 'I took Jack out to see the minefield he rescued me from . . .': www.afp.gov.au/~/media/afp/pdf/r/remembering-the-great-rescue.ashx.

Chapter Eight

Page

107 'I feel so special . . .': Ross D, 'When it comes to fearless courage, Sharon is a star', *Courier-Mail*, 21 October 1991, p 1.

108 'You never dreamt of such gaits . . .': Shephard B, *A War of Nerves: Soldiers and Psychiatrists 1914–1994*, Pimlico Books, London, 2002, pp 2–3.

Chapter Nine

Page

118 Research on perpetual distortions in combat . . . : Grossman D with Christensen L, *On Combat: The Psychology and Physiology of Deadly Conflict in War and Peace*, Warrior Science Publications, 2004.

122 'Railway collisions, their sudden occurrence, their dramatic setting . . .': quoted in Shephard B, *A War of Nerves: Soldiers and Psychiatrists 1914–1994*, Pimlico Books, London, 2002, p 16.

Chapter Eleven
Page
138 'I gloss over anything in a man decorated for gallantry . . .': quoted in Holmes R, *Acts of War: The Behaviour of Men in Battle*, Cassell PLC, United Kingdom, 1985, p 306.
148 'I fell in love with her and she with me,' he explained to the paper.: Hewitt S, 'Hero's haunting past', *Sunday Herald-Sun*, 22 November 1998, p 4.

Chapter Twelve
Page
168 *Courier-Mail* journalist Paul Whittaker had found a former pilot . . . : Whittaker P, 'Ditched plane may have run out of fuel', *Courier-Mail,* 5 November 1996, p 1.

Chapter Fourteen
Page
191 'The willingness to die for another person . . .': Junger S, *War*, Fourth Estate, London, 2010, p 239.

Chapter Seventeen
Page
245 'Or perhaps they had just learned a lesson that Mr Tale-Yax . . .': Sulzberger AG, Meenan M, 'Questions Surround a Delay in Help for a Dying Man', *New York Times*, 25 April 2010.
245 'Thirty-eight who saw . . .': Gansberg M, 'Thirty-eight who saw murder didn't call the police', *New York Times*, 27 March 1964.

245 The question prompted social psychologists John Darley and Bibb Latane to find out.: Darley JM and Latane B, 'Bystander intervention in emergencies: diffusion of responsibility', *Journal of Personality and Social Psychology*, American Psychological Association, 1968, Volume 8(4), pp 377–83.

251 'The majority are unwilling to take extraordinary risks...': Marshall SLA, 'Men Against Fire', *Washington Infantry Journal*, William Morrow and Co, New York, 1947, p 149 as quoted in Shephard B, *A War of Nerves: Soldiers and Psychiatrists 1914–1994*, Pimlico Books, London, 2002, p 236.

251 'six gutful men who will go anywhere and do anything...': Spiller R, *RVSI Journal* 133, 1988, as cited in Graves DE in Charles DA et al (eds), *Military History and the Military Profession*, Westport, Conn., 1992, as quoted in Shephard B, *A War of Nerves: Soldiers and Psychiatrists 1914–1994*, Pimlico Books, London, 2002, p 237.

251 Wigram was killed soon after, leading a frontal assault against the Germans.: Shephard B, *A War of Nerves: Soldiers and Psychiatrists 1914–1994*, Pimlico Books, London, 2002, p 238.

251 In 1973, the Israelis studied high-performing soldiers during the Yom Kippur War.: Junger S, *War*, HarperCollinsPublishers, Australia, 2010, p 236.

Chapter Twenty-One
Page

292 'Guys, I'm feeling crook. I'm going back to the hotel to get some sleep.': ABC, *Four Corners: After Bali*, 15 September 2003, http://www.abc.net.au/4corners/content/2003/transcripts/s946351.htm; Richard Joyes interview with ABC *Four Corners* reporter Debbie Whitmont, http://www.abc.net.au/4corners/content/2003/20030915_after_bali/int_joyes.htm.

298 He knew Bali well but he'd only ever been to the club once. Drinking and partying weren't his scene.: ABC, *Four Corners:*

After Bali, 15 September 2003; Ben Tullipan interview with ABC *Four Corners* reporter Debbie Whitmont, http://www. abc.net.au/4corners/content/2003/20030915_after_bali/int_ tullipan.htm.

306 'I feel guilty that I have found . . .': Sexton J, 'The Incredible Lightness of Being – Bali Beyond the Flames', *The Weekend Australian*, 11 October 2003, p 16.

309 'Heike knew he was "the kindest and most romantic soul" she had ever met . . .': *Real Weddings*, http://blog.realweddings.ca/ paradise-lost-paradise-found/.

Chapter Twenty-Two
Page
315 'It happened so quickly. It was so far from what we'd consider reality.': ABC, *7.30 Report,* 27 April 2006.

Chapter Twenty-Three
Page
326 'On the morning of 22 December 2007 . . . Mr Tanti was . . .': Official citation as per the investiture programme, Government House, Melbourne, 28 October 2010.